THE MAID'S DAUGHTER

The Maid's Daughter

LIVING INSIDE AND OUTSIDE

THE AMERICAN DREAM

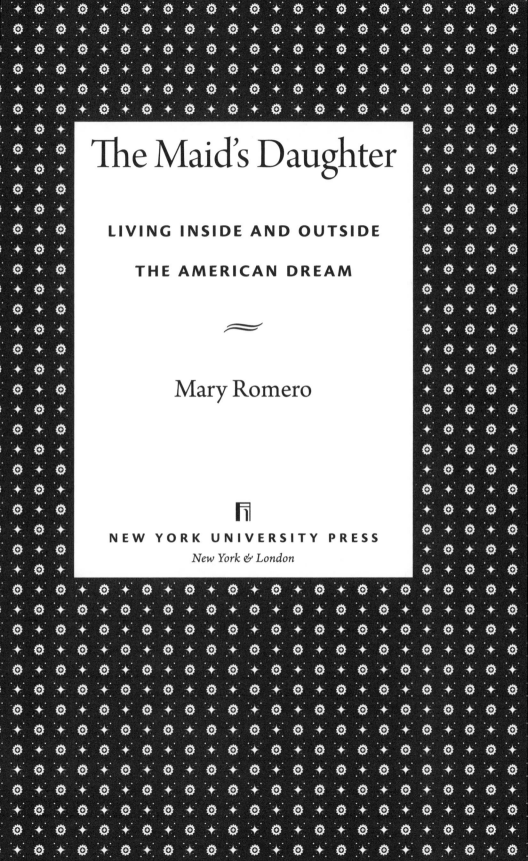

Mary Romero

NEW YORK UNIVERSITY PRESS

New York & London

NEW YORK UNIVERSITY PRESS
New York and London
www.nyupress.org

References to Internet websites (URLs) were accurate at the time of writing.
Neither the author nor New York University Press is responsible for URLs
that may have expired or changed since the manuscript was prepared.

Library of Congress Cataloging-in-Publication Data
Romero, Mary.
The maid's daughter : living inside and outside the American dream / Mary Romero.
p. cm.   Includes bibliographical references and index.
ISBN 978-0-8147-7642-1 (cl : alk. paper) — ISBN 978-0-8147-7725-1 (e-book)
1. Women household employees—United States—History.
2. Hispanic American women—Employment—History.
3. Minority women—Employment—United States—History.
I. Title.
HD6072.2.U5R674   2011
331.4'816408968073—dc22   2011005653

New York University Press books are printed on acid-free paper,
and their binding materials are chosen for strength and durability.
We strive to use environmentally responsible suppliers and materials
to the greatest extent possible in publishing our books.

Manufactured in the United States of America

10 9 8 7 6 5 4 3 2 1

CONTENTS

ACKNOWLEDGMENTS

After working on a project for two decades, the list of thank-yous is incredible. Where do I begin?

The easy start is to list institutional support, which was scarce. The much longer list is of all the persons who contributed to this project by agreeing to be interviewed; colleagues who assisted in helping me make contacts with the children of domestic workers; those who shared useful background information on UCLA and LA and provided sincere interest and insights over the years—I am sure to miss a few, and I apologize in advance. And of course, I want to acknowledge the warriors who took their editorial swords and helped me get to the finish line. I thank Aiden Amos for assisting with all the formatting challenges, Andrew Katz for his copyediting, and Despina Papazoglou Gimbel for her editorial assistance.

I am grateful for the Summer Stipends I received from the University of Oregon and two from Arizona State University. I spent the first stipend transcribing tapes and the second one transcribing and putting the narrative into order. Receiving a sabbatical at Arizona State University is greatly appreciated. However, the real financial acknowledgment goes to Eric Margolis, my husband and soul mate, who was pleased to use our own finances to cover travel for the project over the past two decades.

Several colleagues and research groups provided me the opportunity to get feedback on the project during various stages of interviewing, coding, and analyzing the narrative. One of the first places I found extremely useful comments and support was during my visiting year at Macalester College as the McKnight Professor in St. Paul in 1992–93. Michal McCall offered an intellectual environment that every academic should experience at least once. I was fortunate to be visiting the same year that Darrell Moore was a predoctoral fellow. The Center for Advanced Feminist Studies at the University of Minnesota, Minneapolis, invited me to participate in its Theorizing Female Diversity Seminar. Abby Stewart invited me several times to present at the University of Michigan at Ann Arbor, and every time was a rewarding experience. I am indebted to her for inviting me to participate in the Nag's Heart summer seminars. The participants at the two workshops we directed on narrative offered valuable critique and support. I am grateful to Evelyn Nakano Glenn for inviting me to participate in the 2001 Workshop Series, Center for Working Families, University of California, Berkeley. I thank Julia Wrigley and Annette Lareau for inviting me to participate in the ASA Grant for the Discipline Conference on Pushing the Boundaries: New Conceptualizations of Childhood and Motherhood. Again, I received valuable feedback from both Julia and Annette, as well as from the other participants. Although I have not yet met Katharine B. Silbaugh, I am grateful to her for reaching out to me and inviting me to participate in the Symposium on the Structures of Care Work with feminist legal scholars writing on care work. Joyce Chinen at the Women's Studies Department, University of Hawaii, has always been supportive, and she graciously arranged a brown-bag seminar during my visit to Honolulu in 2002. I had the honor to speak to domestic workers in Mexico City at El Instituto de Liderazgo Simone de Beauvoir in 2003. I thank the Latino Studies Program at New York University for inviting me to present my work in 2005. I treasure the conversation with Renato Rosalto about my work and am thankful that he suggested that I think about family stories in organizing the book. I am grateful for being invited to present at the Andrew W. Mellon Sawyer Seminar on Globalizing the Americas: World Economies and Local Communities, University of Toronto, in 2007. Working with Valerie Preston and Wenona Giles on the Global Migration Systems of Domestic and Care Workers at York University in 2008 was very helpful in pushing me toward finishing the book.

Many wonderful colleagues hosted visits to their campus to present my research in departmental brown bags and classes. The list is long, and I hope I have not forgotten to acknowledge your support: María Soldatenko, Judy Howard, Lora Bex Lempert, Rhonda Levine, Alejandro

Lugo, Ginetta Candelaria, Marixsa Alicea, Jodi A. O'Brien, Vilma Ortiz, Pierrette Hondagneu-Sotelo, Dula Espinoza, Lisa Armstrong, France Winddance Twine, and Maura Toro-Morn. Many of these colleagues provided audiences that included the adult children of domestics or assisted in making direct connections. I appreciate Gayatri Patnaik's interest in the project and her comments.

I want to thank several scholars who took time out of their busy schedules to discuss my project. Along with making me a delicious brunch, Ruth Behar spent an afternoon with me discussing her own experiences writing a narrative. I am grateful to Mike and María Soldatenko for their feedback on my project, and they shared insightful ways to analyze the transcripts. Of course their knowledge of UCLA politics was invaluable. One of my strongest cheerleaders and a dear friend is Marion Goldman, who constantly pushed me to write the book. Thank you for not losing patience and for believing in me. I recognize a promising young scholar and an accomplished artist, Xuan Santos. His masterful painting of the maid's daughter will not be forgotten. I owe you much. I thank Michael Elgin for sharing his photographer's skills and his excitement about the project.

At a moment of throwing out another version of the project, Tom Barone not only gave me encouragement, but his suggestions made the writing move along. I cannot express how important Tom's reading and comments on the first four chapters were. As a leading narrative scholar, his enthusiasm for the book means a lot.

Last-minute assistance includes two graduate students and promising scholars in their own right, Gabriella Sanchez and Sheruni Ratnababalsuriar. Gabriella always responded quickly to my questions about Mexico and about translating Spanish words unfamiliar to me. She always answered my e-mails quickly, and I appreciated her humor. Sher graciously helped me with computer problems. Our hikes in South Mountain fed the spirit while I was writing furiously between travels. One of these travels involved an incredible opportunity to serve on an advisory committee to the National Domestic Workers Alliance. Meeting members of the Domestic Workers Alliance gave me the inspiration to continue writing day and night. Special thanks and *abrazos* to Al-jen Poo and Jill Shenker.

A scholar and writer could not ask for a more supportive and insightful editor. I appreciate Ilene Kalish's sage advice and patience. I am glad she dissuaded me from writing as an invisible recorder and convinced me to use my sociological imagination to outline the book. I am not sure I have completely succeeded in keeping myself visible throughout the project, but I recognize the significance of her guidance.

Needless to say, the project would not have been possible without Olivia. I appreciate all the time she spent with me, inviting me into her home and into her life. She shared her experiences, emotions, and an extraordinary witty sense of humor. Getting to know her family was a special gift that I treasure. Stepping into her life has been a wonderful adventure that has taught me a great deal about the complexity of mother-daughter relationships and friendships that cross race and class divides. She is a brilliant sociological observer and knows how to "read" all the social cues to be in control.

And the most significant person, besides Olivia, in this project is Eric Margolis. He always accommodated Olivia's visits by providing great food and drink. Over the past two decades, he never doubted my ability to finish this project. Even when I had doubts, he was there to tell me that I would write the book when the time was right. The fact that he thought this project too significant to stop gave me the energy to keep moving on—even at my snail pace. Finishing this book would have been a painful experience if I could not rely on his humor, sarcasm, and cooking talents. Facing his own manuscript deadline, he read the complete draft. And, of course, he sharpened his highly regarded editor's fingers and made suggestions that greatly improved the final draft. I welcome them all!

Of course, all shortcomings and disappointments for whatever omission the reader finds say a lot about my discomfort with putting myself at the center and my attempts to protect the identity of Olivia. Any errors are most likely mine.

Introduction

When people exist under one roof, a tiny society forms, ... the stuff of novelas: masters and servants unconsciously dancing in lock step so that, when things go wrong, traumas converge. —JAMES L. BROOKS, *Spanglish*

She's just a displaced person. She doesn't belong in a mansion but then she doesn't belong above a garage either. —SAMUEL A. TAYLOR, *Sabrina Fair*

She had spent her whole life working for de la Torres, and it showed. If you stood them side by side—Mrs. García with her pale skin kept moist with expensive creams and her hair fixed up in the beauty parlor every week; Mamá with her unraveling ray bun and maid's uniform and mouth still waiting for the winning lottery ticket to get replacement teeth—why Mamá looked ten years older than Mrs. García, though they were both the same age, forty-three. . . ."
  "The girls, they treat you well. Doña Laura has a special place in her heart for you."
  "I know, Mamá but they're not our family." —JULIA ALVAREZ, *¡Yo!*

A story of a child growing up within a household where her mother or father is employed as a maid, nanny, or butler can conjure up a plot filled with opportunities for social mobility. Sabrina, in both novel and film, elevates her social status from chauffeur's daughter to wife of the employer's son. In *Spanglish,* Cristina (the maid's daughter) takes a journey all the way to Princeton University. Sarita (from *¡Yo!*) is rewarded for determination and hard work when she becomes an orthopedist at "one of the top sports medicine clinics in the country" (71–72). Indeed, a common plotline for the children of live-in servants is rags to riches. Transformation from the servant class to the employer class is imagined as a result of gaining access to privileges and exposure to the lifestyle of the upper class. Living in the employers' household allows them to see how the upper class lives, creating desires to escape the social status of their birth. Less often does popular culture imagine servants' children rising above their ascribed class as a result of their parents' hard work and of witnessing the working-class capital of entrepreneurship. Nor are the complexities of the daughter-mother bond considered when employers insist that both are "like one of the family." As the daughter is positioned to take advantage of the selected privileges that employers offer her, there is also tension that her upward mobility will leave the parent behind. This is not a surprising theme since social mobility in the United States calls for children to assimilate into the mainstream, leaving their culture of orientation and embracing middle-class whiteness.[1]

As in literature and film, the voices of the children of domestic workers are seldom explored by scholars.[2] Yet many researchers acknowledge that social relationships surrounding paid household labor and care work are ideal places to investigate social inequality.[3] If we adjust the kaleidoscope to include the employees' children, we can see the impact that these inequalities have on the workers' children and how the division of household labor and care work reproduces social hierarchies in society. Frequently negotiated informally behind closed doors, the less appealing work ascribed to mothers and wives is commodified as low-wage unskilled labor. Household labor remains largely the job of women and is structured around class, race, ethnic, and citizenship inequalities.

DISCOVERING THE HIDDEN COSTS

My intellectual journey into domestic work from the perspective of workers' children began in El Paso, Texas, in 1986 when I met Olivia María Gomez Salazar.[4] Olivia was an attractive twenty-three-year-old Chicana who could easily blend in with other Latina students. Her dark hair and brown eyes were highlighted by her light complexion. At five foot three, she did not draw attention with her physical appearance, but rather her assertive speech and posture commanded one's undivided attention. Her wit, humor, and expressive storytelling are marked by her competence in focusing her entire attention on you. As she approached me after a panel discussion and we talked about my research and similar writings on domestic workers, I got a glimpse of her magnetic personality. It was not until a year later that we actually sat down together and she told me about her experiences.

With a great deal of emotion, she told me that her mother, Carmen,[5] was a live-in maid in Los Angeles and that she had lived with her mother in her employers' home from the age of three to eighteen, when she left for college. She lived in the maid's quarters with her mother in "Liberty Place," a gated and extremely wealthy community, for fifteen years. Most of this time was spent in the Smiths' household, which consisted of Mr. and Mrs. Smith and their four children: two daughters, Jane and Rosalyn, and two sons, David and Ted—all older than Olivia. Mr. Smith was an agent in the entertainment business, and Mrs. Smith was a traditional stay-at-home mom. When financial circumstances prohibited the Smiths from hiring Carmen full-time, their work arrangement changed, allowing her to work for other employers in the neighborhood during the week. Although Olivia's entry into the employers' household was first restricted to the maid's quarters, the Smiths moved her out of the maid's quarters and into one of the spare bedrooms when she was ten. Although her mother was relegated to the maid's quarters and she was roomed alongside the employers' family, Olivia was never completely integrated into the Smith family or all their community activities. In Olivia's case, the old adage "just like one of the family" becomes particularly confusing as the social boundaries between "being like one of the family" and "the maid's daughter" became blurred and in constant flux.[6] Each social position demanded completely different expectations. These changes frequently placed Olivia at odds with her mother, even though the only real and legal status within the household was the mother-daughter relationship between Olivia and Carmen. Rising to the surface are the stories highlighting Carmen's fear that she would lose her child to the Smith family and Olivia's fear that she would lose her mother to the employers.

Olivia confided that she rarely revealed her background to other Latinos because her complex circumstances could raise issues of ethnic and class authenticity.[7] I sensed an urgent need in Olivia to talk about her childhood, spending the school year in the Smith household in the gated community and summers in Mexico with her extended family. On reflection, I understand that the process of talking about her experiences and emotions allowed her to contextualize her identity as a proud Chi-cana. I am confident that she viewed me as a Chicana academic who would empathize with her complicated relationships and mixed emotions toward her mother's employers and with her concerns for her mother's health and future.[8] At the end of our first conversation, Olivia was not finished talking, and I was not finished listening. Not yet having a clear research focus, I asked Olivia if she was interested in engaging in a life-history project with me. She immediately agreed and expressed enthusiasm and commitment to the project. I explained that I wanted to tape-record her stories and then analyze and write about her experiences. As a university graduate, she had no problem interpreting my request and gladly gave informed consent to the interviews. She expressed as much excitement about starting the project as I felt about conducting the research. We exchanged contact information, and I agreed to call her in the next few months to work out the logistics for a long visit before the year was over.

Shortly after this first interview, I was approached by another adult child of a domestic worker. Following my presentation at a northern California university, several students approached me. Out of the corner of my eye, I watched a Latina holding back in the line. After speaking to several people, I turned to her, and before she was able to say more than a sentence, the tears ran down her face. I suggested we talk in a more private corner in the room. She immediately apologized and explained that she had never heard a professor frame domestic service as legitimate employment, that is, as work worthy of study or of any importance. As a student at an elite university, she always concealed the fact that her mother worked as a private household worker in the Bay Area. While expressing pride for all the hard labor that her mother did to help her pursue a college education, she also internalized shame over her mother's low-status employment of cleaning other people's dirt. This shame was intensified by sitting in classes each day with the children of employers. Sensing a willingness to share her experiences, I asked her if she felt comfortable about meeting the next day for an interview. She was thrilled. Like Olivia, she had held a secret about her background and wanted to talk to someone who framed private household labor as "real work" with dignity. Encountering an academic researching domestic service validated her experiences and gave her legitimation in a social place where she had felt as an outsider and tried to fit in by concealing her mother's employment.[9]

In the next several years, my encounters with the adult children of domestic workers at conferences and invited lectures increased. Given the venues, the adult children I met were graduate and undergraduate students, law students, faculty, and university administrators. Although they are clearly not representative of all children of maids, nannies, and private household workers, I found them ideal interviewees.[10] Few adults in academia are the sons or daughters of domestic workers, nor are those who are likely to find themselves in the same social space with employers and their children. My presenting research in an audience including employers and children of employers allowed these children of domestic workers to hear uncensored views and attitudes toward workers like their mothers, aunts, and neighbors. After hearing classmates or colleagues make condescending remarks about how workers should be grateful for the opportunity to work and learn skills applicable to moving into the formal labor market, many of these adult children approached me to share their own experiences.

I began recording recollections of their mothers' work experiences from their perspective. Their stories added a dimension to domestic service that I had not found by interviewing domestics or nannies. I shifted the focus of analysis from the employer's home to the worker's family. In my first book, *Maid in the U.S.A.*, the focus of analysis had been the employer's home, without a comparable examination of employees' families. I did compare and contrast the differences in the division of household labor between wives and husbands. Working-class men engaged in more repairs, cooking, and other household activities than did middle-class men, who were more likely to purchase the labor of others.[11] Framing domestic and care work from the perspective of the maid's child provides an important view into the family-work dilemmas that shape working women's lives. Rarely has the dilemma of "women's work" been seen from the child's viewpoint.[12] What does it mean when working mothers are too tired to spend quality time with their children at the end of day? How does the child interpret "work obligations" that extend into family time? How do children make sense out of receiving gifts from their mother's employers instead of employers paying their mothers enough money to improve their standard of living? How do the children of care workers feel about their mother's relationship with other children? And does their mother's occupation shape the way that children are treated by their employers and the larger community?

OLIVIA'S NARRATIVE

I met Olivia in Texas shortly after she agreed to participate in the research project. I arrived at her home with recorder in hand. Without much casual conversation we sat on the floor in front of a fireplace, and I turned on the tape recorder. Without an introduction or question, she immediately began her story.

> My mom was born in a place called Piedras Negras—not the border Piedras Negras but a small town in Aguascalientes, Mexico. Her father was from the state of Chihuahua. She grew up with my paternal grandfather's relatives and spent a lot of time with her aunts and grew up with them.
>
> I understand that my grandmother's parents were very wealthy and had disowned her when she married my grandfather because of the class issue. My mother had very little to do with her mother's relatives. They were very wealthy and had a very large family, about eight children. There was a plague that killed almost all of the family in the early 1890s. My grandmother, whose name is Cristina Hurtado, was one of two survivors, and the other was her brother, Guillermo. He was born with no arms and worked in the circus. He was very talented. He could eat with his feet and worked in the rodeo and did these things with his feet.
>
> My mother spent a lot of time with her father's aunts and uncles in Aguascalientes. They grew up poor—very poor. He later began working for the railroad, laying tracks in Mexico. I guess it was in 1960 when he had a horrible accident. Evidently he was on one of those miniature cars used in the railroad to carry work supplies and had an accident in a tunnel. He came head-on with the train, which cut off his legs from his knees down. He died of gangrene.
>
> I understand that at the time he had the accident, my grandmother and grandfather were already separating because there had been rumors that he had been with other women. So the family had already split up, and my grandmother had moved to a small town about a hundred miles outside Ciudad Juárez in a place

called Moctezuma. My grandfather was still giving my grandmother money, but they were pretty much independent.

My mother's older sister was shy and wouldn't do any work activity outside the home. She was kind of wimpy. She cried all the time and didn't take responsibility for the family. I guess it was just my mother's very strong personality, but she began working. My mother got ideas of things to do to make a living from my father's sisters. Her aunts used to make asaderos and enchiladas. My mother put them in a basket and waited for the trains at the stations to sell to the passengers. Working with her aunts was how she began to travel. She was the first one to get a job and move to Ciudad Juárez. My mother's sisters stayed and did things in the house.

When she was around fifteen or sixteen, she got a job as a domestic in Juárez. Her family still lived in this town that was about seventy or eighty miles from Ciudad Juárez. She got on the train and went to work in Ciudad Juárez during the week. She told me that once when they worked in El Paso, there was a Chicano who didn't like immigrants, and he called the INS on them. So they had to leave. Their employers hid them when the INS came to the door. They got caught by the INS when taking the bus to the Country Club area.

Later my mother had a passport and was able to go across the border to work for different families in what is now called the Country Club area—the wealthy area of El Paso.[13]

My mom got her papers when she was in El Paso, and she was really young. She told me that back then it wasn't hard. All she needed was a Mexican passport, a job, or someone to sign for you. She was in her twenties at the time.

One of the first families she worked for was a family named McLaughlin. They had a couple of kids, and my mother took care of the kids, as well as cooked and cleaned. She had a really good relationship with the kids. Evidently, they were very wealthy, because they had a driver, a chauffeur, and one other woman who worked there—I am not sure in what capacity. My mom stayed there during the week, and on Fridays she'd get on the bus in El Paso and went to Moctezuma to see her family.

Later she worked with this family in El Paso who was very wealthy—upper-class Mexicanos living near the country club. They now own one of the *maquiladora* plants in Juárez.[14] The family had two twin daughters. One was named Olivia, and the other was named María. My mother decided that they had such pretty names, she decided to name me after them. That is how I got my name, Olivia María.

My mother and her sister met some people in Ciudad Juárez, and they got an apartment. My mother had an outgoing personality, and that was how they met people and developed a network. She met somebody living there that had a restaurant. This person brought her friends from Moctezuma to live in Ciudad Juárez and to work at the restaurant. Instead of going out and working as a domestic, my aunt worked at the restaurant. She cooked, cleaned, and waitressed. My mom was the only one in the group that went out and worked as a live-in domestic. She came home sometimes during the week and stayed with them in the apartment.[15]

By this time, her father had already passed away, and she was making most of the money in the family. My mother describes the family situation as never having counted on him for much. I am sure she was already supporting the family when he died. My mother was making eight dollars a week, and most of it went to supporting her family. My mom had already moved all of the family to Juárez and had bought a small little house in Juárez. Then her other brothers and sisters got jobs in Juárez. The house and everything were under my mom's name.

When she was working in El Paso, she met other women working in the Country Club area. She made friends with them, and they later became my godparents. She went with them to Los Angeles after they got caught by the INS and decided to leave El Paso.[16] They convinced my mom to leave with them. One of them had a car, and they drove to Los Angeles. She and her friends rented an apartment in the San Fernando Valley, and they all lived together. There were five of them. There was only one man, Mr. Cordova, his sister, and another two females, and my mother. They were all from Juárez. At the time, my mother was probably about thirty-one. I don't know how traumatic it was for my mom to pick up and leave her family.

Initially my mom worked in the garment industry with the other women. She worked there a short time, about six months to a year. My mother decided that she didn't want to work in the garment industry because she wasn't making enough money and never had inclinations to sew. I don't think she knew anything about sewing, and she decided she wanted to clean houses. That was the kind of work she had originally done in El Paso and found it a lot easier. My mother is a really hard worker. She will work a fourteen-hour day without thinking about it.

She then went to a domestic agency. None of her friends did domestic work. She went to this agency, and she got placed in an area called Liberty Place. It is a private neighborhood with the streets blocked off. She started working there with a family, the Dillards. They had a huge six-bedrooms home. There was another lady working there, Delia. Mrs. Dillard wanted two people to help her. They had eight kids, and my mother had the best relationship with them. My mother always had strong relationships and interacted with the kids.

She lived at the Dillards' house in an apartment above the garage. The houses in the neighborhood were all structured that way for their help. The apartment had a refrigerator, a little kitchen, a bedroom, and bathroom. That is where my mother lived. She lived alone in the apartment. Inside the house there was another room where Delia lived when they were both working there. I think my mother worked there for two years. After Delia quit and went back to Mexico, my mother worked alone in the house.

My mother helped Mr. Cordova find jobs in the neighborhood where she worked.[17] The people who lived there asked my mother if she knew someone to paint, and she would get him jobs. Mrs. Dillard asked my mother to find people to work for her friends. Many of my mother's friends worked in the area. I can't imagine how my mother and Mrs. Dillard communicated, because my mother did not speak English.

Somewhere along the line my mother met my father. He was a construction worker. My father was from Tampalitas. I have never made any attempt to find him. I don't think my mother knew him for a very long time, because she doesn't know very much about his family. She never really talks much about that relationship at all, except that she was never really in love with him and there wasn't much of a relationship. They met at this restaurant, and they saw each other for about a month—not very long. His name was Alejandro Salazar. She never really talks about him. They talked, and they went out. He picked her up on a Sunday, and they went out. Afterwards, he took her back to the house where she worked.

My mother describes it as though she knew that he was leaving. He had a car. My mother made a statement to him about having a flashlight, a map, and certain travel things in the glove compartment of the car. She asked him if he was leaving her or going on a trip. My mother said it sarcastically because she already knew he was going somewhere. He didn't say anything about it, and the next week he didn't come back. I don't know how far along her pregnancy was or whether her pregnancy had anything to do with his leaving. My sense is that he never even knew she was pregnant.

My mother said that she was crying and that is how the Dillards found out that she was pregnant. My mother was really worried about losing her job because she was pregnant. Evidently she had been very small, and you could not tell she was pregnant. She just looked a little overweight. She continued to work up until a week before I was born. She had a really good relationship with Mrs. Dillard. She asked my mom what she planned to do after she had the baby. My mother said, "Just continue working or maybe go back to Mexico for some time." Mrs. Dillard told her about St. Ann's, which is a hospital for unwed mothers. My mom went to St. Ann's, and that is where I was born. It was a Catholic hospital. I was born on June 7, 1963. My birth certificate says my mother was thirty-six.

My mother was still very close with the five friends she came with from El Paso. She had been living with them on the weekends. My godmother and godfather picked my mom and me up at the hospital and took us back to their place. We stayed in Los Angeles till I was about six months, and I was baptized in Los Angeles by Mr. Cordova and his sister. My mom was still working. Mr. Cordova's sister, María Rosa, did not have a job, and she took care of me. I was there probably three to six months, until my mother decided that we were going to leave and go to El Paso. She decided she needed somebody to take care of me. My godfather was driving back to Juárez, so we got a ride with him.

❊ ❊ ❊

My mother didn't tell my grandmother that she was pregnant. She just arrived at the door with this child in her arms.

I asked my mom, "Did my grandmother ever say anything to you or ask you anything?"

"No, we never talked about it."

I don't know what my grandmother's reaction was. My grandmother had a different relationship with my mother than with any of her other kids. My mother had been supporting her and the family while she was in Los Angeles. My mother got away with doing certain things because she was the one who supported the family. Nobody ever said anything—not "How did you get pregnant?" or "How did this all come from?" or "Why?" My mother supported the family. So if she wanted to come home with her baby, that was her business.

By then, my mother was not the only single parent in the family. My mother's oldest sister had gotten married and had two children. The first child died of some illness. After she had her second child, her husband was murdered. She was a single parent with a son, who is ten years older than I am. My mother's other sister is named Ofelia. I am not sure if she ever got married or was living with some-body. He was an Asian Mexicano. Somehow he had Asian ancestry, because his last name was Wong. My aunt had moved in with his parents, as was the custom among the Asians. Evidently her mother-in-law didn't like her. She finally took her baby and left the family and her husband. So when my mother came back to her house in Juárez, her two sisters had children living there as well.[18] So my grand-mother wasn't really going to say much, because that was pretty much the way things were. There were five in my mother's family. Her younger brother and sister were not married—so three of them were single parents.

❋ ❋ ❋

My mother immediately started working in El Paso once again. She left me with my grandmother and her sisters who weren't working. I stayed there until I was two. My mom crossed the border into El Paso and worked as a domestic. This time she worked as a day worker. My aunt, my mother's older sister, Ofelia, spent a lot of time with me.

One thing I remember from my childhood is going to Aguascalientes on the train with *mi tía* Ofelia. She wanted to take me with her to Aguascalientes for a month or two because my mother's younger and only brother, Ricardo, was get-ting married. He lived in Aguascalientes and worked as a taxi driver. My aunt was going to go and help prepare for the wedding. She wanted to take me with her. I was about a year and a half.

My grandmother was very much against it. She told my mother, "*Carmen, si se lleva a esa nina, no te va a conocer ni va a tener nada contigo.*" [Carmen, if she takes the child, she will not know you, nor will she want anything to do with you.]

I don't know why my mother decided to let me go, but she went against my grandmother's advice.

She said, "Go ahead. Take her."

I went with my aunt. I remember we went on the train. The train derailed and tipped over. We had to walk a great distance before we were out of danger of an explosion.

Aguascalientes was a really small town at the time. It had maybe ten thousand people. We stayed there for about three months. I was always with my *tía* Ofelia, and I called her "Mama." To me she was my mom.

Right before the wedding they kept telling me that "Your mother is com-ing. Your mother is coming." I didn't understand, because my mother was right here.

I remember that my mother came on the train. It was so strange because she had a hat box. She was a completely different image to me. I remember the hat box because it was so significant. She was so cosmopolitan, so different, so worldly. My aunt was so traditional, with her little dresses and skirts. She looked like all the other *señoras*. But my mother had this whole different appearance to her. It was really strange.

I didn't want to sleep with my mother. I cried and cried and cried because my aunt made me sleep in the same bed with my mother. I felt her at night and realized that my mother was skinnier than my aunt. I would say, "*¡No con esta no me duermo! ¡Con esta no me duermo!*" [No, I am not sleeping with her! I won't sleep with her!] I didn't want anything to do with her. I didn't let her hold me. I didn't let her touch me or do anything. I remember after the wedding, we all went back to Juárez.

My mother had some agreement with Mrs. Dillard. She had planned to leave for a short period of time and take me back to her family in Juárez, but she intended to return. They wrote to each other. I don't know how, because my mother only wrote in Spanish. My mother only had a third-grade education. I assume that somebody translated the letters. Mrs. Dillard wrote back that she had somebody else, but she could help her find a place to work.

My mother decided that since I was two now, we were going back to Los Angeles.

My grandmother said, "You are crazy. You shouldn't do this."

Everybody said, "You are going to freak the baby. The baby doesn't want to leave this house."

But she said, "I am going to go." And she did.

At the time, people put articles in the paper about sharing rides to Los Angeles. My mother found somebody who was going to Los Angeles in a car and took me with her.

Evidently, it was a horrible experience for my mother, because I cried the entire way. I was so sad. I just stared out the window. I was just heartbroken and cried all the way. I cried and cried and cried. (Interview, January 1988)

* * *

After six hours of uninterrupted recording, Olivia leaned forward and turned off the tape recorder and announced that this was enough for the day.[19] I still recall with amazement the first interview visit. I found myself changing tapes as quickly as possibly as her recollections poured forth.

The rest of the evening we talked about a variety of topics, from university life and local and national politics to the best margarita recipes. The following morning we took a long walk along the Colorado River. She was curious about my interpretations of her experiences, particularly her accounts of growing up with the Smith family. However, I actually said very little before she began reflecting on her stories and linking certain memories that might be key to understanding her feelings toward the Smiths and her relationship with her mother. She seemed to be searching to define the source of conflicts and justifications for the continued anger, hurt, and confused emotions attached to certain events. She had given her narrative so matter-of-factly, along with laughing at the way she has internalized upper-middle-class mannerisms and expectations, that I did not realize how cathartic our six-hour interview session had been. Now it was clear that the intense interviewing the day before had stirred a lot of memories, unresolved issues, and confusing feelings.[20]

CONSTRUCTING THE STORY

This first interview session set the routine, tone, and pace for future interviews. Each of our meetings revolved around the "Olivia in charge" format. She began the interview, determined when to take a break, and announced when the day's session was over. When we returned to work on the project, Olivia did not immediately pick up where she had left off in her narrative but engaged in a similar debriefing period as she did at the first interview. At first, I did not record the debriefing sessions because they were extremely emotional and private. I relied on extensive field notes written afterward. Gradually, as the period between the formal end of the interview and debriefing shortened, I became more comfortable with listening to her analyze emotions and struggle to make sense of her experiences. She also seemed less confused and hurt in the process of linking the present with the past. These debriefings frequently took place while we were walking, driving, or cooking. As our conversation always returned to her experiences as the maid's daughter, I asked her permission to record. She agreed. I trained myself to always carry a tape recorder and plenty of blank tapes. Eventually, the tape recorder was often running as we took walks, cooked dinner, or drove in the car. However, I always turned off my tape recorder when her friends or family members entered a room and asked her a question or when she took phone calls. As the tape recorder became as common as a cup of coffee, the tapes collected random conversations, and the quality was not at its best during activities. At the end of each day, I took extensive notes and transcribed the tapes as quickly as possible in order to capture details and accounts that were not clear and to prepare for our next meeting. When busy schedules and finances limited our visits for long periods of time, we had lengthy phone conversations. She agreed to have these calls recorded.

Since we never lived in the same state, I usually made arrangements to visit her for a few days, or we tried to match our travel schedules to meet in the same city at the same time. She visited and stayed in my home a few times as well. Our arrangements were always made over the telephone, at which point Olivia gave me the updates of stories to add to the project. At times, these stories were recollections she had since our last interview, but more often they were linked to a recent visit, event, or phone call that provided updates on employers and domestic workers in Liberty Place. Sometimes she had phone conversations with Mr. and Mrs. Smith, her mother, or relatives in Mexico. Contact with relatives in Mexico also stimulated memories, particularly reminders of her mother's position as the breadwinner and their constant obligation to respond to family crises.[21] Depending on our travel arrangements, interviews were conducted over one to three days, usually intense and emotionally draining sessions. I also accompanied her on a visit to Liberty Place.

The visit to Liberty Place took place in the late '90s. Although the Smiths were no longer living there, she called another resident who had been one of her mother's employers to gain access into the gated community. After a short visit with this elderly widow, we drove around the neighborhood, and Olivia pointed out the houses of various families she had discussed over the years. Then we went to the Smiths' former home, where she grew up. This was probably the smallest house in the community and sat alongside a tall chain fence. With her engaging and disarming charm, Olivia convinced the current owners to walk us through the house. I saw the kitchen, her mother's bedroom, and Olivia's bedroom and was able to actually "see" many of the incidents she had already vividly described.

After the first decade of interview sessions, we fell into a rhythm. When Olivia experienced pauses in her own story, she turned to me and asked, "What else?" I was always prepared for these moments with a handy list of items assembled from my field notes. Only after a crisis did she pour forth without allowing interruptions for questions of clarity or detail. In these moments, she frequently recalled an event that she had mentioned in numerous interviews before and either added details previously not shared or placed the story in a context that called for additional interpretation—not necessarily a different interpretation but rather identifying the event as symbolic of an overarching tension or contradiction in her life between maids and mistresses.[22] However, she never failed to surprise me by mentioning an event that placed her emotions in an entirely different context. On reflection, I think that some of these family "secrets" were revealed as she became more comfortable with me or as she had resolved and dealt with painful memories. A few were obviously new revelations from conversations with her mother, or an event may have challenged her previous assumptions; and aspects of the experience that was previously perceived as trivial now became more significant. Certain events took on special defining moments, and she reflected back on these many times in the course of our interviews. After years of interviewing, Olivia reflected on many of the family stories she had shared:

> I can identify turning points. For a while I was really upset at how I felt that I was put in a really tough position with my family. I remember how angry I was at myself and at my mother that I was put in an unrealistic position with my family and with the Smiths, that it was a no-win situation. (Interview, July 1997)

After two decades of interviewing, I no longer found myself listening to an angry voice but rather the expressed emotions of a woman who had gained perspective on her life, even wisdom. She had no regrets but had become very content with her life as a consultant, daughter, and mother. And of course I was hearing her from my own changing perspective. Perhaps most important, as she and I grew up, we came to see and understand our own childhood experiences from different vantage points in the life process. When I began interviewing Olivia, I was an untenured assistant professor. Olivia grew from a college student to become a married, successful career woman with two children; I moved from college to college, got married, and was a dean at Yale and then a full professor. Mr. Smith died. Olivia's mom moved in with her. Lifetimes passed while we talked.

Over the years, Olivia joked with me that I was her therapist. On reflection, the role of a therapist probably does characterize our relationship at the beginning of the project. Although I do think we have become friends and have both enjoyed the project, we certainly do not share the same life experiences, nor have we made the same choices in our lives. As a consequence of the research process, our relationship became routinized in the research roles. As the researcher, I was the listener, the recorder, and my actions were primarily limited to asking questions and observing. Olivia was the focus of attention during both the formal interviews and the debriefing, and even other activities never completely moved away from the research project. I found myself observing her behavior with her mother, partners, friends, and children through the lens of the research project. Even our jokes and points of comparison were always based on her life story. In her conversations about daily activities, Olivia conceptualized her descriptions and accounts from the standpoint of the maid's daughter, especially highlighting the influences her experiences with the Smith family have had on her mannerisms, expectations, and behavior.

After our first interview in Austin, Texas, I did not imagine decades of interviewing and writing about Olivia. She is an extremely engaging storyteller and frequently moves into the character in her story and imitates both voice and gestures. The more I interviewed, transcribed tapes, wrote research memos, and coded and analyzed the data,[23] the more I found myself unable to establish an end point to the data collection and organize the final project as a book manuscript.[24] Writing journal articles and book chapters for edited collections was easy.[25] I found myself frozen, however, at the prospect of taking over five hundred pages of transcripts, field notes, and research notes to construct this life story of the maid's daughter.[26] I have written this book many times over the past decade, and each time I was dissatisfied with the direction and started the task over. Searching for a method, I read dozens of life stories conveying a smooth chronological sequence of events in storytelling.[27] I was frustrated and marveled over an author's ability to present a neatly constructed story.

Yet I know that a life narrative told over a period of time is never straightforward and is quite messy. In the end, I am glad that it took me almost two and half decades to finish the project because I would not have seen Olivia as a well-respected consultant who had blended the Mexican-immigrant community into her professional life and embraced her lessons as the maid's daughter, establishing an unbreakable bond with her mother and blending parenting styles in raising her two children. However, to reach this stage of the project has been a long journey.

Early in the project, colleagues urged me to interview the Smith family; but such a project would have required Olivia to submerge herself back into the gated community, and that was the last place she wanted to be. Olivia and I agreed this was also not possible because her mother still worked there when we began the project. We also agreed that the master-mistress story had been told many times over the centuries.[28] Other academics urged me to interview Olivia's mother and compare and contrast their experiences and interpretation of events. I considered this and decided to attempt it in 1989. Olivia called her mother, and she agreed to be interviewed. The one and only interview I did with Carmen was one of my worst research experiences. At the time, Carmen was in her early sixties. She was shorter and darker than Olivia and extremely energetic. She met us for brunch wearing her work clothes—a tee-shirt, jeans, and expensive walking shoes. She spoke only in Spanish but clearly understood English, since Olivia spoke English when she talked to both of us, and Carmen had absolutely no problem responding back in Spanish.

I began the interview by asking her about her experiences working in the gated community. Each attempt to direct the interview to her relationship with the Smiths and working in Liberty Place quickly elicited an apology for placing Olivia in the employers' household and having little time to care and raise her. Embedded in the apology were reasons why she thought she had made the best choices in raising Olivia. Her narrative was a familiar and emotional family story that Olivia and she had argued over for many years, and she could only respond to Olivia's grievances as a child. I ended the interview as soon as I could. I had never intended to make Carmen feel guilty about the difficult choices she made as a mother or to validate Olivia's grievances. The session was terribly painful. I never attempted to interview her again. When I do see her at Olivia's house, we never talk about the project.[29] As uncomfortable as the interview was, the experience made me aware of the painful impact that living at the Smith household had in shaping their mother-daughter relationship. Carmen's experience as a mother had almost always taken place within the confines of her employers' household. I recognize that Carmen struggled to interpret the meaning of her employment as a financial necessity and wanting the best for Olivia's future, but in the end Olivia constructs her own meaning from her standpoint as the maid's daughter.

I also abandoned the idea of writing a traditional life story written in only Olivia's voice and becoming as invisible as the faithful recorder. A narrative recorded over decades cannot be written without editing and selecting the transcript to include or delete. I chose to keep my sociological perspective at the forefront of the project and to develop the project around the issues that attracted my sociological interest in pursuing this narrative in the first place.[30] I use my researcher's voice to analyze Olivia's stories, and her voice is overwhelmingly present in the many excerpts taken from the transcribed interviews. Thus, the two of us participate in a complex of hermeneutic circles—she interprets, I interpret, and over time the understandings being developed morphed and changed. I made the decisions to use the same formal and informal addresses that Olivia used, which are a reflection of the power dynamics of domestic service. Over the past two decades, I have only heard Olivia refer to Mr. and Mrs. Smith by their first name once. None of the employers or their children referred to Carmen as Ms. Sanchez. When I called Carmen to make arrangements for the interview, I asked to speak to Ms. Sanchez, and after a long pause, I got the following response: "Oh, you mean Carmen."

In the end I have organized the book around the themes that emerged from stories told over the past decades. Olivia's being the maid's daughter as a child is quite different from her adolescent years, and both of those periods differ from her life as a working mother; these periods appear in separate chapters in this book. Her interaction with the Mexican maids employed in the gated community and her visits to Fernando Valley and Pico Union and to Mexico are all outside the presence of employers. Here, Olivia's status is not so much as the maid's daughter but as Carmen's daughter—a single mom who has a steady job, is able to assist other Mexican immigrants obtain jobs as household workers and landscapers, and is the primary supporter of her family in Mexico.

OLIVIA'S STORY

As I reflected on the themes emerging from Olivia's narrative, the first interview session began to take on a crucial role in constructing this book. Olivia started with the family story you read earlier; she began with her grandparents and her mother's birth and identified the economic circumstances that initiated Carmen's entry into domestic service. She recounted stories transmitted down as family lore. Later her family stories included reminiscences of events she witnessed and sometimes incorporated details of the circumstances or explanations adopted in the retelling among family members. Rather than examining and researching the accuracy or "truth" of the stories, I treat them as cultural constructions of real individuals, as well as of mythical ancestry.[31] As Olivia was positioned in the Smith household as "one of the family," her family stories are not limited to narratives of lineage and ancestral bloodlines, childhood and adolescent events in Mexico, but include significant events that mark turning points such as migration to the United States and later her journey away from the employers' gated community. Olivia's family stories are interwoven with her experiences growing up as the maid's daughter, particularly the conflict created by the employers' insistence that she assume the role and appropriate behavior of "being one of the family" when called upon. This is evident in many of the monumental events that involve the tenuous ties of fictitious kinship with the Smiths that exposed the economic basis for their relationship and Olivia and her mother's subordinate position.

By analyzing Olivia's family stories of the Smiths and her extended family in Mexico, I foreground the themes that frame Olivia's search for identity and belonging, as well as their significance in highlighting the contradictions in mainstream notions of social mobility and meritocracy. I organized her narrative around these turning points and the circumstances leading up to major family stories that explode the fragile homework boundary and highlight the embedded tensions and contradictions in maintaining the class-based racial and gender social order. I begin with

Olivia's recollections of entering the world of employers at the age of three and learning the rituals and practices of being the Mexican-immigrant maid's daughter. To a monolingual Spanish-speaking child raised in a female-dominated, Mexican household in Mexico, the employers' homes and their English-speaking families in a gated community in Los Angeles were a complete contrast. Her live-in arrangement became more stable when her mother accepted a position with the Smith family. Next, I turn to the contrast that the migrant workers' world posed for her. This social space includes the physical area within the employers' gated community but does not include their physical presence. Along with maid's social gatherings, I examine Olivia's visits to immigrant families in California and summer trips to her extended family in Mexico. Next, I focus on her adolescent years, which were marked by stories of passing as one of the family, as well as her growing resistance to her employers' values and norms and her struggle to embrace her Mexican identity. This discussion includes an examination of the consequences of exclusion and inclusion involved in the Smiths' decisions about when Olivia is to assume her place "as one of the family" and when she is to revert to the appropriate behavior of the maid's daughter. Here lie the recollections of significant events that threaten to tear the mother-daughter bond. I then analyze the unexpected barriers to Olivia's moving away from Liberty Place, the challenges of being a first-generation working-class Mexican American with the cultural capital of an upper-middle-class student, and her pursuit of a career. The following chapter moves into her adult life, including her career and family choices. As Carmen gradually moved toward retirement, both mother and daughter developed different relationships with the Smiths and with each other. In the epilogue, I discuss my last visit with Olivia as I prepared to end the project.

Before turning to Olivia's story, I begin with the question, "If the maid is caring for the employer's children, who is caring for the maid's children?" I review the literature on contemporary parenting models, highlighting the ways that inequalities between families are produced at home and rely on the low wages of women. This is followed by my research findings on the impact of domestic service on the maid's children. Building from this foundation, I discuss the significance of Olivia's story.

Who Is Caring for the Maid's Children?

The classic question, "Who is taking care of the maid's children?" is key to understanding that the employee's children go without care or are less likely than the employer's children to have a full-time adult paid to provide the same quality of care. Globalization of child care is based on income inequality; women from poor countries provide low-wage care work for families in wealthier nations.[1] Even with the low wages and variability in the market, hiring a nanny is recognized as the most expensive child-care option there is.[2] The largest number of domestic workers are located in areas of the country with the highest income inequality among women. In regions with minimal income inequality, the occupation is insignificant.[3] Particular forms of domestic labor affirm and enhance employers' status,[4] but employers shift the burden of sexism to low-wage women workers[5] and relegate the most physically difficult and dirty aspects of domestic labor.[6] However, little attention has been given to the ways that privilege is reproduced through parenting styles and child-care arrangements and the significance that Third World immigrant women's labor plays in reproducing privilege.

MOTHERING AND THE BOUNDARIES OF PAID CARE WORK

Contrasting motherhood and childhood in the employer's and employee's families, the divisions of work and family are revealed as structural issues that transcend the purely personal. Both employer and employee families have child-care needs, but their purchasing power presents completely different options—placing the children of domestics at an enormous disadvantage. Contemporary child experts advocate two types of ideal parenting, commonly referred to as *intensive* and *competitive* mothering. Intensive mothering is based on the ideology that mothers need to devote themselves to raising their children and that mothers should ultimately be held responsible for the welfare of their children. In order for working women to fulfill this function, time is differentiated between quantity and quality, with quality time being most valued. In addition, financial resources are required to assure an abundance of cultural and educational opportunities. Competitive mothering involves providing children with activities that assure their ability to be successful. Intensive and competitive mothering revolves around individuality, competition, and the future success of one's children.[7] Competition and individualism are values embedded in children's activities.[8] Sociologist Annette Lareau refers to this version of child rearing as "concerted cultivation" geared toward "deliberate and sustained effort to stimulate children's development and to cultivate cognitive and social skills."[9] Concerted cultivation aims to develop children's ability to reason through their negotiation with parents and by placing value on children's opinions, judgments, and observations.[10] Family leisure time is dominated by organized activities for children, such as sports, clubs, and paid lessons (e.g., dance, music, tennis). Most children's time is structured by adults rather than child-initiated play. "Play is not just play anymore. It involves the honing of motor skills, communication skills, hand-eye coordination, and the establishment of developmentally appropriate behavior."[11]

Aspects of intensive and competitive mothering are at odds with demanding careers. Everyday practices of intensive mothering require immense emotional involvement, constant self-sacrificing, exclusivity, and a child-centered environment. These mothering activities are financially draining and time consuming. Mothers with disposable income often use commodities to fulfill aspects of intensive and competitive mothering that enhance their children's education experiences.[12]

Hiring a live-in immigrant worker, for those who can afford it, is the most convenient child-care option for juggling the demands of intensive mothering and a career.[13] "As care is made into a commodity, women with greater resources in the global economy can afford the best-quality care for their family."[14] The most burdensome mothering activities (such as cleaning, laundry, feeding children, and chauffeuring children to their various scheduled activities) are shifted to the worker. Qualities of intensive mothering, such as sentimental value, nurturing, and intense emotional involvement, are not lost when caretaking work is shifted to an employee.[15] Employers select immigrant caretakers on the basis of perceived "warmth, love for children, and naturalness in mothering."[16]

Different racial and ethnic groups are stereotyped by employers as ideal employees for housework, for child care, or for live-in positions. Stereotyping is based on a number of individual characteristics—race, ethnicity, class, caste, education, religion, and linguistic ability—and results in a degree of "otherness" for all domestic servants. However, such a formalization of difference does not always put workers in the subordinate position, and employers' preferences can vary from place to place. Janet Henshall Momsen has noted that "professionally-trained British nannies occupy an élite niche in Britain and North America."[17] Interviewing employers in Los Angeles and New York City, Julia Wrigley observed that Spanish-speaking nannies were identified by employers for their ability to broaden the cultural experience of their children, particularly in exposing them to a second language in the home.[18] Employers referenced the growing Latino population in their community and the long-term benefits for their children to learn Spanish.

Cultural standards for contemporary mothering are geared toward reproducing the family's place in society. This is partially accomplished through socialization into class, gender, sexual, ethnic, and race hierarchies. Employment of immigrant women as caregivers contributes to this socialization. Children, reinforced by their parents' conceptualization of caretaking as a "labor of love,"[19] may assume nannies' natural abilities for care and service. Growing up in race- and class-segregated communities, these children are likely to learn a sense of entitlement to receive affection from people of color that is detached from their own actions.[20] As children move from their home, located in class- (and frequently race-) segregated neighborhoods, to school (also likely to be segregated), power relationships and the larger community's class and racial etiquettes are further reinforced. Child-centered homes with full-time nannies will tend to raise children to be consumers of care.[21] Privilege is learned as children acquire a sense of entitlement to have a domestic worker always on call to meet their needs.[22] Children are likely to internalize images of themselves not as members of a community or society but rather as independent individuals who are not responsible for the care of others. Nannies are rarely given parental authority over the child but follow employers' instructions. Parents reprimanding nannies in front of their children or treating them as nonequals conveys the message of inferior status between worker and family members. Systems of class, racial, ethnic, gender, and citizenship domination are taught to children by witnessing "the arbitrary and capricious interaction of parents and servants; moreover, sometimes they are permitted to treat domestic servants in a similar manner."[23] Caretaking without parental authority does not teach children reciprocal respect but rather teaches the treatment of women of color as merely means and not as ends in themselves.[24] The division of labor between a mother and a live-in caretaker or domestic is reinforced by allocating the most burdensome and manual labor to immigrant women of color. This gendered division of labor serves to teach traditional patriarchal privilege as well as teaching class, race, and citizenship inequalities.[25]

Immigrant women of color employed as domestics are likely to be exposed to exploitative working conditions, particularly if they have live-in arrangements. Live-in conditions are most vulnerable for workers because they have less control over their working hours, may not be given adequate food, may be denied privacy (e.g., sharing a room with the employer's child), may barely receive minimum wage or benefits, may lack job security, and may be exposed to emotional, physical, and sexual abuse. Exploitative working conditions for immigrant domestics and nannies increases opportunities for "learned helplessness and class prejudice in the child" and teaches "dependence, aggressiveness, and selfishness."[26] Conditions under which immigrant women of color are employed in private homes are structured by systems of privilege, and consequently, employers' children are socialized to these norms and values.

Third World immigrant domestics experience inequalities of caregiving firsthand as they provide labor for parents in rich, industrialized countries while leaving their own children at home.[27] Sarah Blaffer Hrdy equated mothers leaving their children with relatives in their homeland to European infants left in foundling homes or sent to wet nurses during the eighteenth century: "Solutions differ, but the tradeoffs mothers make, and the underlying emotions and mental calculations, remain the same."[28] Bridget Anderson has noted that immigrant women's "care for their children is demonstrated in the fruits of hard labour, in remittances, rather than in the cuddles and 'quality time' that provides so much of the satisfaction."[29] Transnational mothering cannot provide the "physical closeness, seen as healthy and 'normal' in the Western upbringing of a child . . . because most of the women are not allowed to take their children with them."[30] These conditions reduce mothering to the basic function of economic support. In research on Filipina women in Rome and Los Angeles, Parreñas observed the impact of economic ties rather than affective ties between mother and child separated from each other over a long period of time.[31] The absence of retirement-benefit pensions assures that workers will not be able to contribute financially to their children's future but rather will need their adult children's assistance.

In the case of the children of day workers, their life chances reflect low minimum wage, lack of health-care and child-care benefits, inflexible work schedules, mandatory overtime, and citizenship restrictions. In the case of the children of migrant workers, the loss of a parent or parents, the lack of family stability, and the commodification of their mother's love is all too common. Although these conditions apply to the children of working-poor and lower-middle-class workers who occupy a wide range of low-wage and dead-end jobs, the children of parents employed in domestic service and the low-wage caring industry frequently experience the exchange of inequities knowing that their parents are caring for their employers' families while they go without similar care. The costs of globalized care work are experienced by workers' children and thus remain invisible to families who purchase private care.

EXPLORING THE COSTS OF DOMESTIC SERVICE

Caring for children is not priceless in our society but usually relies on the cheapest labor available. Immigration policies and declining welfare benefits assure professionals of a ready pool of low-wage workers.[32] Child-care policies and programs that are not inclusive for *all* mothers, regardless of class, race, or citizenship, maintain and expand a system of privileges that relies on subordination. In this section, I report comments by some of the children of nannies and domestic workers whom I interviewed for side projects as the interviews with Olivia continued.

Like other mothers employed outside the home, private household workers and nannies are faced with the problem of child care. Child-care arrangements made by private household workers and nannies are similar to other poor and working-class mothers in the United States: mothers and fathers juggle work hours so one parent is home with the children; they call on relatives or siblings, give older siblings responsibility for child care and domestic labor, leave children alone, or in a few cases, take their children to work.[33] In my own research, second-generation Chicanos, who were more likely than other groups to live near relatives, relied on their assistance for child care:

> My uncle and my aunt came from Mexico to live, and they moved into one of the back apartments. So I think that was a big help too for her [mother] 'cause my aunt would take care of my brother. When he'd come home from school, she'd give him something to eat and stuff. (Rosa García, Mexican American child in the '60s in Los Angeles, Interview, February 1995)

Growing up in south Texas in the early '70s, Raquel Ruiz recalled learning to take responsibility for preparing meals out of necessity and the backup support provided by women relatives living nearby:

> I used to pull a chair up to the stove, and that's how I learned how to cook 'cause I'd watch my mom. If it got late enough, I would start dinner. So when mom came home, dinner was already started. And she'd *echaban las tortillas* [make the tortillas], and then my father came home really late—'cause he worked two jobs. Some days she was home early, some days she wasn't, but we had *nenas* [godmother] and *tías* [aunts] to watch us. (Interview, November 1994)

When the options for mothers was taking their child to work or leaving their child alone, some were able to get their employer's permission to bring the child to work for the day. Interviewees who were the oldest in the family recalled accompanying their mothers to their day jobs:

> I remember going there [employer's house], and it was a fancy place—kind of impressive and a lot of work. . . . I just tried to stay out of the way. I only went on days in which, you know, for some reason I couldn't go to school or was home

alone. (William Taylor, African American child in the '50s in Pittsburgh, Interview, June 1995)

The absence of available and affordable child care frequently limited options to unpaid labor. Changes in work and school schedules required flexibility and contingency plans. The irregular hours of domestic service, resulting from employers' last-minute requests, placed an additional burden on mothers to find adequate child care. Stories about child care from the perspective of domestics' and nannies' children capture nuances that are frequently glossed over or remain invisible.

In some cases, fathers worked different shifts to be home with the children; in other cases, female relatives stepped in and assisted. However, the most common impact was the shift of domestic labor and care work to the children. Interviewees described having to rush home to care for younger siblings, start dinner, and do a wide range of household chores, including cooking, laundry, and house cleaning:

> I was responsible for all the housework. Except my sister Josephina and I would draw little papers of who gets what [the household chores to do]. I did the cooking because she couldn't cook, and I was like the supervisor. Whatever she cleaned I had to make sure it was right, because my mother, given what she does, was a perfectionist. (Rosa García, Interview, February 1995)

Although at first glance the chores of these children hardly seem significant, in comparison to the employers' children, replacing their mothers' unpaid labor meant missing extracurricular activities, sports, and time for homework:

> In my eighth grade, I got into what was our drill team. I tried it for a while, but they [parents] kept saying, "You need to come home because this needs to be done, and that has to be done, and you can't stay after school to practice." So I missed too many times, so I finally dropped out. (Antonia Samora, child in the '50s in Arizona, Interview, April 1994)

The burden of household duties, particularly providing child care for the younger siblings, sometimes impacted the elder children's educational opportunities.

Most of the interviewees recalled spending a few hours alone in their homes. During this time, children were expected to contribute labor for the benefit of the household. Alex Conrad's description of his household duties was typical of all the interviewees:

> Basic rule was that we'd get home and our room had to be clean, the house had to be straight, those kinds of things. My mother would cook dinner. She would get home between six and six-thirty, put her bags down, and head straight to the kitchen to fix dinner. So our job was to have the house basically civilized when she got home. Our biggest responsibility was our room and keeping it straight, and not messing up what she had already taken care of. We had jobs like vacuuming and taking out the trash, those kinds of things. There were periods as we got older where we had dusting responsibilities, those kinds of things. She basically took care of the house, did the laundry, and all those kinds of things. She cooked, we did dishes and cleaned up the kitchen afterwards. And there was always kind of tension because we were kids and didn't want to do it right after dinner, and she wanted the kitchen cleaned up after dinner. She had a sense of "I did my work, I came home, I fixed dinner—come on now." She was absolutely right. But we were kids being kids. (African American child in the late '50s in Cincinnati, Interview, February 1996)

I interviewed one son and four daughters of immigrant women who took live-in positions. Live-in positions impose severe restrictions on domestics' ability to mother their own children. Women frequently accept live-in positions during periods of economic crisis or occasionally as a transitional process to residing in the United States. The circumstances forcing working mothers to accept live-in positions underscore the irony that Shelle Colen has pointed out: "to be good mothers, women leave their children and migrate."[34] Four interviewees were separated from their mother for a period of time. Edward Miller's mother left their home in the South during an economic crisis to take a job as a live-in domestic in New York. Since his father was unemployed, the higher-paying live-in domestic position in New York was lucrative enough to warrant separating the family. Ricardo Olivas, a Latino growing up in San Francisco in the '50s, was separated from his mother while she took a live-in position in the city. Since she was a single mother and her relatives had not yet immigrated to the United States, she had few child-care options to accommodate her working situation. However, she was able to enroll her sons in a boarding school in the area. A few children spent a number of years with their grandmothers when their mothers worked in the United States as live-in domestics. For instance, when Sophia Miller was twelve, her mother migrated to New York from St. Vincent, leaving her for four years. Once her mother obtained a green card, she was able to send for her daughter and son. Years later, as a college student, Sophia still felt the loss and rupture in their mother-daughter relationship. The following quotation points to the personal cost of transnational mothering:

Those four years I went through a lot of changes, and she wasn't there. I think growing up I didn't really need her as much as I needed her during that four years when she left. There's things I would've liked to talk to her about, and she wasn't there. Now she's around me, I really don't have that need for her as much as I did back then, and that's something I can't get over.

I've kind of resented her at first. . . . "Why isn't she coming back?" [I asked my grandmother]. "She said she was going to be gone for a month." She was gone for four years. We resented her for that for a while. I really did. (Child in the '80s, Interview, November 1994)

Two of the mothers employed as live-in workers were able to keep their children with them full-time, and one kept her daughters only on weekends:

It was extremely hard for her to spend the weekend away from us where we didn't really know anyone here. I spent most of the time during weekends with my father, but so then as she got to know the *Patrona* [mistress], we were able to go there with her and spend the weekend with her. And she really liked us, and she actually liked us to talk to her two children—the little girl was five and the little boy was two or three. She liked us to speak to them in Spanish. They were fluent in Spanish and French and English. (Gloria Salas, a child in the '70s in Texas, Interview, January 1993)

The two children who were permitted to live with their mothers in the employer's residence both began by sharing the maid's quarters with their mothers as small children, and as the employer's children went to college and vacated their rooms, they moved into their own rooms—the same path Olivia and her mother followed. In each case, the employers were unable to pay a full-time salary to the children's mothers, thus requiring the mothers to do day work throughout the neighborhood. After working for other employers in the day, they returned to the employer with the maid's quarters and continued working for their room and board and a small salary. The arrangement was maintained through most of their working lives because living-in with one employer and doing day work allowed the workers to enroll their children in some of the best schools in the country.

> My mom decided the atmosphere of the house was very good to bring me up in. That Jackie [the employer] said it was fine: "Please bring your son here. He can grow up here. He can go to the schools in the neighborhood." They were very good schools.... I even had my own room. It was the room of the oldest sister, who moved out of the house. Initially I lived with my mother. I had a crib and everything. But once I got old enough to have my own room, I moved up there. I was seven.... After the second divorce she [Jackie] was concerned about finances. Jackie didn't have that much money. She [mother] thought that the environment was good, ... even though a lot of her compensation was pretty much just room and board for the two of us with a very nominal salary. I think it was very low. It was like forty dollars a week. She decided it was better to stay and to do day work so that I would have enough money to pay for things, like day camp for me in the summer, clothes, stuff like that. (David Duran, Latino child in '70s in San Jose, California, Interview, April 1990)

However, in each case, the boundaries between family and work were blurred, and the distinction between paid and unpaid labor disappeared. Live-in versus day work is the major factor shaping the kind of mothering workers engaged in.

Boundaries marking paid and unpaid caregiving were significant in identifying the divisions between work and family. Acting as a mother-manager, or making decisions and arranging events, was a distinguishing feature of parental activities.[35] William Taylor noted the employer's requests that he perceived crossed the line from paid child care to parenting activities:

> My mother took care of these kids. I think the girl and I were the same age, and I used to go over once in a while. This woman [employer] just kind of turned over her house to my mother, and she ran it. This woman kind of depended on her [mother] for all these little things in life that we normally take care of. She [employer] would say, "Look, could you take the kid out"—I don't remember the kid's name—"and get clothes, school clothes?" So then my mother would get in

the car, and they'd go out, and she'd buy her school clothes for the year. She [employer] would leave them money. (Interview, June 1995)

Edward Miller concluded that his mother had indeed been the principal caretaker throughout the lives of the employer's children:

She [mother] actually raised their kids. And she knew more about what was going on in their lives than they [employers] did. I only experienced her [mother] from I guess five-thirty to eight at night, for three hours of the day, because we had to go to bed at that time, at eight or eight-thirty at night. And the little white kids got to benefit from her all day. (African American child in the '40s in North Carolina, Interview, March 1993)

Employers' requests for employees to work longer hours decreased the time mothers spent with their own children, leaving children to perceive aspects of parenting as a privilege. Time spent at work, the demand to work late,[36] and requests to take work home are all factors influencing the rearing and socialization of workers' children. Circumstances of child rearing for immigrant and poor women employed as household workers differ from those of their employers. Middle-class children may not spend much more time with their working mothers than the children of domestics do, but they are provided a parental substitute. An employer's request for employees to do work in her home changes the quality of time she can spend with her own children. This sometimes involved employers' requests for domestics to cook particular kinds of ethnic food that were not readily available and took hours to prepare. Sal Lujan remembered his mother cooking tamales for her employer's party in Texas. Luis Chavez recalled that the employers' grown children occasionally spent the night when he was growing up. As he returned home from college, Luis resented the fact that the employers' requests to his mother were now extended to their grandchildren.

When she was cleaning houses, she was also doing that type of chore [child care]. She might even take children into her house for a weekend. And now it's taken a strange twist. During football season, the admiral [employer] flies in his children for a big football party. And while they're at the football games, all of his children's children, the young kids, are at the house, and my mother is there babysitting them. Still, to this day. (Mexican American child in the late '70s in San Antonio, Interview, March 1993)

Ironing, cooking, sewing, and child care may not be entirely opposed by workers because they can care for their own children while earning money. However, these tasks extend the number of hours the worker is engaged in paid labor; shift the cost of production (e.g., cooking equipment and electricity, food for the children) to the worker, and may include the labor of the worker's children. They also contribute to uncertainty about the length of the working day.

Several interviewees expressed feelings of competition with the employer and their children. After leaving home, they occasionally worked with their mothers in order to have more time to do family activities. For instance, Luis Chavez described working with his mother during his leave from the army in the early '80s:

> I went with her to help her clean so we could get it done faster, because I wanted to spend more time with her. (Interview, March 1993)

Feelings of competition were not entirely eliminated after the children grew up. Edward Miller provides an example of such a case:

> When I go home now and I bump into these kids who knew my mother when she was, you know—it's still a first-name basis. "Oh, yes, Darlene, I know your mother. Oh, she raised me," and all that, you know. I want to say, "Yeah, she raised me too, you know!" (Interview, March 1993)

Alex Conrad resented employers pressuring his mother to work after she retired, particularly when her sons were home from college for the weekend:

> I remember some calls from one or two of them after my mother no longer did that kind of work: "Could you come on Saturday and do some work for me?" And she would do it sometimes for a while, though it meant massive protests from me and my brothers. I don't know if our protests were the reason she didn't do it, but we certainly voiced our opinions when she no longer needed to do it. (Interview, February 1996)

The lingering presence of work relations entering the family space is evident in both Edward's and Alex's stories.

Rituals and practices of deference that characterize servitude are powerful tools of instruction for teaching privilege. Embedded throughout the adult children's stories were illustrations of how children learn about privilege. One of the most poignant and painful lessons was recalled in Edward Miller's image of the employer's crying son clinging to Edward's mother and the knowledge that the son was allowed to express such ownership over his mother:

> I remember going with my father—I guess I must have been four years old, because I could actually physically stand up on the seat—back then they didn't have car seats and seat belts and all of that. So I would drive with him standing up on the seat, the front seat of this '47 Chevy we had. We went over to the house where my mother worked—the white family that my mother worked for—and this little boy, this little white boy about my age, was crying his eyes out because my mother was leaving. I remember feeling a twinge of jealously and downright anger because I had been taught never to cry when my mother left because that was something she had to do. So I had already been trained not to express that kind of emotion. "Get used to it. Your mother has to go to work." And here is this little white boy expressing all of this anguish and emotion because my mother was leaving him. My father had gone to pick my mother up from work, and she was trying to excuse herself from the little brat, and he was crying his eyes out. And I am sitting there watching this, and I couldn't cry; I wasn't supposed to cry. So that was the first hint of caste and class differences and culture and all that.
> (Interview, March 1993)

Edward's memory harbored powerful messages of class and race domination, as well as privilege.

Class, race, and gender hierarchies were conveyed to the workers' children through rituals and practices commonly discussed and analyzed in the literature on domestic service: linguistic and spatial deference and practices such as giving old clothes to workers' families.[37] Workers' children were additionally exposed to their mothers' relationship to employers' children when they accompanied them to work. My interviews included two incidents in which employers requested the presence of workers' children in order to provide companionship for their own children. Edward Miller and Rosa Garcia each recounted employers' request that they play with the employers' children or grandchildren. In both of these cases, they did not feel they had a choice to refuse. Edward Miller was expected to play with the employers' youngest child. He felt the request reduced him to a "toy" for the employer's son:[38]

> As a child I met the children of a couple that my mother was working for, and the little boy, Danny, who was about six and a little spoiled brat. I was his pickaninny, and he just wanted to play with me. So anytime he would act up or demand what he wanted, my mother would call me, or my father would come and get me: "Danny wants to play with you." So I would come over, and I would play with the kid. Danny was the little brat who saw me as a huge big black toy to play with. (Interview, March 1993)

Growing up in Los Angeles three decades later, Rosa Garcia's mother was also asked by her employer to bring her daughter to work in order to play with the employer's granddaughter:

> They [employer] had a granddaughter, and so they asked me to spend the night. My mom was gonna pick me up the next day 'cause she had apartments to do in that building and stuff. What a nightmare that was. I really don't know why she [granddaughter] got so mad at me. She was really mad at me. When her sister came over, I could hear them talking about me. I was just waiting for my mother to pick me up. It was a horrible experience. Really bad. (Interview, February 1995)

Both of these accounts appear to be more stressful than the numerous recollections other interviewees recalled about babysitting employers' children when the interviewees were adolescents. Clearly, Edward and Rosa were placed in an uncomfortable situation by being forced to play with children close to their own age who had far more privileges. Two additional examples demonstrate the class and race awareness that interviewees recalled about their interaction with children their own age. Again, Edward Miller recalls an encounter with another child under his mother's care:

> No, we didn't speak. It was, like, we wanted to. It was, like, we just didn't know what to say, or we knew that if we did, we would be crossing some invisible boundary that we weren't supposed to. So whether they were boys or girls my age, we just kind of stared at each other, and that was it, you know: no expression,

no smile, no ugly faces. Nothing. Just a kind of look like we were both aliens from another planet. And we could see each other, but we couldn't understand each other. (Interview, March 1993)

Jackie Wilson recalled similar encounters from her childhood memories of growing up in Mississippi in the '50s:

I was too young to really ask my mother about a lot of things about her being a domestic. But I did see her get out of the car and seen a little girl [employer's daughter] and knew I couldn't play with her. I went to the car. The little girl would be yelling out the window, "Hi, hi." I went up to the car to play with her, but, you know, you kind of get the feeling that that's not where you belong. It's just like— "don't touch my car"–type feeling. (Interview, February 1992)

The children of private household workers did not necessarily understand the class and racial stratification, but they learned their place in it.

Luis Chavez felt the stigma of serving others while his mother was at work. He focused on protecting his dignity:

I went into the house. I just detached myself from whose house it was. I didn't put a face to any of the people there. I just followed her instructions as to what she wanted done and did it. Get it out of the way and get out of the house. (Interview, March 1993)

Mothers' low wages frequently resulted in enlisting children into the labor force at an early age. The male children were more likely to be hired by the employers to mow the lawn and to do other yard work. Since most of the work arrangements were already part of the underground economy, there were no child-labor restrictions enforced. As children and later as adolescents, daughters and sons worked alongside their mothers. Raquel Ruiz remembered specific tasks she did when she worked with her mother:

On occasion I would go with her if I wasn't in school or if I was out sick. I remember going with her to help her clean houses. I'd dust—mainly try and stay out of the way—pull stuff out of the dryer. Then I got older—fifteen, sixteen, thereabouts—I would wash windows in the summer. I would go and take the screens down, like spring cleaning kind of thing. My sister and I—we'd wash the windows and wash the screens and stuff like that. (Interview, November 1994)

Like middle-class parents who use their networks to help their children get a summer job, private household workers used their available social networks. The interviewees who had firsthand experience working as private household workers began as children with their mothers and continued as adolescents during vacations and summers. Children who did not accompany their mothers to work also had access to learning about the etiquette of race, class, gender, and citizenship. Some learned about everyday practices between employers' children and their mother through stories they heard. Learning about linguistic deference emerged in accounts of the lack of respect that employers' adolescent children gave their mothers:

> As they got older, their attitude became exceedingly patronizing. That is what I couldn't handle. When they really owed her a lot for all she did and sacrificed for them. I guess I don't know how else I would expect them to act. Just a little more respectful, that's all. (Edward Miller, African American child in the '40s in North Carolina, Interview, March 1993)

Knowledge about the lack of respect given their mothers was reinforced in their phone interaction with employers and their children. Nightly telephone calls were the most common type of employer intrusion. The purpose for the calls ranged from negotiating times and days for working to renegotiating verbal work contracts and arranging additional hours. Employers and their children also called workers at home to inquire about misplaced clothing and household items and to ask advice. For instance, William Taylor knew the range of phone calls his mother received from employers:

> I remember a lot of the younger women that she would work for would call her for child-care help—"Look, my baby is this. What do I do?" I mean, it was kind of like, "You're the only person I know that can tell me these things." I remember those kinds of calls. There would be on occasion someone would call and complain. (Interview, June 1995)

Interviewees expressed displeasure with the number of calls they received and the late hours employers called their mothers. Rosa García commented on the employers' lack of regard for their employee's family time:

They'd call for her at any hour of the night to ask her if she happened to see such and such, or if she happened to have broken something—at all hours of the night, you know, at ten thirty at night. (Interview, February 1995)

Workers' children similarly became aware of linguistic deference through evening telephone calls from the employers. For many, the phone calls were the first time they had heard their mothers treated as an inferior or disrespectfully. Rosa García remembered the calls and her mother's attempt to downplay the employers' tone.

They [employers] were very rude. They were just nasty over the phone. "Well, where is she?" One woman in particular—I can't even remember what her name is—but my mom would just say, "Oh, she's just crabby. She doesn't mean anything by it." We [siblings] couldn't stand her. I think in fact my little sister told one of these old ladies off one time. It's like they owned her or something. It's strange. They could call at any hour and be, you know, nastily demand to know where she is. It was horrible. (Interview, February 1995)

Phone calls also exposed workers' children to the linguistic practice in domestic service for the employers to refer to the domestic by her first name—regardless of her age or the age of the employers or the employers' children. Household workers had socialized their children to address all adults formally as a sign of respect. They had heard their mothers refer to employers as "Mrs." rather than by their first names. As a child growing up in Pittsburgh in the '50s, Alex Conrad was raised to refer to adults as "Mr." and "Mrs." He was shocked to hear the employers' son refer to his mother in a familiar manner:

I can remember my reaction of calling my mother at one job she was on, and a kid answered the phone, and I asked for Mrs. Conrad. I heard this kid, who had to be my age, call my mother by her first name. (Interview, February 1996)

Elizabeth Carter grew up in New York in the '50s and heard her mother referred to by her first name. She was also aware of the added insult of employers referring to the worker as "girl" or "my girl."

I don't remember them [employers] calling her "Mrs. Carter" at all. It was always "Jessie," and she was always "the girl." I remember her saying she didn't like that when they called her "the girl" or "my girl"—that sense of attachment that they tried to make out of it. (Interview, March 1996)

Latino children were exposed to another common practice in domestic service. Employers unfamiliar with Spanish names and unwilling to learn the correct pronunciation simply changed the workers' names for their convenience or Americanized them:

This is such a joke with my sister: we'd always say, "Is Molly home?" It's Amalia [mother's name]. But of course they can't pronounce it, so they call her Molly. (Carmen Hernandez, Latina child in the '80 in Chicago, Interview, May 1997)

Gloria Salas remarked on the common practice of employers referring to all Latina domestic workers as María:

Judith [employer] would call mom María. My mom would always say, "My name is Laura, not María." And I remember one time I went to go help at Judith's place, and she goes, "María, how's school?" And I immediately told her, "My name's Gloria, not María." (Interview, January 1993)

In the case of Raquel Ruiz's mother, whose name is Mary, her employers also insisted on calling her María:

They always called her María. Even my mom doesn't call herself María. She calls herself Mary. (Interview, November 1994)

As these children of domestics moved away from home and began to experience social mobility, they were less willing to accept the deferential behavior employers imposed on their mother or family members. For instance, Edward Miller was home for the holidays and was outraged by an employer's intrusion into their family time. He confronted her:

I remember one Christmas I was visiting. I was an undergraduate then, back in 1978 at Berkeley, and I was visiting home. Mrs. Jones called my mother, and my mother had taken the day off in order to be with me. This woman called up, and she was just exceedingly rude. She acted like she was talking to a dog. I picked up the phone. She asked, "Where's Darlene?" I said, "Just a minute," you know, "Who is this?" She said, "This is Mrs. Jones. I want to know where your mother is!" I said, "No, no, Mrs. Jones. No, you do not speak that way—not when you call this house and not when you're talking about my mother." Needless to say, I knew that kind of conversation or her attitude, her manner of speech was not that unusual. What was unusual was that I had picked up the phone that time. (Interview, March 1993)

Afterward Edward's mother made him realize that he might have jeopardized her job and placed her in an awkward position. The adult children of domestics I interviewed were frequently reminded that the social mobility they had achieved was not shared with their mothers, particularly those who were still working as private household workers.

The custom of employers giving away used clothes and other discarded items to their employees is unique to this occupation. The nonreciprocal nature of this type of interaction and the quality of the exchange has been written about extensively.[39] All but one interviewee recalled their families being recipients of this custom. They recalled their mothers bringing home old clothes, furniture, books, and even leftover food. The meanings attached to the custom, that they were nonreciprocal "gifts" in lieu of wages, did not vary. Some interviewees remembered the practice as important during periods of economic crisis and as a means of making ends meet:

> As time went by, they didn't want their clothes anymore. They would want to throw them away. Sometimes she'd [mother] ask for them. After a while they were just given to her, and I wore some of those clothes, especially when Alice [employer] wasn't paying my mom [a live-in domestic]. And my mom was doing day work. I think that was part of her way to supplement the cost of things that I needed. (David Duran, Latino growing up in the Bay Area in the '80s, Interview, April 1990)

However, Edward Miller held the employers responsible for the family's economic circumstances because they paid low wages and did not provide benefits. The following quotation captures the reality of needing the clothes while recognizing the symbolism of the gift:

> I [laughs] had to wear that garbage. That happened quite a bit: hand-me-downs, old clothes, second-hand presents that they probably got from their rich relatives and couldn't use them, so they rewrapped them and gave them to my mom. My mom would bring that stuff home. You know, we did pick through those clothes to see what we could use because we damn sure needed them, but it wasn't anything that we were proud of. Even back then we had pride. It was no buffalo exchange where it was kind of neat, you know, like after the '60s to wear this Annie Hall stuff and to have the kind of worn clothes to identify with the down-trodden. We were not romanticizing being poor. Not at all. No. That stuff

was second-hand. We knew it was second-hand. It was worn. It had the smell of someone else's sweat in it. No matter how many times you washed it, you didn't [get the smell out]. It was a statement about your class. It was a statement about your economic level, and it was a statement about who was keeping you there. And so we weren't at all happy about it at all. (Interview, March 1993)

Other interviewees remembered wearing hand-me-down clothes and having mixed reactions to this practice. While none of them was proud to wear the employers' castoffs, some children were not angered by the practice:

I always wanted to be a Boy Scout. But being a Boy Scout cost a lot of money. But I always had a Boy Scout shirt right. I had my Cub Scouts' shirt, and then I had my Boy Scouts' shirt. I always had one because my mother always seemed to work for someone who would give them to her. Everyone knew I wasn't a Boy Scout, They knew I got those from the fact my mother worked and got these clothes. If my mother got clothes that couldn't fit, she'd say, "Do you know anybody who can wear them?" She said, "You ask them first, because not everyone will wear used clothes." I never did understand that, 'cause up until even graduate school I would go to the Salvation Army and buy used clothes. Other people were like, "Used clothes! You wear used clothes?" Hey, I've worn used clothes all my life. (William Taylor, Interview, June 1995)

While many of the interviewees recognized that domestic service offered employment in a labor market that held limited options for their mothers and saw generosity in additional clothing, they still felt strongly that their mothers were frequently manipulated. For instance, in the following account, Alex Conrad describes how the employer pressured his mother to work on the holidays by implying she owed a debt:

This judge [employer] I mentioned, he was instrumental in our lives. My brother got a scholarship to college because he pulled strings. My brother's very bright, but it helped that he could pull some strings. But years later, this woman—the judge was dead—this woman [judge's wife] would call my mother and say, "Would you come out on Saturday and work?" One time she called, it happened that we were home for the holidays, and I got angry and my brothers got angry and, "No. We don't want you to go." And this woman would invoke "after all the judge did for you." Our response was, "Tell her that your son the college professor and your son the lawyer said that we want you home for the holidays and not going out cleaning her house." There was this real tension between just the fact that we felt that early on, but we could play her elitist games now and argue back. My mother felt obligated, and she felt bad for this woman. (Interview, February 1996)

Alex understood that workers' rights had given way to some feudalistic notion of servant-master relationship and wanted an end to the hold of loyalty and gratitude represented in a debt that never seemed to get paid.

Embedded throughout the interviewees' accounts were the distinctions between "good" employers and "bad" employers, as well as ways their mothers maintained their dignity on the job. For instance, Raquel Ruiz's work experience with her mother offered significant differences between the employee's and the employer's lives that countered some of the negative impressions that domestic service usually conveys:

I remembered when we [daughters] went to work with my mom on one occasion. One of the *señoras* said, "Well, have whatever you want in the refrigerator for lunch." "Okay." We thought, "Oh, great!" As soon as the woman turned her back and walked off, mom rolled her eyes. She told us, "*Ven pa'ca*" [Come here]. And she opened the refrigerator door. There was a six-pack of Tab and a can of tuna fish in the refrigerator. She said, "*Éstas señoras no saben como comer.*" [These ladies do not know how to eat.] (Interview, November 1994)

In taking Raquel and her sister to the refrigerator, their mom exposed the lack of generosity in the employers' invitation. Her comment pointed to the employers' incompetency as human beings and made it clear to her daughters that these were not women to admire. Characterizing employers as silly, unreasonable, and lazy was common in many of their mothers' comments.

Several mothers were critical of employers who did not pay a fair wage, Social Security, or taxes, while attempting to increase their work load and hours. Carmen Hernandez noted, after recalling the beautiful clothes she received from her mother's employers and their invitation to housesit during their vacation, that her mother always made a clear distinction that her Christmas bonus was money she had earned rather than a gift:

"They're not giving me anything. This I have earned." That was very clear to her. "This is not charity. This is what I have earned." Around Christmas they would always give her a three-hundred-dollar bonus or something like that. But it is curious to me how my mom feels. She is grateful, but she has kept the sense that "I've earned this, and it's not about charity." It's interesting to me to see how clearly that is for her. She worked in too many houses and doing too much, because these are not houses—these were mansions! (Child in the '60s in Chicago, May 1997)

Sophia Cliff celebrated her mom's stories, emphasizing how she was assertive and demanded her rights. Arriving from Barbados, her mother was determined to earn her green card as quickly as possible in order to reunite her family.

I remember the first couple she worked for. She wanted to pay taxes, but they had to go through a process in order for her to pay taxes, and they were dragging their feet about it. So my mom threatened to take them to some bureau or something. That's how she started to pay taxes. (Child in the '80s who moved to New York City, Interview, November 1994)

Like employers' children receiving middle-class privileges by accident of birth, the children of domestics are also ascribed their parents' status. Ascribing children their parents' social status illustrates forms of social reproduction that link family and work.

COUNTERNARRATIVES TO THE AMERICAN DREAM

The sons and daughters of domestic workers and nannies consistently attributed their academic and career success to their mother's hard work. Memories of their mother's value of education was supported by her efforts to obtain the best opportunities for her children. Not only had their mothers contributed wages to their children's education, but they instilled a strong work ethic and a sense of personal and familial responsibility. Moreover, these mothers served as an ideal role model, working tirelessly and not depending on others for cleaning, cooking, laundry, or other household chores. Exposed to their mothers' accounts about some employers' inability to maintain semiclean carpets, floors, bathrooms, ovens, and refrigerators, the children did not internalize feelings of inferiority but viewed these employers as incompetent in the most basic everyday tasks of life. The one-sided intimacy of the service relationship meant that domestics and nannies knew a great deal about the family life of employers, while employers knew next to nothing about their "help." My interviews with adult children captured descriptions of the employers' pampered lifestyles maintained through consumption of goods and services. Memorable criticisms of employers home life included alcoholic parents and adolescents smoking pot, wrecking cars, failing classes, and being promiscuous. Mothers told stories of employers' children who took advantage of prestigious private programs to gain entrance into Ivy League schools. On the other hand, other employers' children were applauded by longtime household workers for having spent their inheritance well to further their education or to start a new business. The adult children of domestics were particularly aware of employers who treated their mothers with respect and demanded that their children demonstrate the same respect. Some employers acknowledged their employee's added expense of driving long distances to their homes and offered to reimburse travel. A few paid vacation wages or for last-minute cancelations that would otherwise create unexpected loss of wages. A few interviewees recalled employers' cultural influences that were brought home by their mother, commonly recipes, household decor, and rearranged furniture.

When I have given presentations on Chicana household workers, I frequently heard academics espousing employers' views, arguing in question-and-answer sessions that domestic labor provided workers with valuable cultural knowledge about middle-class lifestyles, the work ethic, and the opportunity to learn or improve their English, and served as a bridging occupation to better-paying jobs. However, I was completely caught off guard to hear this same argument used to claim the academic and career success of the children of household workers. The most vivid encounter with this attitude occurred at a lecture at UC-Berkeley. In response to my presentation of my research on the children of domestic workers, a graduate student asserted that these children benefited from their mothers' experiences of cleaning and caring for upper- and middle-class families. She argued that exposure to middle-class lifestyles served as an aspiration for their children. In addition, the work experience provided immigrant and minority families access to learning social skills required for social mobility. This graduate student made assertions that completely ignored the significance of inheritance, wage discrepancies, discriminatory lending practices, inadequate health care, and the lack of educational opportunity.[40] Her understanding of the working class, minorities, and immigrants was based on distortions about these populations and shaped by a white, middle-class ideology about social mobility. To attribute these children's successes to exposure to upper-middle-class lifestyles erases the hard work and sacrifices their mothers made for them to get ahead, as well as the additional labor done by individuals who did not have access to the same opportunities as white, middle-class students.[41] Only by ignoring or denying economic structures' effect on educational opportunities can the assumption be made that their paths to the university were no different from those of the employers' children.[42]

The belief and attitudes expressed by the Berkeley graduate student reminded me of the cruel irony of the Ms. Foundation's annual "Take Our Daughters to Work Day," which was established with the goal of boosting girls' self-confidence by exposing them to career women in the workforce. This is all well and good for girls in the middle and upper classes. The fourth Thursday in April may encourage them to enter highly paid and prestigious fields currently dominated by men. For sheltered children of the well-to-do, the world of work is indeed often a hidden and a mysterious realm. But for girls whose mothers are among the majority of women laboring in the low-paid service and manufacturing sectors, going to work with mom is more likely an everyday experience—one that will probably lower self-confidence, reduce expectations, and damage self-esteem. I interviewed children whose mothers had a long history of taking their daughters to work—sponsored not by the Ms. Foundation but by low wages and the lack of after-school care. Consider Olivia's recollections:

> I started to realize that every day I went to somebody else's house. Everybody's house had different rules. . . . My mother says that she constantly had to watch me, because she tried to get me to sit still, and I'd be really depressed, and I cried, or I wanted to go see things. And my mother was afraid I was going to break something, and she told me not to touch anything. (Interview, January 1988)

"Take Our Daughters to Work Day" makes sense only if we are ignorant of social class and assume that individual choice and rational decision-making explain gender segregation and discrimination in the workplace. The practice is based on an ideology that if the next generation of girls can individually break the glass ceiling, they will also eliminate segments in the labor force in which women are underrepresented. More important, it requires a great leap of faith that these individual choices will somehow simultaneously eliminate gender-segregated, female-dominated, low-paid occupational categories such as maids, laundresses, waitresses, and so on. The status that children are ascribed is ignored in order to maintain illusions of meritocracy, opportunity, and social mobility.

Assimilation and equality of opportunity lie at the core of the master narrative that outlines a one-directional journey of integration and eventual success of immigrants in the United States.[43] The script claims that hard work produces upward mobility—assimilation completes the transformation from immigrant to a member of the American family through equal opportunity and a democratic process within an assumed meritocracy. While numerous social scientists have challenged the basic assumptions supporting the assimilationist ideology and have pointed to its serious limitations, mainstream academics continue to argue its legitimacy.[44]

As many poor and immigrant students arrive at elite universities without having experienced an array of special athletic and musical instruction or summer vacations in Europe, trips to the museum, and so on, they lack the cultural capital received in upper- and upper-middle-class families and are marked as outsiders.[45] Children of care workers, with knowledge about both social worlds, are made conscious of the privileges and entitlements received by the children of employers. They live with the sense of a "double consciousness," as first described by W. E. B. Du Bois,[46] remaining rooted in their working-class and immigrant experiences while gaining competency to maneuver within the mainstream. But incongruities between the classes are constantly illuminated. The positionality of these interviewees placed them in events and situations in which the two social worlds collided. The conflicts experienced in these social interactions are likely to expose the ways that social inequalities are constituted.[47] Keeping "one foot" in their communities of origin while negotiating work and family, children of domestic and care workers are "marginalized people" likely to reject taken-for-granted assumptions generated by mainstream ideologies.[48]

OLIVIA'S NARRATIVE OF SOCIAL BOUNDARIES AND INEQUALITY

Similar to the interviews I conducted with the college-educated sons and daughters of domestics, Olivia refused to have her mother's hard work and sacrifices disregarded and to attribute her own exposure to upper-middle-class style as key to her success. Olivia shared Edward Miller's childhood memories of longing for more time with her mother and of having employers' children refer to her mother by her first name, claiming her as their second mom. Like Alex Conrad, Olivia experienced the persistent obligations employers use to obtain additional labor from her mother. When the employers' children participated in expensive summer camps, European trips, and prestigious internships, Olivia was ascribed the same social status as her mother and was hired to babysit and walk dogs during the summer. She was also quite familiar with spatial deference, as William Taylor described while accompanying his mother to work. Olivia shared the maid's quarters with her mother and knew that Carmen only ate and sat in the kitchen or her room. Olivia also rejects the notion that domestic service serves as an entry-level job for immigrant and low-income women workers. And she has worried about her mother's declining health and the economic realities of a lack of health insurance and an inconsistent record of Social Security benefits. However, Olivia's experiences living with her mother in the employers' household provide additional insights into the contradictions of meritocracy, opportunity, and social mobility.

To frame Olivia's experience as an American success story invokes the American assimilationist ideology that erases important structural details behind the tensions and contradictions among and between the classes and racial or ethnic groups.[49] Like so many recent narratives depicting the racial, ethnic, and immigrant experiences of Black, Latino, and Asian Americans, the story of the maid's daughter names the kind of exclusion that intersects class, race, gender, culture, and citizenship.[50] Her life history captures the fluid exclusionary processes of race relationships and social structure—accomplished in the economy, family, and schools. Litmus tests for an "authentic" ethnic narrative, faced by the Black and Latino middle class, become as limiting as the assimilationist story itself. Both these narrative structures involve ignoring complex realities—combining factors over which individuals have little control: physical traits (e.g., skin color, hair texture), political circumstances (refugee or illegal immigrant status, U.S. foreign policy), and historical circumstances (expanding or declining economy). The complex negotiations of arrangements that develop between worker and employer reveal everyday practices in which systems of domination are embedded as well as the use of ideological constructs to maintain illusions of meritocracy and equality in an American Dream. The assimilationist story is a slanted and distorted version because successes are erected as the triumph of rising above ethnic and class roots by embracing middle-class values and opening the doors of opportunity available through education, instead of acknowledging the hard work of immigrant parents, building on the social capital from their ethnic culture and collective action.[51] When dominant ideologies are challenged, and contrary evidence is presented, members of marginalized groups are attacked as ungrateful or accused of demanding special entitlements that previous immigrants did not receive.[52]

Becoming the Maid's Daughter

We got to the Dillard's house. We moved into the apartment above the garage. It had a little kitchenette, a refrigerator, and everything. It was upstairs. I was just terrified.

My mother took me to work with her. She didn't cook dinner, but she served dinner. When my mother was working, I held onto her apron the entire time. I just hang onto her. Then my mother basically locked me up in this room. She told me to stay in the room or I was going get in trouble. "Take a nap." I hated taking naps. I'd just stayed awake the whole time. When I woke up from a nap and she wasn't right there, I got scared. I was just horrified at being there. One time I woke up from my nap, and I went to go look for my mother, and I fell down the back stairs. They had the washer and dryer down in the basement. They had a three-story house. I woke up terrified and ran down the stairs. I went all the way down the stairs—fell all the way down the stairs. My mother really felt guilty because she thought I had died. I was just frightened from falling down the stairs.

After my mother had been there for a while, she started to work *por días* [day work]. Instead of working the whole week with any one person, she would work Monday with another family. She got a job with the Smiths, which was in the same park area. She continued to live with the Dillards in their apartment and took me to work at the different houses. My mom worked for the Smiths, the Carsons, and the Joneses.

The Smiths lived down about a block and a half. They had four kids who were little at the time. My mother ironed for them. She started out just doing one type of job for them. Shortly afterwards, we moved in with the Smiths.

Our room in the Smiths house was downstairs. There was a breakfast room when you walked in, and there was a kitchen and a bathroom, the one my mom and I used. Then there was a little bedroom in the back of the house near the kitchen. This is the room where my mom and I slept. The refrigerator was right by the door. This was a really key issue. My mother used to get really upset because in the middle of the night when the kids got something out of the refrigerator, they woke up my mom. She used to get pissed off and say, "Goddamn it! It is night time. Why do they keep getting up at night to use the goddamn refrigerator?" The whole ice machine started up and woke up my mom. (Olivia interview, January 1988)

I begin this chapter on "becoming the maid's daughter" with Olivia's chronology of her mother's employers to frame her physical location in this new social world. Leaving her grandmother and aunts in Mexico to become Carmen's daughter in this gated community connects her identity directly to her mother's employment. The work world of mistresses and maids not only took Olivia away from the familiar physical surroundings she knew as home but locked her in a rigid schedule and routine shaped by the demands of Carmen's employment. Although Olivia never became a maid, she began her introduction to this social world by occupying the deferential space of sleeping in the maid's quarters and restricting her movement in the employer's house that is embedded in domestic service.[1] As Olivia and Carmen moved from one live-in arrangement to another, the area of the house was clearly marked off as the maid's quarters.[2]

The first "permanent" live-in arrangement for Olivia was in the Smith household. There, she joined her mother in the maid's quarters. To maintain boundaries between the maid and the employer's family, Carmen's bedroom and bathroom were in a separate part of the house. The rooms were located in an area of the house that was the maid's major work area, the kitchen. As Carmen's complaint about the refrigerator noise illustrates, employers and their family are not expected to provide the maid with the same privacy as they expect. Such disruptions of night sleep are not uncommon in live-in arrangements.[3]

Throughout Carmen's employment as a domestic with a child, she retained a live-in arrangement with one employer, because a room in the maid's quarters is guaranteed and eliminates the logistics of finding child care and commuting to work.[4] Like the Dillards, the Smiths negotiated live-in help without paying for a full-time live-in maid. The arrangement began as room and board, along with two days of full-time work with a small monetary compensation. Given the necessity to earn a full-time income, Carmen did day work throughout the gated community and in a nearby neighborhood that is part of a social network of employers belonging to the same private clubs. Carmen's combining day work with her live-in situation required Olivia to adjust to living in the maid's quarters in the evening and at night and accompanying her mother to the various day jobs throughout the week.

"DON'T TOUCH THIS. DON'T TOUCH THAT."

The major transition involved in Olivia's move into the employers' houses consists of drastically repositioning her cultural behavior, including a new language. Having spent her first three years in a female-dominated and monolingual Spanish-speaking household in Juárez, Olivia had a great deal to learn about the foreign environment presented by her mother's working conditions as a live-in maid. In some settings, her physical movement was restricted to sitting and looking at books or napping. In other houses, she was allowed to play in a designated corner of a room, and at times Olivia was asked to serve as entertainment for employers and their children. Olivia's vivid memories were sometimes painful, as the socialization process included learning deference, particularly the forms of spatial and linguistic deference that are traditionally found in domestic service.[5]

> The Dillards tried to teach me English. I really resented that. They had an aquarium with fishes. They would say, "Olivia, can you say 'fiiishhh'?" I would just glare at her, just really upset. Then I would say, "'Fish,' no. Es 'pescado.'" You know, like [they are] trying to change me.
>
> I did not want to speak their language. I did not want to play with their kids. I didn't want to do anything with them. Mrs. Dillard tried to teach me to speak English. I hated it. My mom says that I went through immense culture shock. The kids wanted to play with me! To them, I was a novelty, and they wanted to play with the little Mexican girl. I think I just had an attitude problem, as I describe it now. I didn't want to play with them. They were different. When my mother told me to go play with them, I would return a little while later and say, "*Mamá, no me*

quieren aguntar." [Mama, they do not want to include me.] Well it was obviously a communication problem. We couldn't communicate.

I got really mad one day at these girls because *no me querian aguntar.* They did not understand what I was trying to say, and we couldn't play. So I decided that I was going to go home. I didn't like this anymore. So I just opened the door, and I walked out. I went around the block, and I was going to walk home to the apartment where we lived. I went out of the house and walked around in the opposite direction around the block.

The little girls came to my mom and said, "Carmen, your little daughter left!"

So my mom dropped everything and was hysterical. One of the older daughters, who had a car, drove my mom around. They found me on the corner. My mom was crying. She was so upset.

She asked me, "Where were you going?"

I said, "I'm going home *porque no me querian aguntar.* I don't want to be there anymore. I am going to walk home." So my mother really had to keep an eye on me.

I went to the Smiths, and they had kids. There were different rules there. I couldn't touch anything. I mostly sat and played with their toys, but I didn't try to interact with them. They tried to teach me English.

The first thing that I learned was "No touch. No touch." "Don't touch. Don't touch." "Don't touch this. Don't touch that."

I told everybody, "Don't touch."

At different houses I slowly started picking up different things.

From the time I was little, my mother said, "How come you can't just sit in that chair and read?"

"Mother, because I'm bored. I've been reading for three hours."

"Well there's lots of books. Pick out another one."

"I'm tired of reading. I don't want to read anymore."

She was always really frustrated. When I went to work with her, I was expected to sit in a chair and read. I could only watch TV for an hour or two because my mother would tell me, "Oh stop. You're watching too much television. You're gonna turn out like the Smiths' kids."

There were even different rules when Mr. and Mrs. Smith were out of town and left my mother in charge.

I remember that my mother also worked for a Jewish family, the Altmans, when I was about five. Mrs. Altman had this little cast-iron stove set. It had little pans. I was allowed to play with that one toy, but only right there where it was. She let me play with it. Immediately after arriving there, I sat down in my designated area, and I played there. They had this cat clock, an old '50s one. The cat was black with eyes and a tail that turned. They gave me that clock. Sometimes Mrs. Altman took me to the market with her. She tried to talk to me. Sometimes I talked. Sometimes I just sat there in silence.

One day Mrs. Altman had a tea party. She asked me to please come out from my play area and say hello to the people. They all thought I was so cute. They threw pennies and change on the floor for me and expected me to pick them up. I didn't want to pick up the money. I went into the kitchen where my mother was working, and I told her, "I'm not picking up that money."

"Oh, yes, you are. You're being nasty. They're just being nice. Go pick up their money off the floor."

I had to pick up people's pennies and nickels that they had thrown on the floor! I just thought that was so disgusting. That was devastating to me.

I had once thought the clock was really cute, but after that I didn't like it and didn't want it. (Interview, November 1992)

Olivia's account of her early years in the employers' homes is clearly described from the perspective of the maid's daughter. She was an outsider and had to learn the appropriate behavior for each setting. Her emergence into the employers' social space is marked with do's and don'ts. Olivia's recollections of this childhood period were marked not only with learning the rules of behavior but also with her resistance to language and behavior unfamiliar to her. At times she enjoyed employers' attention, particularly since her mother was not in a position to play with her or to make her the center of attention as her aunts did in Mexico. While her interaction with employers and their children broke the monotony of spending the workday alone, Olivia also risked unpleasant interactions. Employers' and their children's attention were not always welcomed, particularly when they framed her as an object of amusement or a defective object in need of repair. She experienced humiliation at being treated as a pet or street beggar when thrown loose change and expected to get down on the floor and pick up the coins. Isolated in these monocultural environments, she experienced treatment as "the other"— the little, working-class, Spanish-speaking, Mexican child among the upper-middle-class, English-speaking, white employers and their children. Rather than attempting to learn Spanish, employers and their children insisted that she speak English. Her ability to speak Spanish was not rewarded or considered a skill; only her ability to learn English was valued in this environment. While attempting to acquire English-speaking skills, her accent became the basis for laughter and teasing by the employers' children, and sometimes by the employers themselves. Olivia was socialized to conform to the monolingual environment and to be treated as the "other." Carmen reinforced the distinction between Olivia and the employers' children by placing limits on the amount of TV that she could watch and telling her when she was "being nasty."

Olivia's account of going to work with her mother as a toddler is not a story of a child running freely and receiving intensive mothering.[6] The emphasis in her socialization within employers' homes was quite different from that of employers' male children; rather than the adults in her life advocating independence, individuality, and adventure, Olivia was socialized to conform to female sex roles, with her movement being restricted and her playing with gendered toys.[7] Learning the restrictions that limit her behavior—"No touch. Don't do this."—served to educate Olivia about her social status and roles in the employers' homes. She was clearly different from the other children, "a novelty," and bound by rules regulating her use of social space and linguistic behavior. Olivia's resistance to changing her language points to the strong self-esteem and pride in her culture and Mexican identity, inculcated during her experience in her family's Mexican matriarchal household. Olivia's early memories are dominated by pressure to assimilate and to restrain her movement and activity to fit in as the maid's daughter.

While her mother continued to talk to Olivia in Spanish when they were alone, Carmen was not able to defend her daughter's right to decide which language to speak in the presence of the employers' families. Furthermore, Olivia observed her mother serving and waiting on the employers' families, taking orders, and being treated in a familiar manner. While Olivia referred to the employers formally, by their last names, the employers' children called Olivia's mother by her first name.[8] The circumstances created an environment whereby all monolingual,

Spanish-speaking women, including Carmen, were in subordinate positions. The experiences taught Olivia about social stratification—the negative value placed on the Spanish language and Mexican culture—as well as teaching her to recognize the lower social status that Spanish-speaking Mexican-immigrant women have in this community. An analysis of the socialization process Olivia experienced as the maid's daughter reveals the way that knowledge about the social order is acquired. Exposure to the social world of upper-middle-class Euro-American families in Los Angeles under such marginal conditions gave Olivia a political analysis that stayed with her.[9] This became more evident when she moved in with the Smith family.

Olivia's move to the Smith residence was much more significant than any of the other employers Carmen had during her career in Liberty Place. Olivia remained in this employer's household until she left for college at the age of eighteen. She experienced elementary, middle, and high school there. Before starting school, Olivia had memorized her mother's work schedule and learned the rules that were stipulated by each employer:

> Some days I went in a different car pool because my mother was working at the Joneses. Then I had to get in a different car-pool line, and they dropped me off at the Joneses. I went to wherever my mom was working. I was really alert about what day it was, because each day my mother worked at a different place, and the car pool was different. One day I went to the Joneses, and another day I went directly home. (Interview, January 1988)

As Olivia grew into the larger employers' community and network, her position in various families became a curiosity to her classmates and to other employers' children. Her routine change of car pools and movement in and out of so many households was a source of private information about various families:

> I remember that the other kids wanted to know what my association was with the Smiths. "Why do you go home with the Smiths' kids?" "Why do they treat you like another one of their sisters?" I don't think they ever explained it to the other kids. They just said, "She is my sister. That is how it is."
>
> When I spent time over the Joneses', the Smith kids [David, Ted, Jane, and Rosalyn] asked me about the Jones kids. It was better when the kids didn't know

that I also hung out with other kids. The Smiths' kids were jealous of the Joneses' kids' relationship with me. They always tried to find out about the Joneses. They wanted to know what I did with the Joneses—how they treated me, and did I like the Joneses better than I liked them? I played dumb a lot, or I downplayed things. If I didn't want to talk about them, I didn't. I was not that close to the Joneses. I didn't like them being so Catholic.

When the kids came to dinner parties, they played games that I really didn't like. They liked to go cat-walking. They went into the neighborhood at night after dark and walked on the walls. There were walls that connected the back of houses. They climbed the wall and walked on the top of the wall, going through the trees. I didn't think that was very fun. You could fall and hurt yourself! And it was stupid! I didn't want to do it. So I only went for a little while.

Sometimes I felt really different from them. I felt like the other kids didn't want me to play with them, but David and Ted told them to. They were the ones who said, "Let's go do this. C'mon, Olivia." When they played different games, the Smith kids always put me on their teams. I felt that nobody else wanted me to play. The Smiths' kids had to teach the other kids how to deal with me. They had to say, "She is on my team, and we are going to do this." I joined them, and one of the Smith kids helped me play the game.

I just never felt like I belonged to anybody's family. I just didn't belong. I was just traded from one family to the next family. In one family, I was somebody else's sister, if that is how they treated me. Later I was somebody else's, until it got to the point that all the networks crossed over. (Interview, January 1988)

Entering various households as the maid's daughter in the afternoon after attending school alongside employers' children during the day oriented Olivia to the subordinate but unique place she held among her peers. Her daily movement to various car-pool lines and the location where she stayed a few hours in the afternoon waiting for her mother changed, but her social status and position did not. Olivia's movement from one employer family to another reinforced the fluidity of the relationships and the lack of permanency in claiming family, home, or a sense of belonging. It also gave her insights into life in the gated community that none of the other children had. Nonetheless, even as a child, Olivia's strongest and most enduring feelings remained for her mother and her relatives in Mexico.

Unlike the previous employment environments that Olivia experienced as a toddler, in the Smith household she observed her mother interacting with the employers' children. She overheard interactions and watched them engage in activity that she knew her mother would never tolerate from her. Like other immigrant mothers employed as live-in nannies responsible for both her child and her family in Mexico, Carmen was restricted to the most basic mothering agenda—earning a living.[10] Providing for Olivia was her primary financial responsibility; however, she continued to be the breadwinner for her own mother and sisters as well. Supporting and assisting her family in Mexico was constant and ongoing. Unfortunately Olivia did not yet understand her mother's employment as fulfilling the most basic parenting obligation. Instead, she was exposed to a close-up look at upper-middle-class mothering, supported by a maid and engaged in as a full-time activity. From her perspective as a child, she compared and unfavorably contrasted the mothering she received from Carmen with the way her mother treated the Smith children. Her first telling of these accounts was filled with anger and emphasized the differences between Mrs. Smith's and her mother's parenting. It was years before she developed an analysis of the different social and economic conditions involved in each situation.[11]

> My mom got home about five-thirty or six. Sometimes she cooked, but Mrs. Smith usually did all the cooking, and my mother picked up. The kids came home and threw their books all over the floor. My mother picked them up and took them up to their rooms. When my mother came home from work, she acted as if it was her home. She picked up and cleaned up. She was still working. She didn't go to her room and close the door. (Interview, January 1988)

Olivia's referencing Carmen's arrival at the Smith residence as "coming home" blurred the reality that work done in this space was done as an employee and not as a family member. Defining the place as "home" implied that time spent there had the potential to be "family time." However, the blurred boundaries between home and work also confused relationships and interactions between persons in the household. Olivia's recollection of dining patterns illustrates the changing boundaries that were largely determined by the Smiths. Carmen's position as worker was reinforced because she ate her meals outside the company of the Smiths and in the kitchen, not in the dining room. However, Mrs. Smith and Carmen frequently had a glass of wine together while they prepared dinner together. Another gendered factor of these curious intersections is that Mr. Smith's schedule determined when Mrs. Smith dined because he never dined alone.

When dinner was prepared for us kids, we sat and ate. Sometimes I sat down and ate with the kids. But sometimes there were two dinner schedules. When Mr. Smith wasn't home, the kids ate. Then when Mr. and Mrs. Smith ate, my mother ate, but she ate in the kitchen. Sometimes she ate with us [the children]. We all ate whatever Mrs. Smith cooked.

Sometimes the Smiths didn't have a sit-down dinner. Most of the times when Mr. Smith came home late, they ate while they watched TV. "Let's just do a buffet style." Then everybody ate wherever they wanted to eat in the house. Dinner was just very relaxed, and it wasn't structured. They never sat together. My mother never had to serve them. Everybody just ate on their own.

After I finished eating dinner, I went into my mom's room, or I did my homework with everyone else. Afterwards I watched *novelas* [or *telenovela*, a TV melodrama] with my mom. Sometimes she ironed while watching *novelas*. Instead of ironing on Saturday, which was her day to work for the Smiths, she did it while watching TV or when Mrs. Smith was cooking dinner.

Sometimes when they had guests or parties, they had a formal dinner. Then they ate in the dining room. My mother helped serve. I never wanted to eat with them at these dinners. I always wanted to eat with my mom in the kitchen.

I didn't look forward to Thanksgiving. It was always an awkward situation because I never knew until dinnertime where I was going to sit—every single time. It depended on how many guests they had and how much room there was at the table. Sometimes, when they invited all their friends, the Stuarts and the Taylors—who had kids—the adults ate dinner in one room, and then the kids had dinner in another room. Then I ate with the kids. A lot of times, I didn't like eating with the kids, because they drove me crazy. They were too obnoxious. Everybody screamed, and I wanted to sit down and eat. I didn't want anyone messing with my food or harassing me. I just didn't think it was fun. I didn't enjoy a lot of what they did.

Sometimes I ate with my mom. It really depended. My mom always ate in the kitchen. She liked it that way because she didn't want anybody staring at her. We

closed the door and sat at the kitchen table. We talked about them. We ate whatever we wanted. There were different rules. We closed the door, talked, and everything was fine. (Interview, November 1992)

As this comment indicates, the only time and space that mother and
daughter found to have "family time" without intrusion occurred when
the Smiths decided to exclude Olivia because there was no room for
non-family members. In general, Olivia did not want to be included,
because the time alone allowed mother and daughter to be a family—
making their own decisions about what foods to eat and conversing in
Spanish. Her recollections of growing up frequently included memories
of trying to find private times with her mother, away from the Smiths
and other employers. Since the blurring of work and family boundaries were an ongoing battle, Olivia constantly begged her mother to take
time to visit friends and relatives in Pico Union, where Carmen was not
the maid and her work obligations were not present.

Receiving and giving gifts was uncomfortable for Olivia because she
did not want to be entangled in the web of obligations and paternalism.
The act of exchanging gifts crossed family boundaries, and she knew she
had no control over these constantly changing social boundaries or the
increased debt owed.

The grandparents were very, very wealthy. At first, Mrs. Smith's parents bought
me gifts, toys and stuff. But as the kids became teenagers, they just gave them
money instead. They gave us these little envelopes with fifty dollar bills in them. I
told my mother I didn't like getting money from this old man.

My mother said, "Well, you don't have to take it, except that he's going to get
really mad."

There was always this Catch-22 answer. My mother never helped me out of any
of it. Then they stopped giving me presents and didn't give me money or anything.

I don't know if my mom felt like we were on their equal level, but when I was
fifteen, she thought we should buy presents. We spent all this money. I really
hated the whole idea. I told my mom it was really stupid for us to buy them presents. They had all this money. "Why are we going to spend the money?" It was a
money issue to me. I didn't think it was appropriate for us to be buying them gifts.
But my mother cornered me into these positions and told me I had to. I remember going downtown and buying them gifts. I didn't buy them real expensive, but

it was just the idea that we were buying them gifts. It took a lot of effort to find something for each one of them. They never bought us gifts themselves. I always felt that they never did their own shopping. That bothered me. Mrs. Smith bought us gifts from them. I felt that I had to put in not just the money but my time and effort to think about what to get, and yet they never did that.

Then we gave Mrs. Smith this big plant for her birthday. She really liked plants, and so we started giving her plants. We usually didn't buy Mr. Smith anything. But I remember we used to buy him this Aramis cologne for his birthday. We never bought anything for Father's Day, only on his birthday and for Christmas. For three years we did that.

Mrs. Smith took me shopping to buy my mother presents for her birthday and Christmas. We talked about what I should get her. If Mrs. Smith decided she wanted me to get my mother something really expensive, she paid for it. A couple of times we got her canaries. I didn't like the fact that she was buying the presents, except that I knew my mother really wanted a canary, and they were fifty-five dollars. She bought her a cage and a canary. We did that about four times, because each one died.

I felt like Mrs. Smith gave me presents because she felt guilty. I felt like she was trying to buy my affection. I made very conscious decisions about the things—how I felt about them—and she knew that I didn't like to be very close to her. (Interview, June 1990)

In recounting the ritual of exchanging gifts, Olivia expressed the way that she felt caught between the expectations of work and family. She had difficulty understanding why her mother worked for them and then used her salary to purchase them gifts. Their financial status was far below the Smiths', and the Smith children were not asked to put any effort into selecting a gift for Olivia. The inequities in the time and effort involved in the gift exchange highlights social inequalities that were masked by participating in this family ritual. Mrs. Smith incorporated herself into Carmen and Olivia's family gift giving when she took Olivia shopping and paid for the more expensive gift.

When Olivia was young, she found the blurring and changing of work and family boundaries difficult to comprehend. Not only did she not control the Smiths' expectations of her behavior, but her mother's actions did not appear consistent. Her mother's interaction with Mrs.

Smith often led Olivia to assume that they were best friends, maybe even like sisters. Their relationship seemed much more personal than Carmen's relationship with other employers did. Like many stay-at-home moms, Mrs. Smith was looking for a confidant; as Carmen was their maid, she didn't have to worry about her sharing confidences, since they did not have the same social networks.[12] However, keeping informed about the stability of families in the neighborhood was crucial to Carmen's own network of Mexican immigrants seeking employment. To know if another live-in maid might lose her job or if there was the potential for a new position opening up required listening to employers' gossip—who was complaining about their marriage, who might be getting divorced, or who was planning to move. However, as a child caught between mistress and maid, Olivia thought the relationship curious and confusing.

> My mother and Mrs. Smith talked in the kitchen. My mother chopped things up and helped put dishes away or washed the dishes that the children used when they came home from school. They were like buddies—best friends—and talked about everything. Mrs. Smith told my mom things about me. My mother gossiped to Mrs. Smith about the Steins and the Joneses. My mother had the whole scoop on the entire neighborhood. She knew who was doing what and who was getting divorced. They talked all evening and exchanged information. My mom just had this network. She and Mrs. Smith got together and drank wine.
>
> My mother was really particular about Mexican food. I remember she didn't like to share Mexican customs. Mrs. Smith would ask me, "So, in Juárez, what does your family eat for Easter?" Then I tried to explain to her what *capirotada* [bread pudding] was, and my mother would cut me off. Or Mrs. Smith would ask me, "Well, have you ever eaten goat before in Mexico?" My mother would look at me indicating that she didn't want me to say anything. I just felt like it was so absurd. Here my mother supposedly had this intimate relationship with Mrs. Smith, more than I ever wanted it to be, and she treated me like I wasn't allowed to speak except when she wanted me to.
>
> I guess my mom thought Mrs. Smith would think eating goats was gross. I don't think that she would have thought that. Mrs. Smith had a really good sense that different cultures eat different things. She used to go to Japan a lot and talked about the things that she ate in Japan. I never thought that Mrs. Smith was necessarily

ethnocentric or even anti-Mexican, as my mom thought. Maybe she just felt like it was too intimate, too personal a thing. And that's where it used to really confuse me. Like one time, she told Mrs. Smith that her brother's wife wasn't very nice. I thought, "Here you don't want me to talk about Mexican food, and you're telling Mrs. Smith about how my aunt is a bitch." (Interview, November 1992)

Olivia was always caught off guard when her mother instructed her not to share certain information with Mrs. Smith, especially information about their food, culture, and life in Mexico. In this case, Carmen clearly did not want her culture and life in Mexico to become shared knowledge with the employers. She was willing to engage in gossip with Mrs. Smith, with whom she shared information about her neighbors' children and marriages and complained about her sisters' unwillingness to work as domestics and become financially independent. However, elements of her culture were considered a part of her that was not for employers' entertainment.[13] Carmen actively managed the separation between social worlds by prohibiting Olivia from talking about their summer trips to Mexico and suppressing information about their "Mexicanness." She discouraged Olivia from answering Mrs. Smith's questions about life in Mexico, including the kinds of food they ate, cultural practices at holidays, and Carmen's economic assistance to her family, which included the purchase of property and vehicles. Carmen controlled the kind and amount of knowledge Olivia could share with the Smiths. Olivia learned to avoid such conversations or to give vague answers. Carmen experienced employers' questions "as a form of prying rather than the sincere interest of a friend."[14] Like many domestic workers, she was protective about not selling her personhood.[15]

Olivia's expectations of motherhood were heavily influenced by living in the Smith household and observing the way that Mrs. Smith, a stay-at-home mom, engaged in mothering. Adhering to contemporary views on socially appropriate mothering, she used "a gendered model that advises mothers to expend a tremendous amount of time, energy, and money in raising their children."[16] As a preschool child, Olivia observed that Mrs. Smith's mothering activities began by preparing the children for school, picking them up at the end of the day, and taking an active role in their educational and social experiences.

Everybody [Smith children] was able to have their own separate thing for breakfast. Jane didn't want to sit and eat breakfast. She went to Lexington—this is a private girls' school. She got a special breakfast. She got to have a BLT for breakfast to eat on the way because it was a forty-five-minute commute. David had corned-beef hash because he didn't like eggs. Rosalyn hated food altogether and wouldn't eat anything she was given. She was never happy. The two boys had braces at the time, so they were always complaining that they couldn't eat certain foods.

I remember everybody was frantic in the morning. Everybody bitched and complained all morning. Somebody forgot to brush their teeth. Rosalyn didn't do her homework, or she couldn't find it. David and Ted used to fight all morning because they wore each other's clothes: "Goddamn you! These are my jeans, and you shouldn't be wearing these!" Everybody was always mad. My mother had to help David find his clothes. He always asked, "Carmen, where are my pants? Where is my shirt?" My mother practically dressed him every morning. That was a big joke—my mom had to dress David.

I went with Mrs. Smith to pick up the kids when it was her car-pool day. We picked up all the neighborhood kids. The Gibbs, who lived around the block, were even worse than the Smiths' kids. One of them would always come to the car crying because he couldn't find his shoes. He just cried hysterically. He was like in fourth grade. He was old enough to find his own shoes. I didn't understand why they had to be this disorganized and yell and scream. There was always one of the Gibbs who didn't have something—their shoes or something. We were always late for school. In the afternoon, I went again with Mrs. Smith. We picked them up and took them all home.

Mrs. Smith was really good about talking to the kids. In the morning she talked to them all the way to school: "How was school?" "What are you doing in class, Rosalyn?" "What do you have to do for homework?"

There was always a lot of interaction. When we picked them up, they talked about what everyone did that day. When they were in the car was the time that children talked with their parents. That had a really big effect on me because my mother couldn't do this with me. (Interview, November 1992)

Living with the Smiths, Olivia was presented with an image of mothering in the form of intensive mothering. Olivia observed Mrs. Smith talking to her children and, in doing so, "developing their educational interests" and "playing an active role in their schooling." She followed parenting experts of the time who advised "the importance of reasoning with children and teaching them to solve problems through negotiation rather than with physical force."[17] While Olivia was clearly attracted to the adult attention the children received about their daily activities, she was critical of their inability to be more self-sufficient and to take charge of their belongings. Given the long periods of time in the employers' homes, particularly when compared with rare trips to Pico Union or two months of the year in Mexico, concerted cultivation was the dominant form of parenting that Olivia was exposed to.[18] Consequently, she juxtaposed the mothering she received with the form that the employers' children received. As Olivia began school, Mrs. Smith gradually assumed some of Carmen's mothering activities, because of Carmen's lack of familiarity with schools in the United States and her uneasiness about speaking to monolingual English-speaking teachers.

> My mother was there for me to some extent, but she was too preoccupied with dinner and everything else to sit and play the role that Mrs. Smith did—"How was school?" "What did you learn?"—and go through that whole process. I immediately recognized that my mom didn't do it because she was working. But later, when I was about ten, I really resented that. Why didn't my mother relate to me the way that Mrs. Smith related to me? Why did my mother always yell and scream? It was easier for me to go to Mrs. Smith and say, "I don't understand this" or "This teacher is not nice to me." I had a sense that Mrs. Smith understood.
>
> I remember that everything I went through I had to tell the Smiths. Then the Smiths explained it to my mother. She talked to me in a different way, whereas my mother said, "¿Es que tu eres mu tonta?" [Is it that you are stupid?] It was always my fault when I had problems with the teacher. Whenever I had problems at school, it had to be my fault. So I was more afraid to talk to my mom about things that were going on. (Interview, November 1992)

Carmen's parenting was not influenced by her exposure to employers, since she was privy to all the "backstage" behavior and observed their children's rude behavior, inability to pick up after themselves, drug and alcohol use, and irresponsibility. Instead, she relied on her working-class background in mothering Olivia.[19] Instead of encouraging children to negotiate, Carmen used a working-class approach with Olivia, giving "clear directives" and "more autonomy to manage" her "own affairs in institutions outside the home."[20] Living-in at the Smiths and doing housework and child work throughout the area, Carmen did not have the time to engage in long exchanges when she needed Olivia to do something. After waiting hand and foot on the employers and their children, Carmen needed to end her day with a child who is self-reliant and respectful.[21] She also recognized that employers are not likely to embrace the maid's daughter into their home and community if she is needy or a problem child.

As Olivia grew older and began attending the same school and social activities as the Smith children, Carmen's interactions with the Smith children became increasingly distinct from her interactions with her daughter. Carmen's expectation for her became conflicted by the permissive standards applied to the employers' children. Olivia did not, at that time, recognize that the employers established the standards for their children and that Carmen simply worked within those parameters. As the maid's daughter, Olivia learned that employers' children have different rules and privileges (even though at times it appeared that they had no rules at all). Olivia also noted that her mother granted the Smiths' sons male privilege. In the following story, Olivia recalls preadolescent memories that illustrate the double standard:

Mrs. Smith and the kids tell stories about how overprotective my mom was toward the boys. I don't know why she was. When Mr. and Mrs. Smith were out of town, my mother always asked the boys what *they* wanted for dinner. So when the Smiths were out of town, we always had tacos, because that was what the boys wanted to eat. If David was out playing, none of us could eat until David came back. My mother sent me and Rosalyn to find David to tell him it was time for dinner.

When they got into trouble, they were sent to their rooms without any dinner. My mother made peanut-butter sandwiches and put them in the laundry in plastic bags. Then she took the laundry upstairs and gave them peanut-butter-and-jelly sandwiches. They got into more trouble. Ted got kicked out of Academy High for smoking cigarettes. He was constantly being kicked out of these private schools.

When the Smiths weren't home, Ted and Jane got stoned in their room. Even though my mother was downstairs, she knew they were getting high. She smelled it in the house. She said, "Open the windows! Air out the room! And don't leave the house!" My mother knew she wasn't going to change them or their habits. My mother even cleaned around their pot. They had a shoe box under the bed with all their pot and their paper. My mother took it and cleaned around the box and then put it back. She never threw it away. If she found pot in the pockets of David's pants, she put it where it was supposed to go—in the shoe box under the bed. David had one friend, Joey, who I knew was Chicano. He came over and talked to my mom in Spanish. Joey and David planted a marijuana plant outside. My mother was just standing there, just watching. I could not understand why she just accepted their rules. (Interview, November 1992)

While the Smith children received intensive mothering from their mother and Carmen, Olivia noted that they did not attempt to treat her mother in a similar manner as they treated their parents. In the following story, she describes a usual pattern of events dealing with the Smiths' adolescent children when Carmen was left in charge of the household. Olivia observed them accepting Carmen's norms that elders are to be respected. However, she also observed the way that both her mother and the employers' children negotiate the least compliance with the rules, which allowed Carmen to fulfill her obligations and the Smith children still to get their way.

She always spoke to them in Spanish, and they always understood everything my mother said. They had a lot of respect for her. They *never* talked back to her. They never said, "No." They had more respect for my mother than they did for their parents. They talked back to Mrs. Smith and said, "No, mom. I'm not going to do it!" But they never said anything back to my mom. They never spoke to my mom like that. If they were mad, they were just mad and held it inside themselves.

As the kids got older and were driving, the big thing was who was going to take the Mercedes. My mother would hide the keys, and they come and beg my mother for the keys. "Give me the keys for the car." "No! Your father said no. I'm not going to give them to you." Then they were frantic looking for them. They would find the keys somewhere where my mother would hide them. Then my mother knew they had won. They found the keys, so my mother let them take the car. But she would say, "Your parents said they were going to call at nine o'clock, so you better be home." So they came home by nine. They sat there waiting for their parents to call. They talked to them on the phone, and as soon as they got off the phone, they took the car and left. They abided by the minimum rules that my mother set, and that was fine.

She'd yell at them, "Jane, you said you were going to be here at six o'clock. I'm waiting for you." They were silent. They never talked back to my mother. They asked me, "How come your mom is so mad?" "Because you said you were going to pick her up and you didn't." They were infamous for saying they were going do something and not do it, or say they were going to come back at a certain time and not be there. (Interview, July 1997)

As Olivia observed the various parenting techniques and ways that the Smiths' college-age and adult children navigated each to get what they want, she too experimented with various strategies. Knowing the contrasts in standards and modes of parenting, she learned that getting her way involved negotiating with her mother in Mrs. Smith's presence.

I tried to play a lot of games between Mrs. Smith and my mom to see who was going to take control over certain things—like losing my homework and saying I forgot it. My mom got really pissed off. Mrs. Smith always said, "It's okay."

Then I realized how Mrs. Smith's kids turned out. Ted had to go to summer school in order to graduate from high school. He went to three different schools and got kicked out of three different schools. He is going nowhere. Rosalyn first went to Bradford College in Massachusetts, and then she and David decided to move to University of Tennessee because the Smiths knew the governor of Kentucky. That is the only way they can get into college. Rosalyn decided to be a walk-on for the volleyball team. She played, traveling all over the place, and failed her courses. David decided to be a sophomore for three years and to be in a fraternity. Rosalyn wanted to be an art teacher. She went to the University of Michigan. I don't know how she got in there. She was teaching art and taking classes, and then she went to Rutgers for a master's in fine arts. She is evidently very talented. She is painting and selling her stuff. And Jane, God knows what she is doing this month. She got married and went to Portugal and then got divorced, and now she has two kids from two different marriages. I knew the Smiths were not going places. All the other [employers'] kids, like the Joneses' kids, were going places. I compared the Joneses, Steins, and all these families and saw the things that worked.

My mother and I talked about it. "Learn from everybody else's mistakes." So we really learned from the way the Smiths' kids turned out and from the way they were disciplined. My mother felt that they weren't doing well because Mrs. Smith let them do anything they wanted, and they smoked pot and did all these things.

They had no interest in doing anything else. They weren't motivated, and they weren't challenged.

I recognized immediately that I had to make my own choices. I was taught to be really responsible by the Smiths. I had rules. I got to go out to play, but when the street lights came on, I had to come home. If I wasn't home and the street lights came on, I was grounded. I knew if I decided not to go when the street lights came on, I chose to be grounded. I was really taught that way. You think about it, and you make your decision. You think about what you are doing and understand the ramifications to it. That is the way I dealt with the Smiths. (Interview, July 1997)

Olivia recognized that the lack of discipline did not teach the Smith children to be responsible, and they were more likely to make reckless decisions. She recognized that the employers' lenient rules and prioritizing children's happiness over success can have serious consequences. However, embedded in this narrative are the privileges that protect employers' children from facing the same consequences as the children of immigrant workers employed in Liberty Place. If the children of the domestics or landscapers are expelled from school or fail in college, they are unlikely to get accepted into another school and will probably not be able to continue their education. Olivia knew that she had rules and that if she broke them, then she was accepting the consequences.

BLURRING BOUNDARIES OF PARENTAL AUTHORITY

Responsibility and obligation created by the pseudo-family relationship of being "one of the family" were even more firmly established when Mr. and Mrs. Smith decided to pay Olivia's school tuition rather than pay her mother a salary. While the arrangement served to decommercialize the Smiths' relationship with Carmen and allowed her not to pay taxes on the income, the agreement created the appearance that the Smiths, rather than Olivia's mother, were paying her tuition:

I don't remember the discussion about where I would go to school. I just remember that my mother and Mrs. Smith made some agreement that they wouldn't pay her a salary. They had never charged her for room and board. She just lived there and worked one day a week for the Smiths. She got paid for that day. Now my mother wouldn't get a salary. Instead they would pay for my education. I was going to go to school with all of the other kids. When it was time to start school, Mrs. Smith took me. I had to take this test. I remember getting all dressed up, and Mrs. Smith took me to register for class instead of my mom.

At the beginning of the school year, Mrs. Smith took me to buy school clothes with the rest of the kids. She paid for them. We went to a place called Jack and Jill. It was a really nice store. All the help in the store knew my name—just like I was one of the Smiths' kids. We spent hours there. They went kid by kid until we got all our clothes. I got five or six new dresses. I went home and showed my mom: "Look what I got." Mrs. Smith never charged my mom for them. Every year it was always the same procedure. (Interview, January 1988)

By paying school tuition instead of giving a salary directly to Carmen so she could pay for tuition, Mr. and Mrs. Smith strengthened their ability to make decisions about Olivia's education. Although the Smiths were not really taking money out of their own pockets, since the salary was owed to Carmen for housework and laundry, the gesture was framed in benevolent terms, and Carmen became indebted to her employers. The debt was paid not only by doing additional work in the evenings, instead of just one full day a week, but also by relinquishing a degree of parental authority over Olivia.

In kindergarten, parents decided if their kid was going to learn Spanish or French. A language course was required throughout grade school. I really wanted to learn French. I was really upset when the Smiths enrolled me in the Spanish course.

I said, "How come I have to take Spanish? I already know Spanish."

"No, we want you to speak perfect Spanish. We want your Spanish to be like—so you can talk to the queen of Spain. We want you to have perfect Spanish."

It took me a long time to get over it. They made that decision without talking to me. I don't know to what extent they talked to my mom about it. But they were the ones who made the decision and enforced it.

My mother acted really differential with me. It really didn't matter to her. I could take French, or I could take Spanish.

I knew there was, like, an appeal process. I could appeal to my mother. I could tell her, "I think this or I think that." If I convinced my mother, she changed the rules and told the Smiths. But it took a long time. It was a really big grievance process. I knew it would take a long time and a lot of energy to convince my mother. My mother didn't really challenge what the Smiths said.

Those issues that my mother knew she wasn't going win, she went to Mrs. Smith first. Winning was a matter of who went to Mrs. Smith first. I could give Mrs. Smith the other side of the story, and she frequently made the final decision. Then my mother was angry. When my mother won, it was totally different. When Mrs. Smith and my mom didn't agree on something, and Mrs. Smith was adamant about it and said things like, "You know, Carmen, it's just that we love Olivia so much. We don't want her to make any mistakes," she would exhale really deeply and say, "We're just afraid for her." She acted like her voice was cracking with a knot in her throat, like she was ready to cry.

Anytime that anything happened at school, Mrs. Smith responded to the note and asked me, "How did school go? What did you learn? Who are your friends?" I had the same role that everyone else did. We just took turns, and everybody talked.

I remember the teacher-parent conferences in the first grade. I had this little note pad that had information about the conference. Mrs. Smith took the note from me and tried to explain it to my mother. I remember her explaining to me, "Oh! Olivia, this means that you are going to have a teacher-parent conference just like David, Jane, Rosalyn, and Bob, and all the other kids have. We go, and your teacher will tell us how you are doing in school." They decided that for the first one, Mr. Smith, Mrs. Smith, and my mom—the three of them—would go. (Interview, January 1988)

Olivia observed the increasing power Mrs. Smith had over her education and resented her mother for not fighting on her behalf but acquiescing to the employers' recommendations. Conflict that arose from the Smiths' increasing influence over Olivia accentuated the gap between their social roles. Then Carmen got sick. Circumstances surrounding Carmen's hospitalization demonstrate the difficulty in interacting as a mother-daughter family unit under the influence and power employers exert over their daily lives. Over the years, Olivia referred back to that summer and the changes that occurred; they became a significant source of conflict between mother and daughter.

When I was about ten years old, my mother got really sick. My mother said she wasn't feeling good, and the previous summer, when she was in Juárez, she had gone to a doctor. The doctor told her she was pregnant. My mother got really angry because she hadn't been with a man. She felt something in her stomach, something hard. So finally she went to Dr. McDermott, who is a good friend of the Smiths. A lot of the Smiths' friends were doctors. The McDermotts lived around the corner from the Joneses. Mr. Jones was a doctor. I thought that my whole community existed within the three-mile radius because everybody knew each other, and that's how things were.

Dr. McDermott did a whole exam on my mother and found out that she had a tumor in her uterus. Evidently it was the size of a basketball. It was just huge. My mother spoke to me. She was really upset about it. That was the first serious illness in our family. So my mother was really freaked out.

The Smiths had a meeting with the doctors and my mother. They sat down at the table: Mr. and Mrs. Smith, Dr. McDermott, Dr. Morgen, who lived a block away from Dr. Jones, and Dr. Jones, and my mother. Over a glass a wine they talked about what was wrong with my mother. They explained what was wrong with her and told her that she had to have a hysterectomy. They had to get my mother to agree that she wasn't going to sweep and clean. There were things that she wasn't going to be able to do.

Mrs. Smith took the initiative to arrange everything. Dr. Jones worked at Saint Francis Hospital, and they were not going to charge her. Dr. Jones was not going to charge her for the hospital because he was on the board or something important at the hospital. Dr. McDermott, who is a OB/GYN, was going to operate on her, and he was not going to charge her. She never paid for any of it. She paid for the x-rays. Mrs. Smith had told them that my mom didn't have any health insurance or any way to pay for the surgery.

Mrs. Smith never paid for my dentist bill. My mom always paid for my dentist bills. When I had to go see a doctor, I saw the same doctor as the Smiths' children, Dr. Rosenberg. He had my family records, and my mom paid for that too. Once I broke my finger, and I had to go to the hospital. I had to go to the emergency room. My mom paid for that.

Evidently, everybody at the hospital treated my mother like royalty, because all the doctors dropped by to see her. They all knew her by name. They talked to her differently. It was a whole personal thing. The hospital knew that my mother was not paying, and she was to be treated special. She got really good treatment.

The big concern among my mother's employers was that I not be alarmed about the surgery. Instead of going to Juárez for the summer, I stayed in LA all summer and went to summer school. The employers traded me back and forth between them. When my mother was having surgery, the Joneses took me to

Balboa. Then I came back to the Smiths, I attended summer school. I was with the Smiths as my parents for about two months. We had dinner together. The Smiths were really, really supportive. I went to summer school, took math and English. I was in this drama class. I got to do the leading role. Everybody really liked me, and Mrs. Smith came to my play. So things started to change. I got a lot closer to them. After I finished summer school, my mother was still in the hospital.

That summer I started sleeping upstairs. Instead of sleeping alone downstairs in my mother's room, I slept upstairs. One of the kids had gone to college. Rosalyn, David, and I were home. I slept upstairs in one of the extra rooms. It was a really neat room, because Rosalyn was allowed to paint it. She got her friend to paint a big tree and clouds on the walls. I really loved having my own room.

My oldest cousin, Lalo, came to LA and got a job so he could be here for my mother. My cousin was at the hospital all the time. He spent the night there. She had the whole room all to herself, and the nurses let him sleep in the bed next to her in the room. They brought him food. They treated him completely differently. My cousin resented all the time I spent with the Smiths. I went to see her, but I only could stay a couple hours. It was really weird. I didn't like seeing my mother in pain, and she was in a lot in pain. Later I realized that she could have died, and I was out in Balboa vacationing with the Joneses.

Later, my mother always tried to make it seem as though I was never at the hospital. But it wasn't any choice of my own. It wasn't like I could jump on the bus or the car. I think my mother was really afraid that now that she wasn't there, they [employers] were going to steal me from her.

I remember before she came home the Smiths had a little talk with me. They said, "We think it would be a good idea if you stayed upstairs and had your own room now. Your mother is going to be sick, and you can't sleep in the same bed because you might hurt her. It is important for your mother to be alone. How do you feel about that?"

I was really excited about having my own room.

They said, "We don't know how your mom will take it. She probably is not going to like it. She might get upset about it, but we think that we can convince her that it is okay."

My mom was in the hospital for about a month. When she came home, she really couldn't do anything. She understood that she couldn't be touched, and she had to be really careful. But she wanted my move upstairs to be temporary.

She argued with them and said, "No. I don't want it that way."

She told me, "No. I want you to be down here. *¿Que crees que eres hija de ellos?* [Do you think you are their daughter?] *Tu te debes de dormir conmigo.* [You must sleep here with me.] You're going to be with me all the time. You can't do that."

When Mrs. Smith and I went to the market together, she asked me, "How does your mom seem? How does she feel? What does she say?"

I told her, "I think my mom is really upset about me moving upstairs. She doesn't like it, and she just says no." I didn't tell her everything. I didn't tell her exactly what my mom had said.

They talked to her and finally convinced her. But my mom really resented it and was really angry about it.

That was a really big change when I slept upstairs. Everything changed. I had different rules. I was more independent. I did my own homework. They opened the back door and yelled upstairs when dinner was ready. Things were just really different.

My mother never recognized that I had different rules for different settings, and they were always changing. She had no concept of the fact that I had to constantly adapt to whatever was going on. I just had to play it by ear. I never knew if it was going be a situation where my mother was going to want me to go with the Smiths, not go with the Smiths, or who I was supposed to interact with. (Interviews, January 1988, November 1992, and September 1997)

Olivia was clearly delighted to have her own room. Having her own room meant having a real place to call her own in the house. However, she was unprepared for the symbolism in moving upstairs and having a bedroom alongside the family of her mother's employers. This change in sleeping arrangements was one of many that begin to highlight the ways that Olivia and Carmen experienced the boundaries of insider and outsider differently. Olivia was in a position to assume a more active family role when employers made certain requests. Unlike her mother, she was not an employee and was not expected to clean and serve the employers. However, Carmen's responsibility for the housework never ceased, regardless of the emotional ties existing between employees and employers. She and her employers understood that whatever family activity she might be participating in, if the situation called for someone to clean, pick up, or serve, it was Carmen's job. When the Smiths requested Olivia to sit at the dinner table with the family, they placed Olivia in a different class position from her mother, who was now expected to serve her daughter alongside her employers. Moving Olivia upstairs in a bedroom alongside the employers and their children was bound to drive a wedge between mother and daughter. There is a long history of spatial deference in domestic service, including separate entrances, staircases, and eating and sleeping arrangements. Carmen's room reflected her position in the household. As the maid's quarters, the room was separated from the rest of the bedrooms and located near the maid's central work area—the kitchen. The room was not large enough for two beds; Carmen and Olivia shared a bed. Once Olivia was moved upstairs, she no longer shared the same social space in the employers' home as her mother. Weakening the bonds between the maid and her daughter permitted the employers to broaden their relationships and interaction with Olivia.

Carmen's feelings of betrayal and loss underline how threatening the employers' actions were. She understood that the employers were in a position to buy her child's love. They had already attempted to socialize Olivia into Euro-American ideals by planning her education and deciding what courses she would take. As a Mexican-immigrant woman working as a live-in maid, Carmen was able to experience certain middle-class privileges, but her only access to these privileges was through her relationship with the employers. Without the employers' assistance, she did not have the connections to enroll Olivia into private schools or to provide her with upper-middle-class experiences to develop the cultural capital to survive in the elite schools. Carmen only gained these privileges for her daughter at a price; she relinquished many of her parental rights to the employers. To a large degree, the Smiths undermined Carmen's role as a parent, and the other employers restricted the time she had to attend school functions and the amount of energy she had left at the end of the day to mother her own child.

Carmen pointed to the myth of "being like one of the family" in her comment, "¿Que crees que eres hija de ellos? You're going to be with me all the time. You can't do that." The statement underlines the fact that the bond between mother and daughter is for life, whereas the pseudo-family relationship with employers is temporary and conditional. Carmen wanted her daughter to understand that taking on the role of "being

one of the family" did not relinquish her from the responsibility of fulfilling her "real" family obligations. The resentment Olivia felt from her
cousin, who was keeping vigil at his aunt's hospital bed, indicates that
she had not been a dutiful daughter. Olivia's relatives expected a daughter to be at her mother's side providing any assistance possible as a caretaker, even if it was limited to companionship. However, the employers
determined Olivia's activity and shaped her behavior into that of a middle-class child; consequently, she was kept away from the hospital and
protected from the realities of her mother's illness. Furthermore, she was
submerged into the employers' world, spending time at the beach, dining at the country club, and interacting with their friends.

I recognize that the process of Carmen's relinquishing parental control to the Smiths was a gradual one; still, the circumstances surrounding
her hospitalization and Olivia's move upstairs marked a painful rupture
in the bond between mother and daughter.

ASCRIBED ROLES AND ASSUMED EXPECTATIONS

> I always had a role. I could never just sit back and not be part of it. I always had
> a role. I was either an assistant cook, an assistant chef, or cheese grater. Or I was
> somebody's babysitter. Or I was the maid's daughter while waiting for my mother.
> In the employers' minds, my entire identity was the maid's daughter. I guess that's
> one of the reasons that I consciously feared cleaning. I already took on all these
> other roles as my mother's helper by cleaning, babysitting, and caring. I didn't
> want anyone to assume that was my role in life. (Interview, March 1998)

Carmen involved her daughter in doing errands and babysitting for employers. Although these were not activities that any of the other children
in the neighborhood did, Olivia's involvement was normalized by the
fact that she was the maid's daughter.[22] She never actually was employed
as a maid or a private household worker, but she was included in a wide
range of service rituals and practices of deference. From an early age,
Carmen recruited Olivia to assist employers by walking their dogs, tu-
toring younger children with school work, and assisting in the kitchen
when serving at parties. Forced into participating in relationships that
characterize servitude, Olivia created a hierarchy of tasks and ranked

cleaning as the one that she would not do.[23] However, her preadolescent and adolescent years included informal work arrangements that no other teenagers in the neighborhood did.

> When I was growing up, I babysat for everybody. I started babysitting when I was twelve. I babysat for everybody in the neighborhood. My mother got me these jobs. She'd say, "Oh, my daughter babysits." I got really upset. I didn't want to be in their houses, much less actually have to interact with them.
>
> After I babysat for somebody's kid, their parents always wanted to talk to me about their problems, like the Sackses. My mother cleaned for Mrs. Sacks for about six months. I babysat their daughter, Millie. Millie wasn't doing well in school, and Mrs. Sacks was always asking me why. After I stopped babysitting Millie, I went over there to see my mom, who was working there, and Mrs. Sacks would ask me about Millie, "Well, why do you think Millie isn't doing well in school?"
>
> "I don't know. Maybe she doesn't like it."
>
> Millie attended this experimental learning center that was really flexible. There weren't any class periods, but other things. Millie needed discipline. This experimental learning center wasn't what she needed. I told Mrs. Sacks, "You know, it seems like Millie doesn't take her school seriously. She says it's really easy. She doesn't really have to do anything she doesn't want to because it's at your pace. So she figures that out and doesn't do anything. No one ever pushes her. So that's why she isn't doing well in school." (Interview, November 1992)

Unlike experiences other teenagers might have in babysitting for neighbors, Olivia was not treated as their neighbor's daughter but as the maid's daughter. The employers did not ask her about her life or inquire about her interests and pursuits, as she had observed Mrs. Smith do with the neighbors' children. Instead, she was confronted as an employee. They expected her to engage in the same emotional labor that her mother did:

> My mother's employers just expected me to be interested in their problems and to listen to them. (Interview, November 1992)

For years she watched her mother be pulled into employers' personal problems and allow them to call on her assistance at any time. Her mother was a confidant to many of the employers and their children. Olivia expressed annoyance at her mother's involvement and questioned if she had any interest in her daughter's life. As Olivia entered her teens, she found herself being treated as a responsible adult that might help employers address family problems. Both mother and daughter were expected to engage in emotional labor and found their personalities being devoured by employers' greedy families.[24]

As Olivia found herself being submerged in emotional labor, she began to view the employers more through the same lens her mother did. Instead of perceiving the emotional labor as exploitative, unpaid labor or as characteristic of the mistress-maid relationship, Olivia understood the situation more like her mother, who defined the employers as weak, helpless, and unable to deal with everyday life. From this perspective, Olivia and Carmen rejected the servitude characteristic of emotional labor and defined themselves as strong, mature, and responsible and as having the ability to solve problems.[25] Many of these issues are apparent in Olivia's story about the Kingstons. At first she was hired to babysit, and then she found herself providing Mrs. Kingston companionship, as well as playing a major role in raising the children. As her telling reveals, she had mixed feelings about being treated differently than the other adolescents in Liberty Place. Olivia found herself caught in the web of maids and mistresses.

> I got hired by some woman in the neighborhood, like a companion. I had seen my mom get so involved with them that I felt like it was okay. They knew my mother was really smart, and they always told me, "Your mother is smarter than you, smarter than all of us put together." They knew that she was unruly, and they couldn't control her. She told everybody what to do, and when she didn't like something, she made it really clear. The employers' kids went to her to talk. They all talked to my mother about their problems. She had her own relationship with each one of them.
>
> My mom had a relationship with Mrs. Kingston. They sat and talked for an hour or two. As a result, I felt she had set the tone. Mrs. Kingston invited me to go on trips with her to babysit the kids and keep her company because her husband never traveled with her. Mrs. Kingston was married to Ken Kingston, who had been one of the president's top advisers when he was governor of California. He had gotten a job as the vice president of the —— corporation, the big department-store magnate that owns —— and —— and a whole bunch of different

stores. She got a job working for the president, handling all his correspondence for his campaign. She was a journalist type. They adopted these two kids. First, they adopted David, and about three days after he was born, I was babysitting.

I raised her kids. I babysat David since he was really little, but my mother was Miss Control: she would come over and monitor what I was doing—made sure I was doing things right. I remember he was like three days old, and I took care of him, fed him, and changed his diapers. I remember I used to call my mom when David didn't want to go to sleep. As he started to grow up, I took really good care of him.

It was like a little solitary confinement to me. I got a chance to get away from everybody else and just be in this little environment and just spend my entire time with David. Even when he was six months old, I had these really elaborate things planned for the day. We had picnics. Of course, I took his baby food. We had projects. It was real structured. I took David over to the Smiths, or I went to where my mother was working and took David over there. I had the whole house to myself. I took care of David all through the summer. It was next door to the Smiths'. It was so convenient: if I wanted something from home, I could just go get it. My mom was working very close by and really accessible to me.

David Kingston used to misbehave all the time. Mrs. Kingston didn't handle David very well. In my estimation, it was because she didn't spend any time with him and didn't really know him. These kids played on their parents' guilt. They were smart. They figured it out very young. Their parents were working or caught up in some other activity and didn't spend any time with them. They tried to re-place this by going out and buying them things. Kids acting up was their revenge. They were very smart to try and embarrass them at points when they didn't want to be embarrassed, like in the supermarket. When he got out of control in the su-permarket, I just gave him that little look my mother always gave me. I took him outside and told him, "Look, you little shit, you don't do this when you're with me. You only do it when you're with your mother. I don't think it's cute. So stop it." Then he settled down. We went back into the store.

I went a lot of places with them on their vacations. When the president got elected, she got all this money and gifts for working on his campaign. She decided to take me to Hawaii with her. We and her two kids went to Hawaii for two weeks. I think she wanted the companionship, and she really couldn't handle her kids. They were like terrors with her.

I remember when we were at Liberty Place, they would run away. When David was older, like six or five, he took his bike after dark and didn't come home. Mrs. Kingston would call and ask me, "Can you help me go find David?" That was just ridiculous—that I went next door, and I had total control over these kids next door. I saw how my mother just got totally sucked in.

Dottie was her name. Dottie and I became very good friends. Dottie Kingston and her husband, Ken, were really distant from each other. It was really kind of strange. We talked about all kind of things. Of course, her marriage was falling apart, and he was never around. It became really apparent that they were having serious problems when Ken did not come home for two days.

I remember one time that Mrs. Kingston and I drove to Palm Springs. She talked about her husband, Ken, to me. I was only fifteen years old. She asked me, "Do you think Ken's going out with other women?" I realized there was something really strange because Mr. Kingston had a male secretary when he went to Palm Springs with us. I remember one day we drove up in the station wagon when the kids were like two and four. I remember getting there, and he and his secretary playing tennis. About two or three times that we went up there, he and his secretary were already there. I noticed that there were strange things going on. One time his secretary had just gotten out of the shower and was walking around wrapped in a towel. That was when she started to tell me she didn't understand why she and Ken were so distant.

I asked her questions like, "Oh, so when did Mr. Kingston come up?" And then she started to tell me that she was really concerned. All of a sudden she started talking about all her marital problems. He was gay, and she didn't know. Everybody else knew he was gay.

The next time Mrs. Kingston invited me, I told my mother, "I don't want to go to Palm Springs with Mrs. Kingston. I'm tired of going."

My mom said, "Well, Mrs. Kingston told me that she wants to see if you want to go."

I said, "No, I don't want to go to Palm Springs this weekend because all she did last weekend was talk my ear off about Ken. And I wanted to just turn around and say, 'Look, Dottie, he's a fucking homosexual already. Get over it.' I don't want to deal with it. I don't want to entertain them."

My mother always felt like listening to the employers' problems was so interesting. She didn't understand why I didn't want to do it.

"They're paying you."

"I don't want to be their little Dear Abby."

When I complained about the racist things they said, my mom only said, "Oh, you know how they are."

Then I told her, "They basically think that we're stupid." I spelled it out to her. She said, "No, no, no, no, they don't."

When I was getting ready to go to college, Mrs. Kingston called me and said, "Come move with me to Washington, D.C. You can go to American University. We live right across the street. You can get a job at the White House."

"I don't want to."

Everybody was really disappointed in me. They acted like I had made the wrong decision again. I just couldn't see myself in this kind of situation. I just could not see myself taking these kinds of handouts and accepting all these things. (Interview, March 1998)

Because Olivia was the maid's daughter, the employers around her, including Mrs. Smith and her own mother, did not find these activities with the Kingston unusual for a fifteen-year-old girl. At thirteen and fourteen, she was frequently called on to care for Jane's young son. Leaving a newborn to be cared for by a teenager was certainly not the norm in Liberty Place, but as the maid's daughter, Olivia was perceived as having the skills. Since she had not been around other babies, the assumption about her ability must have been based on some notions of natural ability, given that her mother was a trusted caregiver in the community. Olivia's abilities were racialized as she was ascribed nurturing and caring attributes that all the Mexican women were assumed to have.[26] Olivia's description of the importance of discipline, as well as the scheduled events that Olivia created for the children in her care, demonstrates the way that she combined aspects of both Carmen's and Mrs. Smith's parenting styles. She perceived that the lack of discipline and the negotiating approach were failing because Mrs. Kingston did not take the time needed to gain control of the situation. Instead, Mrs. Kingston found it easier simply to buy whatever the child wanted and in the process to give control to the children. In the face of a temper tantrum, Olivia took the measure her mother took with her. At the same time, scheduling activities for toddlers and young children is a page from parenting framed as concerted cultivation.

At first, the freedom that having a place to stay outside the Smith household offered was attractive to Olivia, and she planned her own activities with the children. She also enjoyed being treated as Mrs. Kingston's friend and companion. Gradually, the lack of reciprocity in the relationship with Mrs. Kingston became apparent. Olivia began to recognize that the familiar social relationship her mother had with employers was being replicated with Mrs. Kingston. Olivia knew the intimate details of Mrs. Kingston's marriage, whereas Mrs. Kingston knew very little about Olivia, not even her Democratic political views. Although Olivia was expected to be a companion to Mrs. Kingston as she traveled, her primary role was to be in charge of the children. Like her mom, who had become emotionally invested in the employers' lives, Olivia found herself in the same vulnerable position. She had invested a lot of time, energy, and care in raising the children and genuinely was concerned about their welfare. Olivia failed to recognize that mothering is an ability to do emotional labor and is a skill that is financially rewarded and can be used to improve working conditions and to assure employment stability. As the role of the confidant became too painful and uncomfortable for Olivia, she no longer wanted to perform the emotional labor.

Olivia's decision not to accept Mrs. Kingston's offer was perceived as a lost opportunity by the adults around her. Yet the employers were unlikely ever to encourage their own children to accept a position as a live-in nanny, with the possibility of eventually getting some kind of employment in the White House, as a path to attending college. Olivia knew that her decision not to accept the offer disappointed the Smiths and other employers, as well as her mother. However, she recognized that she could never leave the position of the maid's daughter as long as she tied herself in debt to Mrs. Kingston. Olivia did not want to have the sense of obligation that she had toward the Smiths and other employers. She wanted to eventually escape the burden of owing employers gratitude and being forced into constantly doing tasks that are framed as "favors" one does on the basis of friendship but that are in actuality a labor of servitude.[27] Her decision not to move to D.C. and be Mrs. Kingston's nanny highlights Olivia's desire to break away from this world of maids and mistresses. She did not want to live her mother's life.

It was at the point that the whole community became completely dependent on my mother for advice. She knew all these people. I used to hate being introduced to all these people because I just knew that at one point in my life, I was going be so different, and I would not have anything to do with them.

I always thought that when I got to be eighteen, my life would change radically and that things would never be the same. I would never interact with the same people that I knew in Liberty Place. I somehow I had this idea that I would be running into them, but it would be a really embarrassing difficult thing—not because I was the maid's daughter but because I didn't like them. I didn't like what they represented and who they are. I just didn't have a lot of respect for them. (Interview, March 1998)

Over the years, Olivia came to recognize her mother's inability to move outside the role of serving and caring for the employers. For many years, she pondered the reasons that her mother assumed the same role in all social settings that included employers, even when she had not been invited to work. Olivia perceived her mother's need to manage families and events in order to elevate her position as the one in control rather than being controlled. In the presence of employees hired to serve at an event, Carmen would assume a supervisory position.

One Easter, one of the Joneses' daughters invited my mom to her house near a lake. I drove out there. They had a beautiful house with horses and a pool. It was huge. We went there for Easter lunch. My mother insisted on helping. Maybe it was her way to gain power or control. She couldn't sit as a guest like they had invited her, but she had to do something. It was clear that they didn't have any expectation of her cleaning or doing anything, because they had other help. Other places we went to visit, she usually sat and interacted with them in the kitchen. She seemed uncomfortable about it sometimes and played the role of instructor, monitoring them and giving them tips. My mom was always telling them that they didn't put things in the right place. We talked to them in the kitchen, and we were guests. That was really strange. (Interview, March 1998)

REFLECTIONS

After interviewing Olivia over the years and hearing similar stories told and retold, I perceive Olivia's childhood memories as recollections that incorporate her mother's stories but that she attaches her own meaning to. Analyzing the early socialization of children is usually tied to their family life. Most children are not that aware of their parents' occupational status and do not usually have access to observing the ways they conform to employers' regulations. As Olivia became aware that her mother's rules for her were completely different from those for the Smith children, over time she learned how her mother adapted to being a guardian without parental authority. Reflecting on Olivia's careful documentation of her socialization as the maid's daughter, I am struck by how infrequently we notice the way that children are ascribed their parents' status. As a child, Olivia was more likely to be conscious of her social position than are working-class and poor children, who rarely have the access to different class social settings. Olivia may not have been entirely clear about the interaction between class and culture, but being able to compare and contrast the same behavior in the context of both wealth and poverty, she was unwilling to accept explanations of cultural pathology or deficiency models. Caught between wealth and poverty, she found her mother's advice most useful: "Learn from everybody else's mistakes." Making the right choices became just as important to Olivia as having the right to make a choice. Her desire to move on in life was not a rejection of her mother, because she desperately did not want to lose her. She wanted to move far away from the world of employers. Olivia wanted a space called home that does not include employers.

3

Being the Maid's Daughter

> It was weird to me that we lived in this private neighborhood. There were gates, huge gates that blocked off the streets so no cars could come in. They had combination locks. It was not open to the public. I knew everybody who lived there. Nobody came in. We went out, but nobody came in. I remember seeing these kids. On one side was a Black neighborhood, and I saw these Black kids. I knew there was something else that I had no access to. At the same time, I was privy to being able to come in. My mother undid the combination, and we locked the door. We were able to lock the door and go out.
>
> We walked up Olympic Boulevard for a while. I saw the high school, and I saw that all the things were different. (Interview, June 1990)

Early on in this project, I found myself captivated by Olivia's recollections of moving across social boundaries and the incredible contrasts of wealth and poverty she experienced. As Olivia told her story from the perspective of the child she was at the time, her joy of experiencing Mexican culture, filled with family and a spirit of sharing, was quite visibly displayed by her laughter and pride. Immediately evident to me were the contrasts between the social world of the employers and her excursions to visit her godparents, joining in the maids' gatherings, and summer vacations with her extended family in Mexico. In her stories about these retreats from the Smith household, I began to know more about Carmen as a skillful entrepreneur. Outside the purview of employers, Carmen engaged in a range of entrepreneurial activities that remained invisible to her employers. Among other working-class Mexican immigrants and Mexicans, Carmen is a role model—a successful business woman. The complexities of moving back and forth from social settings and interactions that are economically and culturally distinct from each other have been experienced differently by mother and daughter. These retreats from living within the Smith household became a significant cultural anchor keeping Olivia from fading into the employers' world. The world of Mexican workers and their children was a crucial path in her search for belonging and maintaining her strong Chicana identity.

VISITS TO THE BARRIO

The bus ride from the gated community to the Mexican community in San Fernando may not have involved crossing national or state boundaries, but the social distance was marked by the different houses, markets, bakeries, people, language, food, music, and family activities. The Cordova family is not Olivia's biological family but is a "fictitious" family that was more formally established when they became her godparents. Being among her godparents' family reminded her of the smells and sounds of her previous life with her grandmother and aunts in Mexico. Her *madrina* and *padrino* spoke Spanish to her, and her Spanish-speaking ability was valued and rewarded in their home:

> The family that my mother came with from Juárez always stayed together in San Fernando, the three sisters and their brother. We took the bus downtown and then got on another bus for a two-hour ride to San Fernando. It really was not far, but we took city buses, and they stopped everywhere. It was a horrible trip. My mom started to meet a lot of people on this trip. Sometimes she met people on the bus, and she helped them find jobs. It used to annoy me that we couldn't just sit on the bus like normal people, talk to each other, and look out the window. She was always trying to talk to somebody else her age.
>
> We spent the night with our friends in San Fernando. We slept on the floor in their house all together like a family. I really enjoyed it because it was like a totally different cultural experience. We only spoke Spanish. I felt like they were like my cousins. We even did the laundry together. I remembered that everyone took their clothes to the laundromat. We all sat and talked at the laundromat. That was real exciting for me to have all these people all around. They were my *padrinos* [godparents]. I was good friends with their kids. (Interview, June 1990)

Visits outside of Liberty Place represented a completely different cultural experience for Olivia. The music and sounds of Spanish-speaking people in a household represented a dream of what family life should be. Along with the change in language was the change in activities. Sleeping arrangements were not separated by dividing persons as "the family" on one floor and Carmen and Olivia in the maid's quarters. Children did not all have their own rooms. Accommodating additional members on weekends required sleeping on the floor in close proximity to each other. With the members of the household not being separated in individual bedrooms like employers' families, Olivia felt like a family member sleeping on the floor alongside her godparents' children. She was particularly excited about the new and unusual experience of going to the laundromat. In addition to finding that not every household had its own washer or dryer, she experienced doing the laundry as a family activity rather than work relegated to maids. These visits structured Olivia's sense of "being normal"—that is, blending in with other Mexican people rather than being the only Mexican child in the neighborhood and dissolving the social hierarchies that structured her life in Liberty Place. Here was a social world completely away from the Smiths and other employers; she joined a network of new friends whom she did not have to share.

As Olivia got older, she found less in common with her *padrinos'* children. As the children reached middle-school, the differences in their everyday lives were influenced by the lack of opportunities and economic constraints, which gradually pulled them toward incompatible directions. Living in a gated community, safe from drive-by shootings or encounters with drug addicts, Olivia's experiences were different. However, her godparents' children faced gangs, drugs, and poverty on a daily basis. Every aspect of Olivia's schooling and extracurricular activities groomed her to be college bound. Unlike the private schools that Olivia attended, the public schools that the children of immigrant parents in San Fernando attended were overcrowded and poorly equipped, and teaching was secondary to discipline.[1] The realities of poverty were the norm, and the impact on life chances became more apparent to Olivia as she got older:

After I started playing tennis, we just stopped spending the night. That was my big activity. Sometimes my godfather's son played tennis with me. But we grew apart because he got into gangs, and I wasn't into it. I was aware of *cholos* [gang members], and I knew he dressed the whole part. All of them did. They were all into the San Fernando gangs. My *madrina*'s oldest son died of an overdose when I was five. The oldest son shot up heroin too. The oldest one ran off with some woman who was a lot older. His parents didn't approve. He had a daughter who was raised by my godmother. She and I were very close. She was about five years younger than I was. She got leukemia, and we visited her all the time when she was in the hospital. They told her she was not going to live. But my mother knew this priest in Aguascalientes who was famous for doing miracles. The doctors had given her only three years to live. My mother arranged for them to take her to see the *padre*. She is still alive today. She got a bone-marrow transplant. They were convinced the *padre* made her get better.

My other godmother had three sons. I was never really sure who the father was because he was drunk sometimes, or he left and came back. The oldest two were seriously into drugs. The middle one was into this gang stuff. He killed somebody and went to prison. We went with my godmother to wait in line at the jail to visit him in prison.

My godfather's youngest daughter was a teenage mother. I remember that little girl. I used to teach her English. My mother was convinced that she was in gangs or doing things because of the way she dressed. She got pregnant at seventeen. She ended up marrying somebody who was not the father but who basically really loved her. He married her and became the father to the baby.

My mother thought it was horrible. I remember being shocked when my mother told me, "You know I just don't understand why Rosie didn't have an abortion." I always thought what would happen if I got pregnant as a teenager, before I was an adult. I was really afraid of what my mother would say and react. I felt like I would want to go have an abortion, but I had assumed her attitude would be different. I just thought that she would have figured, "I had you. Why couldn't you do the same?" (Interview, June 1990)

Rather than experiencing Los Angeles solely in a protected gated community and surrounding upscale neighborhoods, Olivia crossed the class, racial, and citizenship divide with her mother. Joining her mother on these excursions taught Olivia about the social and economic realities of working-class immigrant struggles and the hardships of poverty. She knew that employers' sons and daughters used drugs, but the consequences were completely different. She also knew that the Smith children were sexually active, but pregnancy was unlikely because of their access to contraceptives prescribed by their doctors. Marrying before finishing college was an inconceivable event in the lives of the employers' family. The country club and extracurricular activities at private schools did not exist in low-income communities; consequently, gang life filled a void created by the lack of opportunity. Olivia's access to a wide range of athletic and educational programs that other children of working-class immigrant children did not have shaped her goals and the choices she made. She found her friendship with her godparents' children dissolving, as they had little in common except ethnicity. Juxtaposing the experiences of employers' children and those of low-wage immigrant workers' children, Olivia felt alienated from both, but she felt a strong commitment to maintain her ethnic identity.

Olivia observed her mother's status change as she moved outside Liberty Place. Her status changed again when visiting godparents in San Fernando and the other maids in Liberty Place. Such visiting offered Olivia a window to know her mother in ways that she did not while living in the gated community. She observed her mother being involved in these other people's lives and participating in activities usually restricted to family members, such as giving advice, visiting her friend's granddaughter in the hospital, and accompanying a friend who was going to visit her son in prison. Among the Smith children, Carmen tolerated drugs, sex, and drinking, but she let her daughter know that she did not approve. Olivia was used to learning the rules and boundaries in her life and figured she knew what to expect from her mother. She assumed she knew her mother's views about such issues as abortion, since her mother was a practicing Catholic. But instead, she discovered that her mother views abortion as an acceptable option. Coming to this realization, Olivia wondered why her mother did not choose to have an abortion rather than to be a single mother. Over the years, Olivia not only recognized how strong and smart her mother is but that she is a complex person whose actions and opinions cannot easily be predicted. Crossing cultural and class boundaries, Olivia began to understand her mother's willingness to conform to employers' expectations.

As one of the first Latina-immigrant live-in maids in Liberty Place, Carmen positioned herself to play an active role in finding employers women to hire. She became the hub of a social network connecting maids and employers, and as one consequence the maids came to know one another and form their own support network. Olivia was included in their social gatherings in the neighborhood. They regularly met in the evenings and weekends and cooked Mexican food, listened to Spanish radio, or watched *novelas* on TV. In the shadows of the employers' homes, the maids created a physical space that was Mexican and not white, Spanish speaking and not English speaking, female dominated rather than male dominated, and working class instead of upper middle class. Excluding employers from these activities allowed the women to build support systems of cultural, economic, and social resistance that addressed their needs as mothers, immigrants, workers, and women.[2] These weekly sessions were essential in establishing the means to affirm and enhance their own self-worth and cultural values. Accompanying Carmen, Olivia heard the opinions of working women as they gossiped and shared strategies for dealing with employers.[3] Listening to these conversations, Olivia gained valuable insights into the socialization processes of Los Angeles's class-based, gendered, and racist social structure. Here Olivia was not a cultural artifact but a member of the Mexican community. The regular evening sessions with working-class Mexican immigrant women became essential in reinforcing her mother's cultural values.

> The maids in the neighborhood got together to do a lot of different things, and I went with them a lot. At the end of the week, around six o'clock, when the maids got done with their work, they got together. Time with the other domestics was my mother's support system. After their work hours, they went to different women's rooms depending on what their rooms had. Some of them had kitchens, and they got together and cooked, played cards, and talked. We did things together like a family. When the maids got together, they talked about a lot of issues. They talked a lot about immigration. They talked about their family problems and about things at home. I remember that on those situations they talked about what their employers were like, when they were going to negotiate for raises, and how they didn't like certain things about their employers. The women shared

information about how to deal with the different families, who the kids were, and why they were like that. My mother knew all kinds of things about these families. Then when somebody was going to work for the Nelsons, my mother filled them all in on the background [of their new employers].

My mom kept track of working conditions through her network. She found out how things were going for the domestics: Did they like their jobs? What were they doing now? Whenever the working conditions changed, they talked to my mother and said, "Well, you know, I told them I didn't want to cook. But after a while they asked me to cook, and I did because I didn't like what they were eating." She found out what had changed and if they had acquiesced to it. Then my mother got pissed off and said, "No! No! No! Don't cook for them. If you cook, then you're going to have to get a raise." If they said, "Well, I don't mind." Then she told them, "Well, then you have to get another raise. When's the last time you got a raise?" She didn't keep track on a little book or anything, but she did keep track. (Interview, July 1997)

Olivia recalled these gatherings as significant in building and strengthening a sense of community and solidarity among the maids of Liberty Place. Along with providing companionship, the women exchanged information about job expectations, salary, and strategies for negotiating with employers for raises. Because of their informal working arrangements with employers, their collective agreements were a crucial strategy to maintain wage standards and to make enforcement of those standards more likely. As live-in maids, they always had concerns about dealing with additional labor, limiting the hours that employers expected them to work and the tasks that needed to be done, and protecting their time off, as well as making provisions to attend English as a Second Language classes for those who desired to learn or improve their English skills. Agreeing on the tasks that were to be classified as part of the job helped maids avoid employers' requests to clean garages, do yard work, garden, and do countless other tasks. Carmen equated serving meals as servitude, which also involved placing the maid in the position of waiting "hand and foot" on employers, which was complete subordination. Carmen had clear feelings about this request and expected the women who were willing to do this work to be compensated for it as additional work.

Protecting time off is a constant struggle for live-in maids, particularly for two-career families. When maids are not assertive about their days off, they can easily find themselves working an additional half day or completely losing the time off and not receiving pay for the additional work.[4] In Carmen's case, she negotiated a vacation in the summer to visit her family in Mexico. Since many of her employers spent time at their family beach homes in the summer, and the children attended summer camps and traveled, the Smiths accommodated her request. Some maids had husbands and families with whom they spent their days off. Others relied on friends and family members to assist in providing them a community and home to spend their days off. If maids did not have transportation to visit friends or relatives, they spent their days off alone in the maid's quarters. In these cases, they were likely to find themselves vulnerable to employers' requests to care for children, to help prepare a meal, or to engage in other work activities. Requests by employers for maids to join them on an outing did not necessarily assure that the day was workfree or restful. Networking with the other maids in the neighborhood helped them plan time off together and share transportation or have a friend to spend the day with.

Scheduling regular gatherings was very important in assuring that none of the workers became isolated, which is a particular problem that many live-in maids and nannies experience. The problem of isolation is particularly crucial for maids who have limited English-speaking abilities and who are separated from their own children and family members. Employers and their families frequently maintain boundaries within their homes, and even when maids are invited to participate in family activities, their role as the maid is always present. Rarely if ever did the Liberty Place maids eat with the family of their employers.[5] If the employers' children had a separate dining time from their parents, the maid might sit at the table to eat as well, but her major function was to assist the children. Only maids working for widows were likely to be asked to join their employers to share the same dining table, but even in these situations, the maid served and the employer was waited on. Regular gatherings provided maids with a safety net in case they encountered abusive relations or felt helpless in vulnerable circumstances. Sharing information and calling on their networks with employers, together they were able to assist each other in crisis.

Intimate details about the employers' marriages and family were freely exposed to Mexican-immigrant maids through two common practices found in domestic service: the treatment of maids as invisible and as confidants.[6] Mexican maids were expected to move around the house without interrupting the family's activities, planning their work around family members' activities and acting invisible until summoned by the employer. Consequently, maids were in a position to hear family conversations and arguments and viewed family scenes that revealed behavior and personal characteristics otherwise hidden from the public. Maids are frequently called on to counsel and to console employers and their families. As confidants, the maids became privy to a wide range of information about marital conflict, sibling rivalry, and problems with in-laws, neighbors, and co-workers.

Along with exchanging strategies for asking for raises or dealing with employer problems, sharing gossip about their employers' families was a crucial ritual for creating solidarity among the maids and maintaining distinctions between "they" and "we." Gossiping involved trust in fellow workers. Most important, critiquing the lifestyles and parenting of employers served the functions for the maids of redefining their status as good mothers and strong women who shared a culture that values extended family and sacrificing for your children's futures, and it was a valuable strategy for rejecting the low-status position the women experienced as maids, as immigrants, and as Mexicans.

> I listened and heard different discussions about what was going on in different houses. They talked about family relationships, particularly the way the parents interacted with their kids. At the time, some of the kids were smoking pot, and they talked about how weird it was that the parents didn't care. They talked about what they saw as being wrong with their employers' families. They talked about the marriage relationships and how weird it was that the women went off to the beauty salon, spent lots of money shopping, and the effect that it had on the kids.
>
> Somehow my mother knew all this. People told her themselves. They'd say, "Well, you know, I'm really disappointed with so-and-so because they just haven't been doing that well in school." They told her all these personal things. These

women felt like they had this personal relationship with my mother and felt she was trustworthy. "Oh, you can tell Carmen anything." A lot of them treated her like that, especially at the Joneses' house. She knew the friends of all the sons and daughters. When their mothers came into the kitchen during a party or dinner, she asked them, "Oh, how is your son or daughter?" My mother was big on doing that. Then they told her, "Oh, well, you know, Carmen. I don't know what's going on." They cried on her shoulder. They told her how lucky she was that I was so perfect. Of course, she never told me that.

My mother always brought up that issue of their parenting. She was critical of the way the Smiths raised their kids. She talked about how different we were and how the kids never took advantage of their education. She said it was dumb for Mrs. Smith to tell her kids, "Oh, it's okay, if you don't feel like going to school today, you don't have to go to school if you don't want to." She talked about how Jane was a pig. The last time she had been to her house, she had to step over piles of clothing on the floor. Her laundry never got done until somebody came over and did it for her. She didn't even separate what were dirty clothes from what was clean. She talked about Ted and David smoking pot. I knew she thought that was unacceptable, but she never did anything about it. She never felt like it was her responsibility to do anything about it.

She talked about my aunts and was critical of how they disciplined my cousins. Especially if we were at the market, she thought it was so inappropriate when some Mexicana would profusely beat their child in the market. When my mom hit me, she felt really bad about it—like she was regressing. She didn't hit me very often. She just glared at me. That seemed to work. That look let me know that if I continued in that behavior, it was all over.

My mother also talked about learning lessons from the Anglos. She pointed out that the Anglos don't teach their kids to say bad things, like, "Oh, look. Look how cute: they said 'fuck.'" She had a very strong opinion about families thinking that it was really cute to teach kids bad words. My mother thought, "Now, why don't we teach them their numbers or something? If we really want their attention and want something, why don't we do something that's beneficial?" She thought you should be teaching kids something beneficial. She told them how important the words we teach our children are and the need to give kids positive reinforcement. I would sit there and laugh. Later when we were alone, I'd tell my mother, "Oh, yeah, like you give me so much positive reinforcement."

"Well, you're different because Mrs. Smith gives it to you."

I always thought it so hypocritical for her to tell me that I wanted to be a little rich kid, but she wasn't willing to look at the contradictions in her life. It was weird. I think that my mom thought that as a domestic, she was able to step in and out of it. She felt like somehow identity issues were my struggle, and she was free from that kind of an identity crisis. She wasn't really sympathetic at all. She just assumed that naturally I was jealous and wanted to be the Smiths' daughter. (Interview, July 1997)

Mexican maids are particularly vocal about their disapproval of lenient child-rearing practices and parental decisions. Drug use and the emphasis placed on commodities in the child-parent relationship were specific areas the Liberty Place maids pointed to as the source of family problems.[7] In exchanging gossip and sharing opinions about the employers' lifestyles, the maids reinforced their rejection of employers' values and priorities in life. Through exposure to the maids' accounts about their experiences working in the homes of white, upper- and upper-middle-class families, Olivia learned the cost of white privilege, class privilege, and male privilege. Employers' careers and lifestyles, particularly the everyday rituals affirming male privilege, were made possible through the labor women provided for men's physical, social, and emotional needs. Female employers depended on the maid's labor to assist in the reproduction of their gendered class status. Household labor was expanded in order to accommodate the male members of the employers' families and to preserve their privilege. Additional work was created by rearranging meal schedules around men's work and recreation schedules and by waiting on them and serving them. Carmen was frequently called on to provide emotional labor for employers' families, thus freeing members to work or to increase their leisure time. Unlike the Mexican immigrants employed as maids, who were frequently the sole supporter of their children, Mrs. Smith and the other women employers were financially dependent on their husbands. The maids had a much higher regard for their own duties and responsibilities as mothers than as wives or lovers. In comparison to their mistresses, they did not engage in the expensive and time-consuming activities of being an ideal wife, such as dieting, exercising, and maintaining a certain standard of beauty in their dress, makeup, and hairdo.

Olivia observed the additional time and energy women employers had to nurture their children—time and energy gained by transferring the less appealing aspects of child care to the maids. She saw how maids consoled the employers' children and provided emotional support. She also experienced the lack of time and energy that Carmen had to mother, because she had to work weekends, holidays, and evenings. Olivia was in a position to acquire a much different understanding of the division of labor than the employers' children had. Her intimate exposure to the realities of white, upper- and upper-middle-class patriarchal families led Olivia to question myths about "family values" and society's denigration of Mexican culture and female-headed households.[8] Unlike employers' daughters, who attended cotillion[9] and were socialized to acquire success through marriage, Olivia was constantly pushed to succeed academically in order to pursue a career and become financially independent. The gender identity cultivated among the maids did not include dependence on men or the learned helplessness that was enforced in employers' homes by hiring maids. Rather, Olivia's experience with her mother and the other maids promoted self-sufficiency.

This sharing of stories about the Smiths and other employers in a fe-male-, Mexican-, and worker-dominated social setting provided Olivia with a clear image of the people she lived with as employers rather than as family members. Seeing the employers through the eyes of the employees forced Olivia to question the employers' kindness and benevolence and to recognize the manipulation they used to obtain additional physical and emotional labor from their employees. She became aware of the workers' struggles and the long list of grievances, including no annual raises, no paid vacations, no Social Security or health benefits, little if any privacy, and sexual harassment. In essence, she learned class consciousness.

In addition to serving as a support group and a mechanism for safe-guarding the quality and quantity of jobs in the gated community, the domestics accumulated savings as a communal/collective initiative. These initiatives in the Mexican community are sometimes referred to as a *tanda*. All participating members engage in spending and investment decisions.[10] Olivia described the women coming together to create a rotating credit union:[11]

There was also the financial system my mom created—a pyramid thing. She got all of them to contribute money and help each other—everyone a hundred dollars. Every time you get paid, like every two weeks, you put in another hundred dollars. And that way somebody had a thousand dollars to send home all at once. They took turns. They actually bid for a place, not with money but by saying, "I want to be in third place. I'll do it if I can get the third place, because that's when I need the money." Then my mom would ultimately decide whose claim was legitimate. If something came up, they would all switch turns. (Interview, July 1997)

If one of the women was unable to contribute every two weeks, Carmen contributed for them. Since she earned the confidence of the other maids, they deferred to her age and experience. Having her daughter living in the neighborhood also provided both the other maids and employers with a sense of her stability in the neighborhood and of her extensive network that included employers.[12] Given that Carmen was the oldest and longest-employed live-in domestic in Liberty Place, she had more connections with the employers, and the other workers relied heavily on her to intervene on their behalf.

Olivia took an active role in the maids' community by serving as a translator. Her bilingual abilities offered the predominantly Spanish-speaking maids with an expert translator to negotiate with employers and to assist in business they needed to conduct in English, and her bilingual literacy skills allowed her to assist in letter writing and filling out forms.[13] Most maids had limited English-speaking abilities and managed to understand their employers' requests, but detailed negotiation required a translator. In this role, Olivia learned negotiating skills and reinforced her allegiance to the immigrant workers. In the following excerpt, she illustrates the significance of her reading and writing bilingual abilities in helping the maids control their working condition and salary, maintaining contact with relatives in Mexico, filling out applications, and conducting business transactions:

When new people [potential employers] moved into the area, my mother went to meet them. She went to their house and talked to them about the help they needed. She went and rang the door bell and introduced herself. They invited her in. She sat down to talk to them and asked them if they were going to need somebody to clean their house. She asked how many kids they had and decided who was good to work there. She did that same type of interviewing with all the people who were looking for help. Then she went back and talked to her friends and said, "I have somebody. Do you know of somebody who needs a job?" She would get somebody placed, and they would start working there.

Ever since I starting speaking English, I have translated for my mother. It started when I was in elementary school. My mother always made me go with her and the other women to negotiate working conditions. She took me with her to talk to potential employers that moved into the neighborhood. She *dragged* me along—and I literally felt dragged. She said, "Okay, *mija*, why don't you go with us to the *señora* so-and-so, so you can translate." Sometimes I thought it was a real pain in the ass. But once I was there, I remember feeling really protective. I wanted to make sure that the woman was not going to be abused. I always thought the questions that they asked me to translate were interesting. My mother reworded the woman's answers and told me, "No. You tell him this: They need a TV. All right?" She gave me the evil eye to let me know I had better translate what she had said. I knew whose side I was on. I was not a neutral negotiator. I was not simply translating. I was actually trying to get the best situation for this particular person.

She tried to get the women the days off that they wanted, usually two days—either Sunday and Monday or Monday and Tuesday. Employers usually expected them to be there on the weekends. I always thought that was stupid. Why don't they get off on Friday? They started working at eight.

This was a real weird feeling for me to be playing this role. It was really interesting because the families were always so impressed with me. Since my mother took me along, they all knew my mother as, "Oh, Carmen, the one with the daughter." Not only did she have her own network, but I was the big neighborhood novelty. I went to all these homes and did all this translating. When I was about twelve and was involved in other things, it annoyed me to go translate for my mother. I protested. My mother always thought I didn't want to go because I was embarrassed. Once I was in the woman's living room, I kind of enjoyed it. Then I decided I really liked translating and even thought about it as a career.

I translated for the other domestics too. I helped them write their letters in Spanish. I helped them write the addresses on the envelopes. I helped them fill out papers to go get their Social Security cards. I did stuff like that. I always went to the post office with them. They called me up and asked me to go with them.

I felt close to them. I knew they needed the help, or they wouldn't be asking me. I really sympathized with them. It must have been very hard for them to be away from their families in Mexico or who lived elsewhere in Los Angeles. If it was hard for me dealing with these people [employers], I imagined how hard it must have been for them to be so far away. They were adults and had to put up with this shit. (Interview, November 1992)

Olivia's role as an interpreter for her mother and other Spanish-speaking adults is not that unusual among immigrants.[14] Children translating for their parents as novice interpreters "often find themselves in the role of resource person or local expert."[15] Olivia accepted her role as translator as including negotiation of the best working conditions. Like other immigrant children translating for their parents, she became a trusted mediator who protected the interests of the workers.[16] School attendance and interaction with employers' children provided her opportunities to become fluent in English much sooner than the Spanish-speaking maids and landscapers employed in the gated community. For the most part, their employment did not provide the same level of interaction to learn English quickly. Their social time was spent among predominantly Spanish-speaking persons. As a language broker, Olivia assisted her mother in encounters with doctors, employers, teachers, and other monolingual English speakers.[17] Although some researchers argue that placing children in a translating role becomes role reversal with the parent, Olivia recognized that her mother listened carefully and that she was "simply carrying out tasks that may more appropriately be thought of as analogous to specialized 'household chores.'"[18]

Carmen's remittances were the most significant portion of asset building for her extended family. Carmen assisted in financing a community store, building homes, and paying for her nieces' and nephews' education. Whatever happened to her in the United States, she was always assured a home for herself and Olivia in Mexico. Olivia saw the wide range of asset-building activities that her mother and the other Mexican immigrants were involved in. Translating for her mother and other maids was only the beginning of Olivia's involvement in the daily lives of maids and mistresses. She was included in a variety of economic endeavors negotiated by her mother, particularly taking clothes to Mexico as gifts and to sell.

One of the most unusual practices in domestic work is employers' giving of old clothes and other items that are normally recycled, such as household items, to their employees. Although numerous researchers have noted the practice of employers giving domestics old clothes and other goods, usually in lieu of benefits, Olivia recounted the way that these goods crossed borders and became supplemental income for extended family members.[19] Olivia expressed mixed feelings about assisting her mother in the entrepreneurial venture of selling clothes. Her laughter was sprinkled throughout her narrative about the collection and reallocation process:

> I remember when we lived at the Smiths, my mother had bags of clothes, garbage bags full of clothes that we were either going to give to my cousins or keep them. They were just there in the closet. At some point we needed to make a decision about it. There were always things in the room that my mother had been given.
>
> She had a sewing machine that had a real pretty cherry-wood cover that made a real nice table. I used to tell my mother, "You don't sew, Mom." At one time she started sewing for the Joneses. She did their tailoring. She brought it home. My mom told Mrs. Jones, "I can't do this stuff because I don't have a sewing machine." Then Mrs. Jones said, "Well, we'll get you a sewing machine. Do you want this sewing machine?" My mom said, "Yes, I want this sewing machine." Then we took it. I remember it was a big deal to bring the sewing machine home to the Smiths and put it in our room.
>
> That is how the collecting began. My mother had access to these things, so she took them. It was like a reallocation process. After she got things, she would make a decision about it. Did she want it? Or who else should get it? Which one of her friends needed furniture and needed things? She then gave it to them.
>
> My mother brought everything home. At night, my mother and her friends got things the employers threw in the trash. Later she got to the point where she was up front and just asked for things. "Are you going to get rid of that? Are you going to throw that away? Because I really want it and like it." The Joneses were always getting rid of things, and she always brought it home.
>
> We always had tons of pencils because people threw away their office junk. As if I really needed boxes of pencils or a whole bunch of used pens with a rubber band around them! While I was watching TV, it was my job to check all the pens and keep the ones that worked. There was always more than we needed. But we had to keep them because they worked.

I remember having this awful desk that my mother convinced me that I should have. Mrs. Robertson, who was a consul from Switzerland, was throwing away a bunch of business shit. She brought this desk home that I kept for years. This table was like a mini file cabinet. It had a little door with the key. The fact that it had a key was the big deal to me. It had a little storage place almost like a little safe. That's where my private papers were kept. It had a tacky metal folding table that swung up with this aluminum leg. It was always rickety and falling apart. I didn't like it. But my mother convinced me that I needed it for school and that it was great to have this desk. I finally took the top off and threw it away. I used the little file cabinet and kept all my little private letters, my "boy's" junk, in it.

At one time there was not an inch of space along the wall in this room. We had a queen-size bed where we both slept in. I hated that little room because there was too much stuff in there. There were all kinds of things under the bed, even men's shoes. We kept them because my uncle might use them, or somebody that he knew might need them. Sometimes we took the stuff to Juárez. We had this, like, garage-sale storage stuff.

My mother's attitude was, "Look at all these stupid people. These are really nice clothes." That was the way it was with the Jimenezes [employer]. Once I got a little older, Mrs. Jimenez would wear a dress once, throw it away, or took it to my mom. Then I'd have it. Mrs. Jimenez never really commented. I didn't wear any of the Jimenezes' clothes around her. I didn't think she had given it to Mom with good intentions. Like, the Joneses, the attitude was, "Oh, here, Carmen. If you want this, fine. If not, give it to somebody else who needs it." Whereas Mrs. Jimenez could have given a shit where it ended up. I felt like we were basically getting it out of the trash. It wasn't really a hand-me-down. It was something she wouldn't have worn anymore. It was like with disdain. Mrs. Jimenez left it up to my mom to get rid of the stuff that she didn't wear anymore. I thought that was real strange. She really didn't make conscious decisions about what she didn't want anymore. If she wasn't wearing it anymore, my mother removed it from the closet and put it somewhere else. Then my mother would ask her, "Do you still want these things?" Then she would say, "No." Then sometimes my mother would flat out ask her, "I really like this dress for Olivia. Can I have it?" (Interview, June 1990)

These stories recognize the employee as an agent in the exchange rather than as the subject of this practice. Olivia was aware that her mother was not a passive participant in this ritual of giving clothes in domestic service. She observed her mother taking an active role by periodically going through the employers' closets and pulling out all the clothing and shoes that were no longer being worn and making room for the new school wardrobe. Employers found this task quite helpful, and Carmen was in a position to add newer styles to her inventory of goods. Throughout the school year, Olivia watched her mother bringing home clothes that the employers gave her. The used clothes were placed in plastic bags and were stored in their small bedroom. Their room was only large enough for one bed, and as the bags overflowed the closet floor, more eventually were placed under the bed. I recall my visit to Liberty Place in the late '90s and seeing the maid's quarters. I was shocked to see exactly how small the maid's room was. Imagining a queen-size bed in the room, I doubt there was much walking area left. I can only imagine how crowded the space was prior to removing all the bags and taking them to Mexico.

Many of these items made their way to the families of the other live-in maids who were less assertive than Carmen was about asking for things that the employer was no longer wearing or using. Carmen's friends and relatives also received items that they might need. School materials, such as pens and pencils, were shared with the children of immigrant workers. However, the major destination for these items was Mexico. As Carmen and Olivia prepared to leave for Mexico for their summer visit, Olivia would sort through the clothes with her mother, pulling aside items she wanted to give her good friend Rosalina, a young mother living across the street from her aunt in Aguascalientes. Clothes previously worn to the country club, cotillion, prom, and other middle-class activities were destined to be worn at *los posadas*[20] and *quinceañeras.*[21] Casual wear became clothes for the everyday chores of shopping in the open markets and hauling water. As Olivia's narrative of summers in Mexico illustrates, she had difficulty making sense out of the recontextualization and cross-cultural consumption of these designer clothes, as they embodied new forms and became transnational. The fashions from Rodeo Drive become "reworked in the context of local practice."[22] Olivia's recollections of the entire ritual of employers' giving of clothes and the elaborate sorting and redistribution process that her mother and aunts engaged in capture the expression of social identity and dress, as status is either transformed or maintained through the exchange. The following account illustrates how she learned to value things:

For a while, when I was younger, my mother and my aunts sold clothes in Aguascalientes. It was really strange to me. I did not approve. Some of the clothes they sold were new.

This is when my mother made decisions about what I didn't wear anymore and what I wasn't going to have anymore, and then she sold it. I got pissed off when my mother sold some of my clothes. I was never aware of which clothes she had decided to sell.

I remember I had these obnoxious little shorts that I called them my "Fourth of July" shorts, because they were blue culottes with fireworks and American flags on them. They were my Fourth of July shorts. I thought they were very cool. I remember I was still wearing them. I was looking for them and could not find them.

My mother said, "Oh, no. You didn't bring them."

I said, "No. I know I brought them. They're here somewhere. There in some pile somewhere. I know you took them."

Then two weeks later, I'm in this little town with all these poor people. I look up, and there is some little girl wearing my Fourth of July shorts. I was so pissed off about it.

When I first became aware or conscious of what my mom was doing, I told her not to sell the clothes. I didn't think it was appropriate for her to be selling these things. I felt she should just be giving them away. I knew that we had gotten them for nothing. They had just been sitting in our closet in bags. It's not like they had any value. I thought these clothes had value when they're purchased by Anglos at Saks. Afterwards, there's no value to them. That was my concept of it. They purchased them. Then they belonged to another network. It's our decision how we wanted to handle it. We shouldn't be exchanging money for it. I thought that was a real dirty thing. I didn't care if she gave them away, but I did not want her to sell them. I thought they were giving this stuff away, because sometimes my mom told me, "Oh, we'll give this to Rosalina," or she mentioned another person. But everything that wasn't destined for somebody she sold. My aunt's role was to set a price on each piece of clothing. The price was set according to what they could afford. Nothing was very expensive: a couple bucks for each thing. There was, like, a real market in Aguascalientes.

The night before we got on the train, my aunts and mother packed very secretively after we had gone to sleep. They decided what to pack. My mother had this suitcase that she didn't open until she was alone with her sisters. Together they made joint decisions about these clothes. What clothes were going to stay for my cousins? Who fit into what clothes? The clothes that were too worn out for us to wear were placed in a pile to give away. Then there were the silk shirts. They were kept just because they are silk shirts. They separated all of the clothes into these piles, and then we went to Aguascalientes. In LA, when my mother was putting the clothes into bags, I said, "No. I want this. I'm going to give this to Rosalina." I always thought it was really neat to see these really poor, poor people wearing these really nice clothes. I like the reactions that they caused.

Eventually I became aware of my mother and aunts selling the clothes in Aguascalientes. When I was outside playing with my friends, I began to notice all these people going to my aunt's house. The clothes were all laid out. I started to realize that these ladies were going to my aunt's house in the afternoon to look at the clothes. They only sold clothes when my uncle's wife was not home, because she was very status conscious and wanted to maintain an appearance of being upper class.

Some of these people who went to look at the clothes were girls that I didn't like. I thought it was repulsive that my mother had invited their mothers and them over to go through these clothes. These girls were little rich bitches. I was really angry to see my mother selling clothes to them, because they didn't need it. I had finally accepted my mother selling clothes to the people who were middle class. I didn't like the idea that these rich women were buying these silk shirts. Their families were ranchers, and they were just starting to make all this money. To me, they were like the Smiths or the Joneses in terms of class. I just hated them. They never came out and played with anybody else in the block. They were really prissy. They only wanted to stay inside in the air conditioning and watch TV.

Then they started giving away clothes and selling the shoes. I didn't mind the clothes as much as the shoes. They had all these shoes. To me they looked ridiculous in these expensive ladies' shoes that were all size eight. These women wore them everywhere. A month later, I would see them in the strangest settings. (Interview, June 1990)

Olivia identified the clothes' monetary worth set at the time of purchase by employers in an upscale store. Her discomfort with her mother and aunt's selling of the clothes illustrates the complex relationship between the process of distribution and social relations, as well as the transmission of social identities. When Carmen sold the clothes in Mexico, she took the place of Saks and became the peddler. Olivia advocated for a redistribution process that did not commodify the clothing and transmit American social identities. Olivia's disapproval of her mother and aunt's selling of the clothes may have been a desire to transform the value of the designer label as well as all the meanings attached to the ritual of gift-giving in domestic service and how the clothes are purchased. Giving away the clothes to whoever wants or needs them transforms the original process for the distribution of goods from exchange value to use value. She wanted the clothes to be redistributed in a manner that stripped the clothing of class "status"—that is, stripped of social identity and connection with the world of maids and mistresses in the United States. However, placing a monetary value on the clothes in the exchange reaffirmed their commodification. In order to retain the class status embodied in the cruise wear, sportswear, and weekend wear, the Mexican middle class had to purchase the item. The class status was lost if Olivia's mother and aunt gave the clothes away to the rancher families. Giving clothes away is an act of charity, and the class status attached to the employers' clothes would be lost. Accepting the clothes as a gift reduces them to the same mistress-maid relationship that generated the bags of used clothing in the United States. Olivia's mother's and her aunt's status thus becomes elevated through their generosity. However, in the same way that the mistress might decide which clothes to resell, which to give to the Salvation Army for a tax deduction, and which to give to her domestic worker, Carmen and her sister classified the clothes into gifts to friends, give-aways, and items for sale.

In later interviews conducted in the late '90s, Olivia reflected on the ways she developed a habit of hoarding clothes and household goods to redistribute to her family and friends:

> I don't think I've been conscious of collecting things until recently. My friend John pointed it out to me. He helped me move one time. He said, "Do you realize that you have three truckloads of clothes? We've done three trips just on your clothes." I feel like I adopted a lot of these values that you collect things. It doesn't matter if

you wear them or not. I guess my mother always decided what I was getting rid of and what I was keeping. I never had to make any decisions about things. If I didn't wear them, my mom got rid of them. The clothes just existed there, and somebody was going take care of it—I mean, not so much in terms of washing them but making the decision about whether they stayed or not. (Interview, March 1998)

Every time I visited Olivia's home, I found the collection of clothes ready for redistribution. During one of my visits, her husband teased her about her obsession with putting the caps back on the pen. She turned to me and said,

I have no idea why I can't stand to see the caps off pens. (Interview, July 1998)

I reminded her that as a child, her job was to check all the pens her mother brought home to see if they worked. On many occasions, I saw her salvage items that could still be used. Olivia is, after all, her mother's daughter.

SUMMERS IN MEXICO

Mexico, particularly the border twin cities—El Paso, Texas, and Ciudad Juárez—and Aguascalientes took on mythical proportions in Olivia's search for belonging. Throughout her childhood, she held on to the dream of returning to the border and resuming her life with her extended family, with her mother returning to work as a domestic in El Paso. Spending almost every summer with her relatives reinforced the image of a different life. She enjoyed seeing her mother interact with her sisters and aunts, engaged in fun instead of constantly picking up and cleaning after others. Life was so different than in Liberty Place, where the person next door is your neighbor, not a relative or a godparent, and each house contains a nuclear family, instead of a combination of nuclear and extended family members living together. Families in Mexico are larger and more have women as the head of the household. Spanish instead of English is the dominant language. Everyday labor of cooking, cleaning, child care, and laundry is divided not by race and ethnicity but by gender and age. Olivia held on to the promises of returning and imagined Mexico as a utopia where she really belonged. Everything there was new and different to Olivia. She marveled over hauling water, cooking without the use of electric or gas stoves, and feeding chickens. Some of Olivia's most cherished childhood adventures were her visits to see her great-great-aunts:

We had to walk forty-five minutes to get to this little town. They were very, very poor. Anna [cousin] and I were usually sent to a market to buy meat, eggs, cheese, and *manteca* [lard] to cook while we were visiting. They lived in adobe houses that didn't have any doors. The adobe house had separate rooms, but none of the rooms were connected. We had to walk out of one to get to another. We sat in this one room that was a kitchen. It was black from all the smoke and tar. They had a little *comal* [tortilla griddle]. They made a fire, and that's how they cooked. We sat in this smoke-filled room. This room was really strange, because there was this big stone that was a step. It was all adobe floored. They had all their cups and their plates in an open shelf. There was a big container of water. In the corner they had a surface that was tiled, and that's where they cooked. Everyone just stayed right by this fire all day long. There was this little stone, and that's where my great-great-aunt sat.

They had one room that was their religious room. It was for *la Virgen* [the Virgin Mary]. It was the only room that had a door. It was always real cool inside the room. Sometimes they sat in there. I was just fascinated by the whole thing. Inside the room was an altar. They had this virgin in this big glass case with candles in it. They strung up little paper things.

I asked my grandmother, "Why do you have *la Virgen* in there?" They were real nice and patient with me.

They told me, "Well, it is for *la Virgen* and she takes care of us."

"But why do you have her in this glass case? Isn't that supposed to be in the church? Why do you have it in your house?"

"Well, because she's taking care of us and stuff."

"So what do you think about this?" My great-great-aunt asked me this question. I liked being with her, but only when we were alone. I wanted my mother to leave us alone so we could talk, because when we were alone, she treated me totally different.

My mother didn't like me asking all these questions.

I thought it was real strange that they had all these different activities for each room. In one room we sat in the room while we were eating. We had these clay bowls. I really loved to eat there. I just thought it was so neat that we ate in these clay bowls. The water tasted really good. We sat on the floor and ate. They made handmade tortillas. We ate, and then we went into another room.

We literally spent all day there. My mother and aunts sat there for hours and hours and hours. I felt like they were so happy. They sat there all day long in this smoke-filled room and talked like nothing was important. They just sat there, laughing and talking. I thought it was great to see my mother really relaxed and to see my mother in this whole different environment: not cleaning, not rushing around, but sitting and paying all this attention to them.

The chickens came in through the door, walked around your legs as we sat on these little chairs. I remember sitting there and noticing that my great-great-aunt was wearing Mrs. Jones's shoes. I thought that was funny. I thought, "Yeah, Mrs. Jones has no idea where her shoes are now. How far they've come!" (Interview, June 1990)

Olivia's childhood memories capture the delight she found in the transformation of social identity that the designer clothes went through when worn by residents of Aguascalientes. She recognized how impractical the heels were for great-great-aunts carrying water from the well and feeding the chickens, yet she enjoyed knowing that the shoes had traveled so far—a journey her mother's employers would never have been able to make. The size-eight shoes worn by Mrs. Smith no longer portrayed the wearer as small, dainty, and a member of the leisure class. The clothing did not enclose a body in play and leisure pursuits but one that was active in work. Since the clothing was given by a younger relative far away from the social world of LA mistresses and maids, the social identity communicated in the dress was deconstructed, and the wearers did not become Americanized. Having crossed the border, the clothes now became discarded only when they were worn out and redistributed only when they no longer fit, rather than discarded when they were out of style or simply unable to compete with newer items in the closet.

Embedded in many of Olivia's stories about Mexico were descriptions of events and the environment that contrasted cultures, communities, and families. In the absence of appliances and money, many daily activities focused solely on domestic labor: obtaining and preparing food, cooking, cleaning, and doing laundry. Olivia noted the lack of material belongings but saw contentment and enjoyment in life.

I used to sit and think about my blind aunt in Juárez. I used to think about her situation and how she was content. She's blind. She lives in an adobe house. She's so happy with the money that she has, with her eggs, chickens, and her pigs. Here I am with the Smiths, who are always pissed off about money. They are always fighting with each other. (Interview, June 1990)

Other meaningful experiences involved her friend Rosalina:

When we went to Aguascalientes, I always visited a woman named Rosalina who lived across the street from my aunt. Every morning, I got up and went to this lady's house across the street. I was very close to her. She spent all her time with me. This woman was like my best friend. Rosalina never had any girls. She had ten boys. Every time she had a little girl, they died. I was her little girl. I did things with her that I never did with anybody else.

She had this adobe house that was falling apart. Every morning she made tortillas. She got up really early in the morning, at five-thirty or five, and went to the *nixtamal* [grain prepared to take to the mill to make tortillas] to take the corn that she had cooked the night before. She took it to the *molino* [mill]. She grinded it and got the *masa* ready. In the back of the house, they had cows. In the morning, she tried to get me to milk the cow.

I told her, "No. I will be close to you, but I want to sit on top of the cows and pull their horns." I didn't get into milking cows. She wanted me to be there for that because she knew how repulsive I thought it was.

She'd tell me, "Now, tomorrow morning, get up early, so you can be here."

If I got up late, I hurried up and put on my clothes. I sneaked out of the house, and I went across the street. My mother thought I was asleep, and when she didn't find me in bed, she crossed the street and went looking for me, because my hair wasn't combed. She didn't think it was okay for me to be at Rosalina's so early in the morning.

My aunt or cousin came to get me to go to breakfast. I'd say, "No, no, no, no. I've already eaten breakfast with Rosalina. I'm not coming home. Okay, I'll wash my face and do whatever you tell me, but I'm not coming home."

Of course, I wanted to do everything myself. I wanted to make tortillas. So she bought me a little *maquinita* [machine] to make tortillas. I had a baby one. I made my baby tortillas with her. I had a little basket to put my little tortillas in. I spent my whole day with her. I helped her wash. After we washed, we went to the store to get ready to make lunch. I had my little basket just like she had. I went through every day in the summer with her. (Interview, June 1990)

From her childhood experiences, Olivia concluded that life in Mexico was much simpler and less complicated. She observed a lifestyle that was not rushed and filled with commitments and tight schedules. Spending the day with Rosalina was an enormous contrast to the commotion of starting each day watching a different breakfast prepared for each of the Smiths' children, rushing to car pool or arranging transportation and schedules for extracurricular activities during the school year. In Mexico, Olivia did not have to remember which employer her mother was working for each day and what she was allowed and not allowed to do. Instead, she had much more latitude in planning her own daily activities. She did not feel overscheduled or exhausted from activities organized by adults.[23] Olivia was allowed to hang out with Rosalina, a longtime trusted neighbor, instead of facing a day of child-focused leisure activities orchestrated by Mrs. Smith, Carmen, or another adult.

Olivia slowly learned about another side of her mother that was not apparent in Liberty Place. In LA, she saw that her mom was unable to have the last word in decisions concerning Olivia and deferred to the Smiths. She observed her offer a sympathetic ear to employers and their children, as well as responding to their problems and calls for assistance. Olivia did not see her mother as completely independent. Encountering other Mexican-immigrant women working as domestics, Olivia did not see her mother as particularly unique. However, her encounters in Mexico revealed that her mother had accomplished a lot, particularly for a woman and a single mother. Olivia encountered adults who admired Carmen as a hard worker and an ambitious woman. For instance, she recalled,

Rosalina was real curious about my mom: "God, your mom works so hard." Everybody had tremendous respect for my mother and all she had done. (Interview, June 1990)

Carmen's having migrated to the United States without a husband or a father and remained financially independent, even with a child, was indeed an achievement. During this period of migration from Mexico, women seldom attempted the journey alone or without family members who were already settled in the United States.

As a child, Olivia never fully understood why her mother was so well respected, but she was aware that her status completely changed when she was with her family in Mexico. The power dynamics between Carmen and her family were quite visible to Olivia, who knew that the privileges and obligations she experienced were gained by being Carmen's daughter:

> This is when I noticed that my mom had a different role in the family. She financed everything. My mother made all the decisions. If it wasn't okay with Carmen—that was the joke in the family: "*Lo que diga Carmen.*" [Whatever Carmen says.] It was always "*Lo que diga Carmen.*" All my aunts and cousins talked to my mother about situations or decisions they had to make. They had to talk to my mom first before making a final decision. Whatever my mom said, that was what they did. My mother always had all these discussions about their futures with them. She sat down with them and asked, "What are you going to do in the next two years. Where will your kids go to school?" I used to think, why is my mom doing this, and who cares? Why does my mom do this? It was almost like an interview. My aunts and uncle knew that my mother was going to have these conversations with each one of them. It was as though my mother was trying to get them to plan and to structure their lives differently. And she did.
>
> Again my relatives treated me deferentially. They were so grateful to my mother that I didn't have to do anything. I experienced all of these exceptions to the rules of what girls should do. (Interview, November 1992)

Olivia gained privileges not given to the other children because she was Carmen's daughter. Faced with a different social position, Olivia quickly encountered the privilege as learning a new set of rules. As a teenager, she was more frequently in Mexico without her mother, and the rules changed. Outside the shadow of her mother, she was no longer absolved from the gendered division of household labor:

> When I went to Juárez alone, I realized that when my mother had been around, my aunts and cousins had just put up with my different values and everything I wanted to do. When my mother wasn't there, they told me I was lazy, because I didn't help clean. They changed the rules and said, "Olivia, you have to get up in the morning, and you have chores. You have to either mop or sweep. You have to

put the dishes away, and you have to do these things." There was nobody I could appeal to. That was really hard, being there without my mother, because she established the rules of what I could do and what I couldn't. It was really hard for me to be immersed in Juárez and have to learn by making mistakes. Then I returned to LA and had new rules again. (Interview, November 1992)

Olivia became aware of the unequal distribution of work between men and women in Mexico. In Liberty Place, this was less noticeable, since the immigrant maids performed the gendered division of household labor, and she observed Mexican immigrants employed to do all the household labor, landscaping, and house painting and repairs. Although Mexican women worked as housekeepers and nannies, and Mexican men did landscaping and painting, race, ethnicity, class, and citizenship status were the striking differences to her.

Trips to Mexico exposed the degree to which her mother's position in the family was economically based. She was aware that her mother sent money to her aunts and took clothes for her sisters to sell, but she did not yet understand the considerable sense of responsibility her mother had for taking care of her relatives. For instance, Olivia had difficulty understanding why her aunts, uncles, and cousins were not assuming the financial responsibility for the extended family. She was further confused when her great-great-aunts greeted her mother with open arms and were genuinely excited about her visits and the time she spent with them:

It always really bothered that we were the only ones supporting my great-great-aunt and my great-grandmother. It seemed strange to me. They had other relatives. How come we were supporting them? How come we brought these things to them? I remember asking my mom, "So, you mean, if we don't bring them food today, they aren't going to have any? Are they going to share their food?"

"No, they'll buy some *fidel*. They'll just eat *fideo* [vermicelli] with an egg or something and have a few tortillas."

When we were in LA at the Smiths, my mom called my aunt and asked her how my great-great-aunt—"Did she have money?" My mother sent her money. Every month my mother sent her twenty dollars. My great-great-aunt treated my mother with all this respect. "Oh, Carmen, tell me . . ." I always thought it was really strange that they were so excited to see us, whether we brought them anything or not. (Interview, June 1990)

Although Olivia knew that her mother was strong willed and that employers treated her respectfully and trusted her with their deepest secrets, she did not realize what a successful businesswoman her mother was:

> My mother bought some apartments. I don't know where my mother got this idea of such an investment, but somehow my mother decided that she wanted to buy these apartments and rent them out. This was the way the family could have a steady income when she wasn't there. She no longer had to mail them money every month, and they wouldn't have to wait for a check from her. When Anna was about fifteen, she took the bus to the apartments with my aunts, and they picked up the rent every month. The rent money paid the electricity, the gas, and the bills.
>
> Even after buying the apartments, my mother made a lot of other investments that I thought were really strange. In Juárez, my mother had high-interest banking accounts. She put them in her younger sister's name, in case the apartments needed repairs. There was money for my aunt to draw upon. My mother understood how to do these things. There were separate projects and separate funds available for the upkeep of these things.
>
> My mom decided that she wanted my uncle to move back to Juárez. She sat down with my uncle and said, "Look. You have no opportunities. What are you going to do, be a taxi driver forever?" My uncle had a horrible car accident where he killed this little boy. He was really shaken up and wanted to leave, and he didn't drive. He wanted to get away. My mom said, "Look, in order to be okay, you have to forget this whole accident. You've got to move to Juárez and start all over again, and I will help you. I will buy you a house so you can live there." (Interview, June 1990)

Olivia was astonished to watch her mother as an astute businesswoman and pondered how she gained the skill to engage in so many asset-building endeavors.

As a child not faced with the responsibility of feeding a family or other parental obligations, Olivia tended to romanticize poverty. However, there were times when her memories included recognition of the cost of being poor. For instance, recalling staying with her cousin Anna in El Paso, she remembered the substandard living conditions and the constraint that poor families face in daily life:

My aunt worked in El Paso. She only had a border-crossing card, not a green card. She didn't want the INS to be asking her questions as she came across every day. So she got this little apartment in El Segundo barrio, just a couple of blocks from the border in El Paso. They were run-down apartments, and the bathrooms were outside. It was a one-bedroom apartment with a real little kitchen with a hotplate where my aunt warmed her food. There was no stove, just an electric hotplate. There was just one bathroom for the whole place. It was a horrible, horrible bathroom.

My aunt worked nights at the El Paso Electric Company. When she left for work, she locked Anna and me in the apartment. We couldn't get out of the apartment. My aunt left around five, and we were locked in the apartment after that. We knew we couldn't leave. We had games. We watched TV and played. But we were locked in. My aunt not only locked the door but also the screen door. She had a nail on the screen door to close it, and we couldn't get out by ourselves. I remember one time we sneaked out. Anna's friends lived on the same floor in the other apartments next door. We got the kids who lived in the other apartments to open the door for us. (Interview, June 1990)

The privileges of the middle class became apparent to Olivia as she contrasted the lives of her cousin and aunt in El Paso with the lives of her mother's employers. The vast economic differences were visible not only in the location and size of housing but also in the description of plumbing and major appliances in the home. Even though her aunt was employed full-time, she lived in poverty. Unlike the upper-middle-class employers, her aunt could not afford child care, much less middle-class housing standards. The physical restriction Olivia described in this story was her aunt's attempt to protect her daughter from danger when she left to go to work. Because her aunt was unable to stay home and care for her daughter, her first priority as a mother was to provide financial support. Contrasting her aunt's one-bedroom apartment and the employers' home, Olivia perceived that freedom to enter and leave the house was a privilege. Reflecting on the impact that these experiences in Mexico had on shaping her identity, she summarized that it was useful to know both sides of the class divide:

In some ways I really think it was like an escape, and I really needed to do it. I really looked forward to looking at things from another perspective. I got really sick of all the conveniences. I got really sick of all the whining about all the fighting over a thousand dollars. I got really sick of being in the situation that I was. (Interview, November 1992)

Olivia's initial childhood memories of Mexico were romantic and filled with optimism that this was the place and these were the people who were part of her, and this was the "real" place she belonged. Yet she was constantly faced with interactions that suggest she was no more like others there than she was in Liberty Place. Instead of blending in, her dress, speech, and mannerisms marked her as different and as a curiosity to others. Stories of summer visits were not without their own conflicts and tensions. She became aware of the constraints on women and the unequal status between men and women:

Rosalina thought all my clothes were really neat. My aunts tried to dress me in little dresses. I didn't like to wear dresses. I only wore shorts or jeans, tee-shirts, and tennis shoes. When I did get all dressed up, Rosalina really liked my little dresses. She touched them and thought they were really pretty. I hated that. I hated to be treated like that. So I would go home and take it off real quick. I would either give the dress away or tell my mother I didn't want it anymore.

I wore completely different clothes from everyone else in Juárez. I wanted to wear shorts. I always wore shorts when we lived in California. When I was about twelve, my uncle was against me wearing shorts. He told me I couldn't wear shorts.

I used to tell my mom, "Mom, *mi tío Carlos dijo que no me puedo poner shorts.*" [Mom, my uncle Carlos said that I cannot wear shorts.]

"*No le hagas caso.*" [Don't listen to him.]

My mother told me to ignore him. So I wore shorts anyway. He didn't let my cousin Anna wear shorts. I know the reason this happened. My mother supported her family.

Rosalina asked me, "What's it like to fly in the airplane? What's it like to do these things?" I'd say, "Well, it's really not that exciting. I really don't like it that much." I didn't want Rosalina to glamorize me or glamorize all these things.

Every once in a while, she convinced me to speak English to her. My aunts wanted me to speak English.

"Olivia, how do you say this? And so how do you say . . . ?"

I was treated as a novelty because I had different skills than all the other kids. They were real curious about me. That really annoyed me. They felt like I was this mutant child. They asked me questions about what I thought about things. They were always teasing me.

"So when you go to the United States, do you even speak Spanish?"

"Of course I do. I speak Spanish to my mother all the time."

Then for a while, I had an accent in Spanish. I couldn't roll my r's. My cousins and everybody made fun of me. That really pissed me off. I felt like they always wanted to see the differences in my behavior. (Interview, November 1992)

The world of Mexican workers was not only filled with new adventures but also represented an opportunity to have a "real" family—one not negotiated and controlled by employers. Consequently, this social world became analogous to family life, because it was the only time and place that Carmen did not have to merge home and work boundaries. In Los Angeles, Olivia framed moving back to Mexico or spending more time in Mexico as a way to build a stronger mother-daughter relationship—a real family without the Smiths' interference. Olivia wanted this ideal extended family with her mother. However, the reality of spending more time together was anything but harmonious. Olivia was unable to escape the ascribed expectations of being Carmen's daughter. No longer in the social position as the maid's daughter, Olivia faced a different set of role expectations, which were ascribed to her as the daughter of the breadwinner of a working-class family in Mexico. As she described her time in Mexico, I heard the frustration and disappointment in her voice as she recounted encountering conflict and tension with her mother instead of the domestic bliss she anticipated. Rather than Mexico's being the utopia Olivia dreamt of as a child, she found that a move back to the bosom of her family held other sets of contradictions, tensions, and conflicts. She had difficulty understanding why her aunts scolded her for not taking care of her mother when she was only a child. In LA, the employers viewed her as a model child, but her relatives considered her a spoiled brat. As she entered her teen years, she was even more determined to find a sense of belonging.

Passing and Rebelling

Olivia's recollections of growing up in the employers' home capture complex and seldom examined dynamics of "passing." Passing, crossing boundaries of race and ethnicity, is tied to one's cultural identity and is strongly class based.[1] Passing was required for Olivia to continue to participate in the white, upper-middle-class milieu, but it inhibited her from expressing a Mexican and working-class identity.[2] Olivia had to function as a competent actor in employers' homes and in their neighborhood, private schools, and country club.[3] Speaking only middle-class English and wearing clothes purchased by Mrs. Smith granted Olivia entrance into social circles to which she would otherwise not have had access. However, accepting a place alongside the Smith family placed Olivia in opposition to her mother and the other Mexican-immigrant workers who served and cleaned. She defied the assimilationist cultural script, a defiance that threatened the tenuous connection to social and economic resources that her mother worked to make available to her. In other words, to defy the employers' cultural script resulted in hurting her mother. Yet adopting the employers' cultural script was an "obscene form of salvation"[4] that required Olivia to hide many of her cherished memories and relationships. As she grew into her teen years, Olivia began to resist conforming to behavior and dress used to pass as an employer's daughter. Among the workers of color she encountered, she wanted to be recognized and known as the maid's daughter, not the Smiths' daughter. She wanted the guards at the entrance to Liberty Place, landscapers, maids, nannies, valet, and janitors to know she was not complicit in the class and racial hierarchy but remained her mother's daughter. Yet she did not want to assume the same class position as the workers or to feel a sense of inferiority because of her race, ethnicity, or class origins.

Confronted with employers' stereotypes of the heavily accented Chicana dropout who becomes an unwed mother, Olivia resisted by identifying the contradictions of meritocracy and found value in her cultural roots. Employers discouraged her claim to a Chicana identity, but Olivia fought back, reminding them that she was not one of them. Still, she recognized the consequences of not having educational opportunities or access to class and race privileges ascribed to employers' children. She knew that most Mexican Americans did not join gangs or become teenage mothers (although some in her extended family did just that) but was cognizant of the stereotypes employers had of Chicanos. As an outsider within, Olivia never constructed academic success as "acting white" because she was exposed to plenty of upper-middle-class, white students who failed in school, smoked marijuana, drove drunk, were sexually active, and engaged in a wide variety of activities that would be framed as criminal behavior in the barrio.[5] Therefore, she never equated "Mexicanness" or "Chicanoismo" with juvenile delinquency, dropping out of school, or any other stereotypes that were commonly held by employers.[6] As she consciously cultivated a Chicana identity, she framed this identification as one denied her because she lived in the Smith household. In addition, her emerging identity gradually moved toward opposition to gender-based class and race privilege. Having gained access to the contradictions of democracy, meritocracy, and equal opportunity, her identity formation involved developing racial-ethnic and class traits that placed her in the best position to rebel against Mr. and Mrs. Smith, whose privilege made them ideal symbols of the "oppressor." However, this construction became complicated when she confronted her own internalized cultural values that were unacceptable and incompatible with her desire to find a sense of belonging among working-class Latinos; she experienced her own privilege as instrumental in assisting other Chicanos who did not have the same opportunities. Her journey involved exploring and crystallizing the multiple facets of her identity.

Olivia's straight, black hair and light skin, her strong academic performance, and her white, middle-class dress allowed her to easily go unnoticed in her upper-middle-class and all-white private school. As she portrayed herself as just another student in this setting, from grade school to junior high school, her passing became a journey to self-knowledge that revealed ways that race and class privilege are embedded in meritocracy and that highlighted the hidden costs of becoming one of the elite.[7] For Olivia, the most painful aspect of passing as white and upper class through her performance of "appropriate" forms of speech, mannerisms, and dress was the required separation from her mother. Engaging in the same activities as the other private-school students, who were also the children of Carmen's employers, did not involve concealing that her mother was a maid but did require her to share the same social space as the employers' children. Olivia recalled childhood sleepovers as placing her in a social position that excluded her mother:

> Rosalyn and all the other [Smith] kids were allowed to have friends sleep over on Fridays. Then they played all day and went home on Saturday. When the older kids weren't home on the weekend, I was allowed to do that too. When they came over, we all slept in one of the big bedrooms upstairs that were empty because one or two of the Smiths' kids had left or weren't there for the night. We slept in the big bedroom. I remember going to sleep and thinking how weird it was that my mother slept downstairs. Here I am upstairs with my friends, and we all are sleeping upstairs. I didn't get to spend much time with my mom those days because I had my friends over. It was really awkward. It got to a point where I didn't invite any friends over anymore because I wanted to spend time with my mom. I really didn't enjoy them anymore. I didn't have anything in common with them. (Interview, November 1992)

Olivia began to be more conscious of the ways that passing forced her to choose between her mother and the employers' children. While she was permitted to pass across mistress-maid boundaries, her mother could not. Therefore, she had to spend time either with her mother or with her private-school friends, but not both. Passing required her to remove herself from the social position that her mother occupied.

At the same time, this was a period in which Olivia found herself excluded from some of the activities that the Smith children were engaged in, such as cotillion. Expecting to be the next one to attend cotillion, she was not invited to be a member of that group. Accepting the exclusion as not important and the cotillion as something she did not want to do anyway drew her more to a community in which she would not be rejected.[8] Having been denied access to all the cultural capital that the white private-school students had, she distanced herself from the Smith family; her act of rebellion accentuated the ways that she was not like the employers' children and did not want to be like them. Olivia began to withdraw when she found crossing race, class, and cultural boundaries to be an alienating experience:

> Prep High was an all-girl school in the neighborhood where a lot of the daughters of famous parents went. Everybody who went to Prep High went on to the Ivy Leagues. They had color pastel uniforms. It was like a sorority high school. It bred these same sorority types—the socialites.
>
> I had mixed feelings about attending Prep High. They were all beautiful. Every single one of those kids was beautiful. At the end of the year, I remember looking through the yearbook at the pictures. All the blond hair—they just looked like they should have been on TV. Obviously, their parents had invested money in braces and in how they looked. They constantly told them if they were too fat or too skinny. There was not one that was fat at eighteen years old. They all looked like they were supposed to. They all got educated and did what they were supposed to, except for a couple of them. We always knew somebody who got caught with pot and got kicked out of school. We always heard about them, and they were always Rosalyn's friends.
>
> It was very much the status symbol, Prep High School. You were upper class and elite—performed by these rules and didn't smoke pot. If you didn't do horrible, awful things, you could be the elite. You could look perfect, and you could go to the Ivy League schools. That was success. Then you could go out and meet some other guy from an Ivy League school, get married, have lots of money, and live happily ever after.
>
> All of these important people—I was really not impressed. I mean, they were not different. I just thought, "These guys are idiots like the rest of us." I mean, there is no difference, but they were treated special. Mrs. Smith talked about them as if they were significant.

I thought to myself, "So what?" I had them in my class, and they still made mistakes. They were just normal. I was never really impressed with the status. I never wanted something just for the status. I knew that didn't work. I knew that in the end you still might smoke pot. You could still get caught. You could still make mistakes. They were not perfect. They had the same probability of ruining their lives as any Chicano in the barrio or anybody else. Being rich didn't make them better. These parents had problems with their kids.

But I always wondered what it would be like to be in an Ivy League school. Everybody always talked about how "so-and-so's kid took the PSAT and did well," "so-and-so's kid got a twelve hundred, got a fourteen hundred." They all got over a thousand on their SATs. And they all got into Cal or Stanford, Yale—the top schools." I always wondered whether I would get into an Ivy League school.

In a way I didn't want to go to Prep High. I didn't want to have to deal with all of it. I always said that I wouldn't go to Prep High because I was really scared that I was going to end up like them—looking like them and being like them. I wanted certain things the school offered, but I didn't want to go and have to wear those stupid uniforms and have to go to these stupid parties. I didn't want to play it. But I was really interested in it. (Interview, November 1992)

In addition to Olivia's not wanting to become a sorority type and to separate herself from other children of Mexican-immigrant working-class parents, Olivia began to experience exclusion from rituals that would have marked her as an equal among her Prep High classmates. All of Mrs. Smith's daughters and sons participated in the preparation to attend cotillion, an upper-class ritual involving a young lady, the débutante, being presented at a formal ball. Unlike the Mexican *quinceañera*, which is also a coming-of-age ritual, there is no religious aspect; rather, cotillion presents the young lady to a select upper-class set of families:

All of them went to cotillion. Every Wednesday night, at one of the dance halls, they had cotillion. It was kind of a débutante type of thing. The big thing was buying your daughters really nice dresses to wear to cotillion. It was like a ball every Wednesday. They would teach kids ballroom dancing. The girls had to wear white little gloves, and the boys had suits. Mrs. Smith took all her kids to cotillion. And everybody went to cotillion—except me.

I thought, "If it is significant and important to learn ballroom dancing, why am I not learning to do ballroom dancing?" I remember being kind of disappointed that I didn't get to go. But at the same time, I thought it was really stupid. I don't know why I never went. It was never discussed why I was not invited, and I never asked for anything. I took what they gave me.

I had my own views and attitudes about these things. A lot of things I knew were really stupid and worthless, because I was constantly going to Mexico, and these people were fine, and they didn't need to go to cotillion. It really doesn't make a difference in your life. You were not going to be better or worse because you went to cotillion. (Interview, July 1997)

As Olivia began to navigate educational choices, she recognized that the students taking the route to an Ivy League school from prep school were completely different from her. By birth, they were among the elite and enjoyed powerful political connections. They physically exemplified the qualities deemed beautiful in U.S. society. Perfect bodies accompanied smiles that were the product of braces at an early age and regular visits to the dentist, as well as access to nutritionists, sport coaches, and personal trainers.[9] Peter W. Cookson and Caroline Hodges Persell, in their study of elite boarding schools, found that "to be accepted into a private school is to be accepted into a social club, or more generally speaking, a status group that is defined as a group of people who feel a sense of social similarity. People sharing the same status have similar lifestyles, common education backgrounds, and pursue similar types of occupations."[10] Olivia's limits to passing became obvious when she was excluded from the class and gender cotillion rite that would have anointed her as a young woman from an upper-class family. However, becoming a débutante was not a choice for Olivia to make but involved gaining permission from an established member of the elite. Although she might have had access to the clothes and educational experience of the elite, she did not own the economic or family lineage required to belong.[11] In other words, she was gaining social capital but not social networks. Having been excluded from cotillion and other significant rites of passage into this elite group, Olivia recognized the limits to passing and gaining full membership as elite. At the same time, passing as one of the students at Prep High called her attention to the social exclusion occurring in the structure of private schools. There were no other Mexican American students and no students from poor or working-class backgrounds. While

Olivia remained curious about the Ivy League experience that awaited her fellow students, she seemed to fear the possibility of becoming one of them.[12] If she completely assimilated and passed as a member of the elite, she would constantly need to be on guard to conceal any working-class experiences and Mexican culture, as well as to cut family ties and interactions with Mexican Americans. Since the Smiths' children had taken their inheritance and their opportunities to live alternative lifestyles involving drugs and under- and unemployment, Mr. and Mrs. Smith were invested in Olivia's social mobility. As their only hope for a success story in the family, the Smiths were reluctant to let her leave Prep High and attend less prestigious schools:

> I never tried to stay home from school. I hated being home so much. Even when I was sick, I tried to go to school. When I was in high school, I stayed out as late as possible. I didn't want to have a lot to do with the Smiths.
>
> At school I was totally different. My personality changed. From the minute I got off the bus, it was really different. The bus dropped me off right at the gate to Liberty Place. That is where I left this whole different reality. I went into this other little trance. From the gate entrance, I walked about a half mile home. I walked past the guards at the entrance. The guards were always Black or Chicano. I knew their names. I waved and chatted to them. Then I was on my way home, back to lily-white land. I walked past all these rich houses. I looked at the houses and just thought about my history there. I grew up in everybody's houses. I knew what everybody's houses looked like on the inside. As I walked these eight blocks, I went through a settling-down period. Then I got home.
>
> When I got home, I went upstairs to my room, closed my door, and listened to Mexican music while I did my homework. When Mrs. Smith yelled, "Olivia, dinner is ready," I went downstairs. I ate dinner quickly and went back upstairs until the *novela* started. Then I went into my mom's room to watch the *novela*. Sometimes I helped my mom finish the dishes so we could watch the *novela* together.
>
> I decided that I was going to fail all my classes because I didn't want to be there anymore, and I wanted to get kicked out of school. I went home and told everyone that I didn't want to be there anymore. At the time, there were nine people in my freshman class. I wanted to be in a public school. I wanted to be normal. I wanted to meet normal kids. I was sick and tired of listening to these same nine kids talk

about their families, their parents' marriages, who was getting divorced, and who was doing everything. I just was sick of it! I just wanted to get out real badly.

When I started to fail, Mrs. Smith started to see that I was really serious about not wanting to be there anymore. I used to come home and cry. My mother tried to talk to Mrs. Smith, but she said, "Oh, Carmen, Olivia needs to grow up, and she needs to put up with the situation."

So I just said, "Fine, I'm going do it my own way. I am going to fail."

Then she told me, "Okay, Olivia, if you are serious and don't want to be at Prep, then you have to get your grades up, and then you can transfer someplace else."

I went from F's to A's. I said, "Okay, I'm going to get A's." I just studied, and I went to study hall. I stayed there until six o'clock at night studying. I got all A's so I could transfer. But now nobody wanted to take me. I wanted to go to the Sacred Heart High School, an all-girl school that is racially mixed. There were Chicanas and all different kinds of students there. I couldn't get in because I had F's and then I had A's. They thought I was a real unstable student. Also, I didn't pass the standardized test with a very high score.

Mrs. Smith told me that she found another Catholic school in Santa Monica. It was coed, and it was a pretty good private school. She called them and talked to them about accepting me and found out that I needed to make up my algebra grade. In algebra, I went from an F to a C because I couldn't make up a whole semester of stuff.

Mrs. Smith found out that they were the nuns of the Holy Order. She talked to her father, who knew one of the judges in Santa Monica and was friends with the nuns. He asked the judge to pull strings to get me in. They made an agreement that if I did well in summer school, the school would accept me. I went to the summer school, and I aced algebra. I went right through it. I really liked this school because there were all these Chicanos who had failed algebra and were in my summer-school class. I met new friends, and I was real happy. (Interview, November 1992)

Both the Smiths and Olivia's mother wanted to make sure that Olivia received a college-prep education. After Olivia successfully proved she would only succeed if placed in a diverse educational environment, the Smiths selected a private school that offered an excellent education and had a mixed-race student enrollment. Public school was completely outside the scope of options. The logical choice was one of the most exclusive parochial schools in the city.[13] Without a tracking system and with the ability to select students, parochial schools are able to offer greater college preparation to their students. Olivia felt that this educational setting allowed her to succeed without being the "only one" or being separated from other Mexican American students. She did not have to choose between a good education and maintaining her culture, and she was assured of having a social network that included other students of color, particularly Latinos.[14]

Olivia's passing within the all-white environment of Prep High or in Liberty Place did not pose the same challenges that mixed-race settings did. Watching the way that the Smiths reacted toward people of color made Olivia aware that she was treated as an exception and that an assumption was made that she was not like the "others." These diverse social situations allowed her to observe the way that race and class differences were truly evaluated in monocultural, white, upper-middle-class settings. In those situations, she experienced the way that the Smiths perceived people of color:

> I just knew that the Smiths were racist, *really* racist. When we went out in the Cadillac, and we drove through a Black neighborhood, or when we got out of the car, Mrs. Smith turned her disgustingly huge diamonds. She turned them around. I got really disgusted that she thought that these guys were going to jump her. (Interview, November 1992)

In these settings, Olivia felt exposed as nonwhite and yet felt that she was considered different from other people of color. Olivia's childhood recollections of being treated as if she were a monolingual Spanish speaker unable to negotiate a bus ride gave her pause about truly "fitting in" and led to a comprehension of the construction of "whiteness":

> I remember Rosalyn being super paranoid of Black people. She was not necessarily racist, but she was just super paranoid. I remember saying, "It is really not that bad. I know things are not that bad."
>
> As we were walking to school she was constantly acting weird, even more so because she had me with her. Rosalyn used to do a really weird thing. We would get on the bus. We had bus cards. But sometimes when we came home and it was really crowded, she was weird. There was a lot of *Mexicanos* in the bus, and Rosalyn would relate to me in Spanish. Rosalyn would tell me, "*Sientate. Vente.*

Vamonos." [Sit down. Come here. Let's go.] I could never understand that. She never did that any other time, only when we were on the bus. I don't think she knew why she did. She just did it. I think she did it to show them that she could speak Spanish. Maybe she did it to show that she could relate to me on my level. (Interview, November 1992)

Olivia noticed the change in Rosalyn's behavior as she became aware that "whiteness" no longer dominated the situation. Not being the dominant majority, Rosalyn appeared to be threatened by Blackness and by Mexicans.[15] Olivia deduced that Rosalyn spoke a few phrases of Spanish to pretend that she was bilingual and was caring for a monolingual Spanish speaker. Rosalyn masqueraded and passed as a bilingual speaker in this public "multicultural performance." Olivia pondered in her analysis if Rosalyn's act was performed to bridge the race, class, and ethnic boundaries or to assure the Mexican riders that she could understand Spanish and therefore that they should not assume she did not understand their conversation. Although Rosalyn's motivation may be unclear, the few chosen Spanish phrases did not place Olivia in the position of a peer to Rosalyn. Her words clearly demonstrated that she was in charge and in a position of power over the younger Olivia.[16]

Mrs. Smith, having used her connections to get Olivia into Catholic school, sought to take part in Olivia's school activities and to be informed about her friends and their backgrounds. As much as Olivia attempted to keep home and school separate, Mrs. Smith refused to be shut out. Olivia recalled Mrs. Smith's having a Christmas party for Olivia's friends in Liberty Place and the tensions arising from trying to merge her working-class Latino friends into the employers' social space:

One year, Mrs. Smith decided that I should have a Christmas-caroling party in Liberty Place. She said, "The Christmas party will be your present." Of course, it's seventy degrees in LA in Christmas.

Mrs. Smith was always so interested in my friends and everything that I was doing. Most of my friends were Chicanos, except for Tim, whose girlfriend was Cuban. They were all working class. They didn't know much about me, but they all assumed that I lived in their same neighborhood in Santa Monica. A couple of them had come over when we went to see the play *Zoot Suit*.[17]

I didn't want to do it [have the Christmas party]. My mother, said "Oh, yes, yes, yes, do it. It'll be so fun." Bob, my boyfriend, was really into it, and so were all my other friends. I was not into it at all. Everybody talked me into it.

We were going to have this gift exchange. Mrs. Smith got a ham and this whole big spread of food that she set up in her dining room. Of course, Mrs. Smith had bought all the little rolls, the mustard, and everything had its own little plate and knife. She brought out all this silver and crystal.

The night before the party, I was really horrified and didn't want to do it. I almost backed out of the whole thing. I was sure my friends were going to be shocked. Since Liberty Place has a guard at the gates, I had to give him a list of my friends' names in order for them to enter the neighborhood.

Mrs. Smith wanted to watch us interact. I guess, this party was her sociological experiment.

My friends were not interested in Mrs. Smith at all. My mother wasn't home. I don't know where she was, but she wasn't home. Rosalyn was there, and she was really nice to them. She tried to talk to them and make them feel a little bit more comfortable. After we had our little gift exchange, they basically left us alone.

My friends began joking about the things in the house. They joked about the pictures on the wall.

"Who is this Olivia? Is this your great grandfather?"

They made jokes, like, "God! Is this real silver?"

"This is really heavy, it must be."

They didn't say anything too loud because they knew Bob would get really pissed off.

I laughed at their jokes. I had set myself up for this. I wasn't going to act hurt or act like I was not able to take it.

Then Mrs. Smith wanted us to go Christmas caroling. We weren't going to do it. It wasn't even cold outside. After a while my friends were just playing along. They wanted to watch the reactions of the neighborhood. It was hilarious.

We went out Christmas caroling to one house. We went to the Sackses' house, and she was kind of entertained by it.

Then we said, "Okay, screw this. Let's just go for a walk." We walked around the neighborhood houses, and they asked me, "Whose house is this? Whose house is that? What's it like on the inside?" We walked around, and then we came home.

We had champagne in the crystal glasses, and everybody opened their little gift. Mrs. Smith had made us hot toddies. The Smiths had a pool table. We played pool. Mr. Smith was out of town. Mrs. Smith went upstairs, and then about nine-thirty everybody left.

That was it. I swore to God I never wanted to do that again in my life. I never wanted Mrs. Smith to try to pretend to entertain my friends. My mother was going somewhere with the Joneses, and that's why she had talked me into this, because she wasn't going to be home. (Interview, November 1992)

As Olivia feared, her friends were shocked at the unfamiliar party set-up. However, instead of withdrawing from the situation, they teased Olivia about the table arrangements, photos, and other aspects of the Smith house that were not consistent with the Olivia that they knew at school. She discovered that her friends were just as interested in seeing the reaction they received from the residents in Liberty Place as Mrs. Smith was in watching them interact. While both engaged in ethnographic-type gazing, drawing conclusions about each other, Olivia felt embarrassed in merging her school and home life. Olivia framed Mrs. Smith's concern and interest in her friends as an "experiment" because they represented the "other" who were not part of her social world.[18] Having been urged by her mother to have the party, Olivia was angry at her for not meeting her friends. In essence, she was unable to claim her own working-class background without her mother's presence in the Smiths' home.

Observing the increasing power that Mrs. Smith assumed over her education, Olivia felt embittered that her mother did not fight on her behalf but acquiesced to the employers' recommendations. As a child, Olivia did not understand the personal relationships involved in domestic service and judged her mother's actions accordingly.[19] She knew that her mother was working additional hours to show her gratitude to the Smiths for getting Olivia into a good school. However, Olivia experienced this additional work as her having less time with her mother. Throughout grade school and high school, Olivia rejected the Smiths' assumption of their being in loco parentis and kept a mental note of the changing amount of her tuition and the failure of the Smiths to revisit their verbal work agreement with her mother.

I think that my mother felt indebted because the Smiths had intervened to help get me into the Catholic school I wanted to attend. That favor was the real issue behind my mother working at the Smiths and not getting a salary. I didn't feel like the favor had been such a big issue. I made a big issue about the fact that I felt they weren't paying her a salary. They were using my mother. They were only paying for my education.

I said, "Mother, school costs this amount. Why are we supposed to feel indebted to them, because you could be making all that much more money if they weren't paying for my school? I think you should break this deal and tell them no, you don't want them to pay for my education anymore, and have them pay you a salary. We can afford to pay for my education. Don't think that they're doing us this great thing." (Interview, November 1992)

Mr. and Mrs. Smith attempted to decommercialize their relationship with Olivia by treating her as a daughter when they arranged to pay tuition, purchase school clothes, and pay for her meals when she was invited to the country club instead of paying Carmen a salary. Over the years, Olivia observed her mother at their beck and call and understood that the informal work arrangement was exploitative. Support for Olivia was a debt that Carmen could not finish paying. Consequently, she had very little negotiating leverage to distinguish between the time she was working and when she was not. The tasks she did as a housekeeper and those she did as a "friend/family member" became one in the same.[20] Olivia was conscious of the exchange, because the increase in Carmen's work meant that she always had an exhausted mother.

CONSTRUCTING RACIALIZED GENDER AND SEXUAL IDENTITY

Although tensions surrounding Olivia's educational choices were present when she was in elementary school,[21] high school presented more consternation for the Smiths and for Carmen as race, class, gender, and sexuality became more pronounced in Olivia's new activity of dating. The Smiths' own children may not have dated or married their parents' ideal partner, but their process of choosing mates did not involve encountering "the other."[22] The Smith children engaged in drugs, sex, and drinking and driving without facing the same consequences that Olivia's working-class Latino friends faced. The ways that Olivia performed gender and sexuality gradually became a new form of resistance. In recounting memories of dating in high school, Olivia's narrative became infused with increasing tension over Mrs. Smith's behavior and comments she made about African American and Latino males. Olivia noticed Mrs. Smith's racial attitudes about "the other" and her attempts to steer Olivia toward dating white boys from the employers' social network. Olivia was particularly annoyed that her boyfriends of color were perceived as hypersexual, whereas the white teenagers in the neighborhood were assumed to be "safe." Having access to both social groups, Olivia knew that some teenagers in each group were smoking marijuana, drinking, and having sex. However, adolescents in Liberty Place had much more private space and were unlikely to encounter police officers in their gated community or in the parking lot of the country club. They also had access to health care and were highly unlikely to face an unwanted pregnancy. Olivia resented the assumption that she might ruin her life by dating Chicanos. The more pressure she received from Mrs. Smith, the more determined she was to rebel and "perform" her racial stereotypes of the hot-blooded Latina.

Mrs. Smith talked to me about boys and asked me about all these Anglo guys. I knew that she was implying that I should go out with them. The Smiths were constantly encouraging me to date white guys. I wasn't interested in the white guys. I had no interest in them. It was like, "I knew how stupid you are." I had seen all these whites, and I saw how they were. I was just uninterested. I saw how they lived and in the way they interacted. So I had no interest in them at all.

My mother found it interesting that I was always able to find Chicanos and Latinos to date. I think she always thought that I was going to grow up and marry an Anglo. But she never knew how I was going to turn out.

Sometimes my mom and Mrs. Smith talked about my boyfriends—like my relationship with Patrick. They didn't think it was appropriate that I spent so much time with him. When I was like fourteen, Patrick and I wanted to go to the movies. My mom didn't think it was appropriate because I was only fourteen. We were going to a matinee, not at ten o'clock at night. My mom didn't want me to go, so she took the issue to Mrs. Smith.

I told them, "You guys are really ridiculous. What do you think I am going to go out and do, get pregnant?" That was my favorite line to really freak them out. When I knew they were being super paranoid, I'd say, "What do you think I'm going to do, go out and get pregnant?" Then they stopped questioning me. I told them, "You say how much you trust me, but then when you decide you don't want me to go do something, then you don't really trust me." They didn't have anything to say to that.

I was very confrontational when I had to deal with both of them, because I felt like they were trying to pressure me. So I said real outlandish stuff to them. I tried to embarrass them about their actions.

Mrs. Smith would say, "It's not that your mother and I are unreasonable."

I'd say, "Oh really, what is it then?"

"We just don't want you to grow up, you know. You're the baby."

When my mom and I were alone, I'd tell her, "You don't care about Norman smoking pot."

But I would tell Mrs. Smith, "Everybody else can come home whenever they want to." But my attitude was, "How dare you try to even reprimand me about anything, because I haven't done half the shit your kids have done." So a lot of times I felt like they had nothing better to do. I felt like Mrs. Smith was real over-protective of me, because I think she was afraid that one more kid would go bad on her. Since she wanted to take credit for me, she had to make sure that I didn't do what her children did.

When I wanted to date, I talked to my mother about my boyfriend. My mom and Mrs. Smith acted uninterested in my boyfriends until I actually wanted to go out on a date.

I started dating Patrick when I was sixteen. Once, Patrick and I went to the beach with Mrs. Smith. We held hands the entire time. Mrs. Smith was just so disgusted. She told Rosalyn how pathetic it was that we were hugging and being totally affectionate in front of her. I remember doing it on purpose to freak her out and to see what she would do. She just put on this face. She looked like she was constipated all day. She didn't say anything to me directly but told Rosalyn and Jane. They told me that their mother was completely offended and disgusted that I just couldn't keep my hands off of him. I don't know whether Mrs. Smith told my mother or not. But they realized that if I was going to get pregnant and have sex, it would have happened by now. So no news is good news.

My mother didn't deal with my sexuality. We never talked about sex. She thought my exposure to the Smiths was going to prevent me from being a teenage mother. But they were not that open about sex when it was not heterosexual. Jane created this big scene when she decided to be a lesbian for two weeks. Ted and David were home and opened the door to her room, and she was in bed having sex with some woman. Ted and David came running to me like I was supposed to do something about it.

"So? What do you want me to do about it?"

"Well, go tell her something! Go do something! She's disgusting!"

"No one tells you shit when you're in bed."

Rosalyn had already told Ted and David that she was a lesbian, but they were disgusted by the whole idea and refused to accept it.

I asked Rosalyn, "Well, do your parents know?"

She says, "They can't not know. I mean, they can't be that stupid."

But they are so oblivious. If they had information they didn't want to know, they would make up some lie to themselves. They would find some justification for it not really being that way. Rosalyn was really humored by it. I know her father really liked her, and they were real close. She still did things to really piss him off, like wear bizarre clothing or dye her hair different colors. They always tried to get her to dress up. She played along. She'd wear these wild outfits to the country club. She had this unspoken revolt against them. But she dealt with them and got money from them. (Interview, November 1992)

Olivia described both Mrs. Smith and Carmen as pressuring her to date white males within the employers' network. Olivia viewed Mrs. Smith's pressure as stemming from racial stereotypes of Mexican Americans as low achievers, dropouts, drug users, gang members, and teenage or unwed mothers. Olivia was similarly aware of her mother's bias toward Western definitions of beauty, particularly in terms of height, weight, and skin color. Olivia's breaking rules of proper touching and affection in public in front of Mrs. Smith became a way to bring attention to her sexuality. Aware that her mother did not discuss sex with her, Olivia knew that her mother would ignore her behavior and that she could challenge Mrs. Smith on the basis of the sexual behavior of her own children. Although the family did not object to heterosexual sex, Olivia was aware of their uneasiness about homosexual sex and chose to ignore the sexually of their lesbian daughter, Rosalyn. Olivia responded to Mrs. Smith's concerns by drawing attention to contradictions within the Smith family.

Gradually, Olivia moved toward dating more traditional Chicano males but rejected their attempts to dominate her. Her working-class Mexican American boyfriends who had middle-class ambitions tended to have conservative politics, and Olivia acknowledged that these relationships were short-term. She hoped to meet more politically active Latinos in college:

> I knew that it [the relationship with Larry] wasn't going to last because I was really ambitious. I was going to go to college. What really bugged me about him was he was kind of Republican. His brothers were in the Marine Corp and stuff. They wanted very badly to be American—to be a piece of America. After everything that I had gone through, I did not want to end up dating a Chicano who wanted to be white. Finally I got really sick of Larry because he just was turning out to be this big Republican. He was just too possessive. (Interview, November 1992)

However, Olivia continued to date Chicano males who were not necessarily college bound, because they gave her access to another social world, an escape from the Smith household, and they functioned as a form of resistance. Olivia had always been determined not to lose her Mexicanness.

An event that Olivia reflected on many times over the years is one of the Smiths' dinner parties with a well-known recording artist who was their longtime friend. The dinner conversation represented a strong statement of disapproval from the Smiths of Olivia's decision to embrace a Chicana identity and her refusal to assimilate and "pass" as one of them. During the conversation, her belief that a Chicana can succeed without breaking away from her community was challenged. Again, she was given the clear message that she must "act white" to be a competitive applicant for admission into a leading university and to succeed as an adult:

> The incident where I realized that the Smiths were really trying to change my values and the way I looked at things was at a dinner party. They acted like things were really out of control because I was dating Larry. I was sitting at the table with the Smiths and their guests. They started having a conversation about my boyfriend. Mr. Studio, who was an actor, asked me if I was still dating this Latino guy.
> I said, "Yes."
> And he said, "Well, Olivia how long have you been dating him?"

I said, "I don't know."

"And have you decided where you are going to school?"

I said, "Yeah, I want to go into medical school, and I want to be pre-med. I really want to go to UCLA. They've got the best medical program in the country, and I think that would be a real good place."

Then somebody else said, "You know, Olivia, you really need to move away from home. You are just not going to mature, and you are not going to learn a sense of responsibility until you move away from home. And your grades? I understand they are excellent. You should really go back East. You should go to Harvard or Yale or some really good institution. I am sure you can get in, and you know there is affirmative action—you know, this thing that they let minorities in."

And I said, "Well, I just really want to go to UCLA."

Mr. Studio said, "Olivia, are you sure you are not going to Harvard or Yale just because you are dating this guy? You probably are going to meet all these other guys. I hope you are not making the decision to go to UCLA because of this guy."

I said, "No. He is not going to go to UCLA. He is not going to go to college. I am going to go to UCLA because that is where I want to go."

"Where else are you going to apply? You should at least apply someplace else."

I started getting really upset when I realized that they were basically telling me that I didn't know how to make my own decisions and that somehow I had lost control. I felt like they were checking me for mental stability to see why I really wanted things. I remember bursting out crying, getting up, and walking away. They didn't say anything to each other. I went to the bathroom. I washed my face, and I came out.

Mr. Smith said, "You know, I love you very much." He put his arm around me. "You can do whatever you want to do. I didn't mean to hurt you. We care about you very much. We didn't mean to hurt you."

But I knew they were basically disconnected from what they were saying. They had no idea of the impact of what they were saying was going to have on me. They didn't even understand. As it turned out, the relationship with Larry just kind of ended over a long period of time, I think maybe because I was at UCLA. Things were very different, and he wasn't going to school.

In the end, one of my friends did get his girlfriend pregnant. And Mrs. Smith asked me, "How is Andres? How is Lourdes? How are your friends?"

I had to say, "Well, Andres got his girlfriend pregnant."

It was real hard because it was admitting that, "Yes. They are exactly what you expect them to be. They couldn't do anything else." (Interviews, November 1992 and July 1997)

This memory of the dinner party with one of Mr. Smith's clients in the entertainment business was still extremely painful to Olivia ten years later. Olivia attached several meanings to the incident that reveal the complexity of her relationship with Mr. and Mrs. Smith. First, she was confronted with the realization that the Smiths discussed her dating and selection of boyfriends with their friends. Second, she resented having her dating life a topic of discussion for the Smiths to analyze and discuss with their dinner guest—while she was present, no less. Olivia was "othered" when her dating and education decisions became the topic of discussion and a source of amusement for the dinner party. By being subjected to questions about her relationships and future plans, she felt dissected by persons who maintained racial and cultural superiority and who embraced deep-seated negative stereotypes about Mexicans. She viewed their mentoring about selecting universities as an attempt to prevent her from identifying with the social world that she shared with Mexican maids, friends, and relatives in Los Angeles. Olivia refused (and still refuses to this day) to believe that the only route to a successful career required her to completely pass into the employers' social world and cut all ties to her Chicana class, racial, and ethnic identity. She did not question their sincerity about caring for her and wanting the best for her, but they did not comprehend what they were telling her to do. They had never been forced to pass or even to step outside their own social networks. They were born into the upper middle class. Mr. and Mrs. Smith and their dinner guest had never been told to leave their culture or family in order to obtain an education or to go to college, to have a professional career, or to be financially successful. They treated Olivia's Chicana identity as "a teenage phase" rather than as an essential part of her authentic and meaningful state of being.

The incident was also a painful memory because so many of the Smiths' expectations were later revealed to come to pass. Breaking up with her working-class Mexican American boyfriend because of the difference in their future goals weakened Olivia's argument that she did not need to pass as white to go to college and maintain relationships with her working-class friends. Answering Mrs. Smith's question about Andres confirmed her stereotypes of Latina teenage mothers; moreover, Olivia knew that admitting the pregnancy reinforced the stereotyped image of her friends and added additional fuel to the argument for assimilation.[23] Olivia wanted social mobility, just not on the terms laid out by the Smiths. She knew that not all Chicanas become teenage mothers and fathers; many do go to college and retain a strong sense of a racial-ethnic identity that is class based. She was determined not to make that final passing into their social world, turn her back on her culture, sacrifice ties with her family, and become a stranger to the social world of working-class Mexicans.

BEING CHICANA IN THE EMPLOYERS' WORLD

Having viewed photos of Olivia as an adolescent, I know that she was an attractive teenager with a thin athletic body and wore her hair and makeup similarly to other Chicana youth in the late '70s, with heavy eye shadow, mascara, and bright red lipstick, and she loved colorful platform shoes. As Olivia embraced her Chicana identity, she adopted the appearance of her Latina peers at the Catholic high school she attended. Unlike the adolescent females in Liberty Place, Olivia did not conform to the preppie appearance. While at school, she interacted easily with the other Latino students, as the student body self-segregated by class and race.[24] Upon returning to Liberty Place, she encountered the employers' teenage children—the ones she grew up with—but refused to change her appearance to "fit in." Instead she forced them to accept her as she was and challenged their stereotypes of Mexican Americans.

After working at Baskin Robbins on weekends for a year, Olivia was promoted to manager when she was seventeen. Along with being a disciplined and responsible employee, she was also bilingual, which gave her an important skill to serve the Spanish-speaking nannies that came in with their charges. As the manager, she enjoyed having the employers' sons recognize that she could outsmart them and was as academically gifted as they were. However, unlike them, Olivia had always been expected to know how to sweep, clean, and be responsible. She was in a position to point out their inability to do everyday chores and to observe their failures in handling simple work tasks. Given their privileged and sheltered backgrounds, they had managed to avoid learning basic tasks that working-class children acquire at an early age:

> When I turned sixteen, I started working at the Baskin Robbins. The owners of Baskin Robbins, the Hoerders, really liked me because I was bilingual, and there were a lot of Spanish-speaking maids who brought the kids there. The Hoerders were immigrants from Germany. Their son, Joseph, was really cute and had the biggest crush on me. He didn't want his parents to find out because they wouldn't approve, not so much that I was the maid's daughter but that I was an employee of theirs. They weren't racist. They had another Chicana who had worked for them that became a manager. They had hired other Chicanos before. Joseph and I worked together. He really liked me, and we went out. Then I decided I didn't like him, so I dumped him.
>
> I became the manager and was responsible for opening and closing the store. This was like my big opportunity to get back at all these brats. I always had these intellectual battles with them, outwitting them. I tried to humiliate them and put them in their place by letting them know that they weren't that bright. At work, when we talked about current issues, I always pointed out the weakness in their argument. They were basically very intimidated by me. I don't know if they really saw me as a Chicana and whether that intimidated them. I was smarter than them. I could outwit them. But they all seemed to really like me.
>
> I worked with all these punks that my mother had worked for. Phillip worked there. He was so stupid when it came to common sense. He had a 4.0 and was brilliant. He had the city's record for the Rubik's Cube. I had to teach him how to sweep. He had no common sense. I was just disgusted. All these guys who worked there during the summer had just gotten into Berkeley. They had graduated from Prep High. They didn't know how to work. All these guys were always after me. I got back at them by making them do all this shit work—cleaning the grime under the refrigerator. Taking orders from me—that was my way of getting back at these guys. But they only seem to love me more. They thought it was really great. They were willing to do anything so I would go out with them. (Interview, November 1992)

The range of experiences Olivia had made her strikingly competitive among this group of future Ivy Leaguers. Nevertheless, Olivia took a great deal of satisfaction in demonstrating the importance of working-class "common sense." However, she was only able to do this because she had also had a private-school education that few working-class children gain access to. Managing the ice-cream shop placed Olivia in a position of authority, but the period of time and situation was really insignificant in changing the social order of things. In our interview, Olivia did not consider the possibility that the owners may have promoted her to manager as they did a previous Chicana employee because they viewed her as seeking longtime employment, rather than as simply taking a summer job and then continuing her education in the fall. Although working as a manager at Baskin Robbins might be an important experience in the fast-food industry or retail sales, the work is certainly not tracked into lucrative career advancement but is basically low-wage service work. In acknowledging that the Hoerders would not have approved of their son's having a romantic relationship with her, she claimed the disapproval was on the basis of her employment status rather than class, race, or ethnicity. As evidence that the Hoerders were not racist, she cited their willingness to hire Chicanos, even as managers, as proof. Her familiarity with moving inside and outside employers' social worlds, including employment that brought her into the intimacy of home and family, blurred the division between a willingness to hire someone and viewing that person as an equal. She frames the "white, blond males" who follow her as desiring her, without reference to the hypersexualized image of Latinas that is so common in popular culture.[25] Olivia did not seem to consider the possibility that the employees "were always after" her because they internalized the stereotype of the hot-blooded Latina and may have perceived her as someone they might date but certainly not marry. Since Olivia did not consider marriage as an avenue to social mobility. as the employers' daughters frequently did, she was not likely to consider the motivation of the employers' sons in dating her.

Managing at Baskin Robbins did draw Olivia's attention to the fact that she actually found something appealing to the adolescents from Liberty Place who were social outcasts and who themselves did not succeed in "fitting in." This recognition brought her to a vulnerable choice when she decided to accept an invitation to date an upper-class, white employer's son. However, she was only willing to accept the date on her terms, which meant not changing her appearance to look any different from other working-class Chicana teenagers. Consequently, she proceeded to date him in their social space without wearing the preppie clothing or changing her hairdo or makeup style. Instead, she insisted that everyone would just have to accept her as pure working-class Mexican style. Going to prom with Phillip was a memorable event for her:

Phillip asks me, "Are you going to your prom?"

I said, "Oh yeah I'm going to my prom."

He said, "Well, I bought this prom bid, and I don't have anybody to go with. Will you go with me?"

I felt so sorry from him because he was so pathetic. I said, "Well, let me think about it. I don't know."

"Please, please, please, will you go to the prom with me?"

I don't know why I agreed to go, but I went to the stupid Christmas prom with Phillip. Maybe I went with Phillip to get back at Larry [a previous boyfriend] or maybe because I really wanted to piss off Phillip's sister, who was this bitch. She never spoke to me. The whole family treated me like shit when they went into Baskin Robbins. They were always really rude to me. They couldn't believe that I was Phillip's boss. I hated his family. His parents had a baby when their youngest was ten years old. Phillip was just in love with his baby sister. Phillip's family was so ugly. He looked just like his father, bless his heart. He was ugly. This big, huge, Neanderthal-looking kind of man. His mother was very attractive—thin, of course, a size ten. He had a beautiful sister who always looked like she was turning up her nose. He told me that the other guys were only his friends because they wanted to go out with his sister. He went to St. John's school.

The Smiths were so happy. They were always trying to get me to go out with Phillip. His grandfather had been the very famous coach of the Yale football team when Yale had done something great. Several times Mr. Smith and Mrs. Smith told me the story about how famous he was. It went in one ear and out the other. Anything that impressed the Smiths was not going to impress me.

The night just could not end soon enough. Phillip was just so excited. I mean, he was like this St. Bernard—just so excited. His stepbrother, from his father's previous marriage, picked me up. He had no personality. My mother was really embarrassed, and he was just really embarrassed. When he came over, Mr. Smith said, "Oh, your grandfather this . . ."—all this status bullshit.

I said, "Phillip, let's go." I always told Phillip what to do since we were little. "Come on, Phillip. Let's go. Put the glass down. We're leaving."

Mrs. Smith just rolled her eyes at me. Phillip bought me this corsage, and I had bought him this little boutonniere. Mrs. Smith made me buy it. I wasn't going to buy him anything, but Mrs. Smith said I had to. So I got him a little carnation. He bought me this wrist orchid.

Phillip wanted his parents to take pictures of us. We didn't take any pictures at the Smiths' house because I didn't want any pictures taken. I wasn't going to do that.

He said, "Well, I told my parents that we were going to go back and take pictures. I really want us to go."

I said, "Do we have to? Do we have to go over there?"

He said, "Yeah, we really have to."

We got to his house, and his sister opened the door. Phillip picked up his baby sister, and his older sister pointed to me and said, "Oh, look, look, look." The baby looked at me and started crying. Phillip got really embarrassed, and he said, "I think your makeup scared her." I was wearing eye shadow and red lipstick. My cousin Anna had taught me how to do my makeup, pure Mexican style. But I thought it was very nice. I had even modified it so it was totally me. But Phillip's sister never wore makeup, just some lip gloss.

Then we went into the other room where his other sisters were watching TV. They were rude. Phillip's dad said a rude hello to me and walked out of the room. Phillip's mom took the pictures because he wanted these pictures.

Phillip took me out for a steak dinner. He was always such a pig. He ate so much. I didn't even eat. He took me to this very fancy restaurant. His stepbrother and his wife were so entertained by me. All these people that I know from elementary school were there. They were shocked that I was with Phillip. First of all, nobody at Baskin Robbins could stand Phillip because he was such a nerd. Phillip's sister was completely offended by Phillip because he was a nerd and nobody liked him. She was just a bitch to him. I saw her with her friends pointing us out to people.

I became kind of protective of him. I was really angry at the way everybody treated him. I decided to have a good time with Phillip just to spite everybody. Then I met his friends, who were all sitting together at their table they had bought. I had nothing in common with these guys. The guys were all chemistry nerds, brilliant guys with girlfriends who were stupid little air heads. His friends weren't that impressed with me because I was very kind of aloof with them. Occasionally we danced. It was the longest night.

Then I saw my Chicano friends! I knew them all. I wished I had never gone. "What am I doing here?" I really wanted to be over there with them, but in order to play this little game that I was playing, I had to sit on the other side with Phillip. All these Chicanos, like Jaime, my big heart throb, were on one side of the room with their Chicana girlfriends. I remember Jaime was so shocked that I was with Phillip, this white guy from a very wealthy family. I was so disgusted that I had let my mother and Mrs. Smith talk me into going with Phillip, someone who I had hated for the last eight years. All these white boys always liked me. That was really disgusting to me. I just hated them. Having these real white boys, blond boys, following me around was really pathetic. That's when I really realized I don't like these people. That's when I started thinking about my future: "What am I going to do? Who am I going to date?"

I thought about them across the room and realized that if I did go over and talk to them, they would never say, "God, why are you here with Phillip?" I walked over and talked to them. They didn't even ask me who I was there with. We chit-chatted for a little while, and they invited me to their parties. It [the prom] was all very segregated.

It was a big thing for these rich kids to rent Winnebagos to go to the prom in. Then they would have all-night parties. This was their parents' idea, in order not to be drinking and driving. A couple of them went in on it together. The parents paid for it. They were driven there by their family chauffeur. Then everybody sat in the back of the Winnebagos, got drunk, and had sex.

Phillip said, "Do you want to go to a couple of these afterparties?"

Phillip and his friends decided they wanted to go bowling after the prom. I wanted to say, "Phillip, we're not doing this." But I knew what the options were, so we went bowling.

Here I am with all these nerds going bowling. Then he decides that we need to go to these parties. We went to these parties and drank a little bit. Jack was there. Jack chased me around. I knew all these guys from school. They started following me around, waiting for Phillip to go to the bathroom. They figured they could steal me away from Phillip and then get laid in the Winnebago. We went to one of these parties in this huge, expensive house in Beverly Hills. Everybody was just drinking and had nothing to say to each other. I had nothing to say to any of these people. So I said, "Phillip, let's go."

We went back to the Smith house, parked, and talked until like six o'clock in the morning. Phillip was so happy just to hold me and kiss me. We stayed in the car talking until six o'clock in the morning. Then I got out of the car and left. He went home and called me the very next day to see if I wanted to go to a movie with him. I said, "Okay, we'll go to the movies."

He asked me a lot of questions about the Smiths. We talked about the fact that I lived with the Smiths. I was really up front with him about everything. I said, "I don't like it."

"Well, how does your mom feel living here?"

I said, "Well, I don't know." I didn't give him in-depth answers.

"Well, we've lived here forever, and they're friends." And blah, blah, blah.

We went to see *Raiders of the Lost Ark*. He tried to tell me everything about the movie. People around us told him to shut up. On the way out, we ran into these girls that we worked with and who hated Phillip. Whenever he wasn't on shift, they talked about him. They saw me with him and just pretended not to know me. They didn't even say hello because they were so embarrassed.

Phillip tried to call me. I said, "Phillip, I'm not going to go out with you." I never saw him anymore. He wrote to me when he went to Yale. I had no interest, and I never wrote back to him. Mrs. Smith always made such a big deal about him: "Oh, Phillip wrote you." About two years ago, Mrs. Smith told me Phillip came home for Christmas. "He's now at Harvard Law School. He wanted to know your phone number in Texas and what you were doing." Mrs. Smith proceeded to talk to him for about twenty minutes, telling him that I had been at Harvard at this summer program. I said, "Oh, why did you tell him that?" Phillip tried desperately to find me everywhere. He called all my old phone numbers in Texas. Of course, Mrs. Smith never had the right number. That was kind of the end of that whole thing. (Interview, July 1997)

The story of Olivia's attending the prom with Phillip demonstrates the difficulty of crossing social boundaries and the problems arising from passing.[26] Although Phillip was willing to accept Olivia as she presented herself, he clearly recognized that the rest of the family did not consider her an appropriate person for a long-term relationship.[27] Phillip was completely unnerved when he met Olivia's mother, who had worked in his home and was clearly not representative of his friends' parents. However, the awkwardness of the situation immediately changed when Mr. Smith appeared in a pseudo-parent role and changed the setting to one more familiar to Phillip. Before the Smiths had a chance to feel at ease about the relationship, Olivia broke the gender norms by instructing Phillip that they were leaving, instead of using a more passive method of suggesting that they should leave.

Unlike Phillip, Olivia found herself in hostile and unsettling situations throughout the evening. First, the baby's reaction toward Olivia, which she attributes to her makeup, calls attention to her "otherness."[28] Second, the cold reception she receives from his family lets her know of their disapproval and marks her as unacceptable for their son. In her narrative, Olivia was able to identify Phillip's family's reaction to her "pure Mexican style," but only in terms of racial difference, not racialized sexuality (the exotic erotic), which would define her looks as cheap, easy, and not the kind of girl that you bring home to meet your parents. Obviously these kind of sexualized assumptions were not made about this makeup style in the Latino community; Olivia was determined not to change the "Mexicanness" that she displayed in her appearance. To successfully pass required her to "go in drag" in order to conceal what she believed was her true identity, which she refused to do. Since Olivia had spent her entire life in Los Angeles learning to read social cues about the norms and values of each social setting, she was quite conscious of social signals that she did not belong and was not welcome. Phillip was oblivious to his family's reaction or even to the racial segregation within the prom that placed Olivia on the wrong side of the room.[29] Olivia did not want to give the impression that she had crossed over and was now passing for a white, upper-middle-class girl, and she knew she had no other choice but to cross the racial boundary and acknowledge her Chicana/o friends.[30] Once she did this, she returned by crossing back over the racial and class divide to continue her performance as Phillip's date. She consoled herself by recognizing that she had selected to befriend Phillip, the misfit in the group.

Decades later, she received a call for Phillip, who had recently become a widower with two sons. She agreed to join him for dinner on her next trip to LA. She was curious to find that he was completely aware of her anger as an adolescent and had not at all been put off by it. Instead, he had found it appealing. She was unlike anyone he had ever met, and he was fascinated by her odd living circumstances, ability to compete with the other Liberty Place adolescents, determination not to change her appearance, and unwillingness to give up her Mexican culture. In her midforties, Olivia pondered the question, "How did my other peers view me?"

PASSING AS RESISTANCE

Olivia used passing as a strategy to protest white and class privilege. During her adolescence (always a stormy period), Mr. and Mrs. Smith pressured her to conform to their values and to fit into their class and culture. Olivia's memories of Mr. Smith were framed by his insistence that she learn to converse with adults and develop the skills to "work a room" by blending in and moving around introducing people and engaging in conversations comfortably.[31] As an adolescent, she learned the social skills that Mr. Smith taught her. However, as a teenager, she had little use for these skills in her everyday interaction but figured ways to employ her cultural capital to be an extremely competent actor in the employers' social space and to use passing as a form of resistance. Masquerading in the role of a Smith-family sibling involved adopting a specific posture, manner, speech, and dress. As the only nonwhite person present in social settings with the Smiths, she was distinguished from the other Mexicans present, who were marked as service workers by uniforms and were treated as invisible. In a sense, Olivia also became invisible in her upper-class dress and demeanor in order not to draw attention to her racial identity. Pulling off the performance gained her access to employers' social spaces without others asking for explanations. These social settings then became ideal circumstances for Olivia to resist by revealing herself as passing and disrupting the social interaction.[32] In doing so, she forced everyone present to see the rigid class and racial social boundaries that they were pretending did not exist. Her act disrupted the normalization of interaction between persons with differences in racial, social, and economic background by making visible the forms of behavior used to maintain segregation and social inequalities that privilege allowed them to ignore.[33] Invisible boundary lines allowed generous tipping and formal courtesies that enhanced and affirmed the superiority and benevolence of the upper middle class.[34] Olivia's use of passing to disrupt the social order demonstrates her astute reading of social settings and her competency in performing upper-class norms and values.

One type of everyday action that Olivia used to employ passing as a form of resistance involved calling attention to the fact that she was the maid's daughter and expressing concern over the additional work the Smiths left for her mother to do at the end of the day. Sitting alongside the Smiths at the dinner table, she passed as a member of the Smith family; however, after the meal, Olivia symbolically crossed over to acknowledge being the maid's daughter.

> I didn't like that the Smiths expected her [Carmen] to do the dishes after dinner every day when she came home. I remember making a big issue out of it when my mother was gone at somebody's party. They wanted me to sit there at the dinner table and bullshit with them, entertain them, and listen to their stupid-ass stories. In high school, I started getting up from the table, clearing the table, and then doing the dishes. I knew that made them uncomfortable. Mr. Smith would tell me, "No, no, just leave them there."
>
> I would say, "What for? So my mother can come home at eleven o'clock at night and do them? No. I'll do the dishes."
>
> He told Mrs. Smith that I had an attitude about it. But Mrs. Smith was drunk by then. It's not like she was going to do it. She wanted me to clear the table and stack all the dishes.
>
> It first started was when my mother came home really pissed off about having to do the dishes. She was really tired. So I helped her do them. I took note of how pissed off my mother was. I picked up on it, and I made a big issue out of it. (Interview, November 1992)

Being serviced by Olivia was uncomfortable for Mr. and Mrs. Smith because the action undermined claims that Olivia was like one of their own daughters. Their children had never been expected or asked to engage in household labor. By Olivia's calling attention to doing dishes as labor assigned to the maid, the Smiths' privilege was highlighted. Calling Olivia's action a bad attitude rather than a fair assessment of the extra work the dinner dishes created for Carmen, Mr. Smith disavowed a role in reproducing class and gender privilege.

Being a guest of the Smiths at the country club was a performance that Olivia frequently reflected on over the years, because this setting required special costumes and precise performance to pass.[35] The social constraints Olivia experienced highlight characteristics of her ethnic and class identity that were rejected. Always conscious that she was the maid's daughter, she refused to engage in the same types of action that made service workers invisible. The following narrative illustrates her understanding of her passing as one of the Smith family members. Her narrative of the country club concludes with a scene from a specific Easter dinner with the Smiths. The conversation is one that Olivia revisited many times over the decades. Mrs. Smith's comments became symbolic of her "true" feelings toward Olivia:

> I went with the Smiths to the Los Angeles Country Club off and on while I was growing up. Usually when we went to the country club, Mrs. Smith took me shopping a couple days before to get a dress. Women had to wear dresses in the dining room. Only on certain days were women's days. They weren't allowed in the men's bar.
>
> It was very segregated. They didn't accept Jews and Blacks. Of course, the only people that served were Black and *Mexicanos*. When we got there, they stared at me because I am the only Chicana. They probably didn't understand what I am doing with this white family. They had valet parking, and all the workers were Blacks or *Mexicanos*. When we went to get the keys to the car from the valet, I always said something to the Mexican workers about the car in Spanish. Mr. Smith always pretended that he was deaf. He didn't hear any of it. I talked to them in Spanish, and it just unnerved everybody. Mrs. Smith looked at me. I let her know all the time that I had this identification with them [the workers], and that identification was more important. I wanted them to know that they couldn't dress me up and take me to their country club and think that I didn't know who I was. I was so conscious of all the segregation. I went along, but I didn't really talk to them. I sat in the car with them. I sat in the back seat and just looked out the window.
>
> I talked to the waiters in Spanish. They just smiled, and I thought they were happy to see one of us on the inside sitting at the table. I also knew all the cooks. I knew them by their first name. They were usually treated as if they had no identity. I think I intentionally got to know them because everybody who was white was so rude to the Blacks. So I made a point to sit and talk to all the workers.

Everybody treated them like shit. They knew I was Carmen's daughter, the maid's daughter. And they saw I was Mexican. They knew I was not a Smith.

I made friends with this Black woman, Ruth, who was in charge of cleaning. When I went into the dressing room with Mrs. Smith's friends, I would make them uncomfortable by always talking to Ruth. They got really annoyed that I spent my time chit-chatting with Ruth. I went to the bathroom and hugged her. All these white women were just appalled. I went over, hugged her, and I said, "Ruth, how are you doing?" She was laughing. She knew by then exactly what was going on. We sat there and talked. Ruth was there to wait on these women in the bathroom.

I started to gain a lot of weight intentionally. Everything I did was intentional to spite them. Everybody was so conscious about being skinny. They had this cafeteria in the country club. It was really a very segregated club. The adults hung out with the adults. And the kids had these people there that were supposed to be keeping us entertained. The adults ate their meals in different rooms. The kids had this cafeteria. Everyone knew your account number, and you would charge everything. I hung out with Michelle, who was the Facios' daughter. She was always revolting against her parents because they were alcoholics. She was real conscious of it. She liked to really piss them off. Her mother was always telling her how heavy she was. So we'd go and order like french fries every hour. We'd just pig out on french fries. We just ate all the time and charged all this stuff to the account number.

We went to the country club for dinner. Mrs. Smith got drunk, and I just felt like a glutton. We just ate so much: courses and courses and courses with cream sauce. It was just a pathetic, nauseating situation. I wanted to literally puke. I'm sure they could tell, because I don't hide my emotions very well to begin with. I would just sit there and just be disgusting. Mr. Smith would say, "Oh, smile." I'd just look at him with this stone face. Occasionally Mr. Smith would make comments like, "Oh, don't dip your bread in the gravy," and corrected my table manners. He thought he was going to make us happy by ordering all the kids Shirley Temples. We'd sit there. It was just a mess. The kids [Smith children] all had long hair. They were all stoned. They pretended to go to the car and then get stoned in the parking lot. We all sat there, and I was entertained by the fact that David and Ted were stoned. I just thought it was great. They deserved this.

We were being served, and Mrs. Smith says, "The Fullers have a yacht, and they have a house in Cabo San Lucas. We sailed with them from Tijuana over to Cabo San Lucas one weekend. We got off the boat, and there were all these poor little

kids with no shoes and hardly any clothes. We came out, and they just came running towards the gringos asking us for money and things. They were all begging us
for money. You know what I thought, Olivia? I stopped to think about how lucky
you are. I thought how fortunate you are to have these wonderful things. Olivia,
you don't realize how lucky you really are."

I must have just been livid and physically showed it, because Ted put his hand
under the table and on my leg and just like held it. I knew he was telling me it
was okay; just ignore it. I remember feeling so angry and wanting to cry after she
pulled that shit. I was just like unconscious. I just sat there and ate my meal. Everybody sitting at the table was just disgusted with the parents. I just wanted to get
up and leave. (Interview, November 1992 and July 1997)

Even though the children of the employers removed themselves mentally from the scene by getting stoned, they were still physically present
in white bodies dressed in clothes that clearly indicated their gender and
class. Olivia chose not to join the Smiths' children in getting stoned. For
Olivia, smoking pot only fulfilled an American stereotype of Mexicans
as having a natural weakness or a special relationship with marijuana that
other groups do not. Consequently, getting stoned was not an option
of resistance for Olivia and did not symbolize an act of resistance as it
did for the Smith children. Rather than getting stoned, she was mentally
present, observing all the social boundaries maintained through various
rituals and practices involving bodily movements.

Having noted the norms governing etiquette at the country club, she
set out to violate those that maintained racial and cultural dominance.
Olivia wore clothing that marked her with the Smiths' status, but she
consciously tried to place it on a body size and shape that was not socially acceptable for females.[36] Whereas her friend Michelle's weight gain
was an act of rebellion against her parents' drinking, Olivia's weight gain
was aimed at shaping her body toward an image that was the opposite
of the ideal white, upper-class, and female sexual body image. This ideal
representation of the body as skinny instead of fat is not an economic
question of the price of food calories but rather the leisure activity of
creating and maintaining bodies to resemble the highly regarded skinny,
slightly muscular, ideal body type for women, who then break their fast
to engage in the ritual eating of designer food and international cuisine

in the country club's dining room. Olivia also speaks Spanish in a social space designated as an English-only environment.[37] Her verbal interactions with the valet, workers busing tables, and the restroom attendant cross the border into a familiarity coded not with condescension but with ethnic, racial, and class identity and solidarity. Her social acts of speaking Spanish to the workers, knowing their names, touching their bodies, and acknowledging their presence as social equals rather than low-level service workers were clearly forms of resistance as well as symbolic reminders to the employers that their interpersonal relationship with their immigrant Mexican maid's daughter did not dissolve the racial, ethnic, or economic differences between them.[38] She begins to turn passing into a form of masquerade to gain entrance and inclusion into the employers' social space; then, unlike the male transvestite, whose interest is in maintaining the illusion, she reveals her performance as an illusion.

Breaking norms of speech and touch, Olivia's social behavior was intended to reclaim identity with the racial, ethnic, and class status of the workers of color.[39] The adolescent Olivia showed the Smiths that she had a strong solidarity with the workers and that this identification was more important than the one she had with her mother's employers. However, in the end, Mrs. Smith turned the tables on Olivia by recognizing her identification with the Mexican workers and comparing her to the "poor little kids with no shoes and hardly any clothes" whom she encountered while sailing to Cabo San Lucas. The point of her story—and the message to Olivia—is, "Yes, you have the same racialized body as other Mexicans, but your economic and social situation is different because of your relationship to us." And the hard work and sacrifices that Olivia's immigrant mother made in order for her daughter to have these wonderful things are denied and reduced to luck—"how lucky you are." In this struggle of wills, Olivia was reduced to a subservient position as well as being reminded of the Smiths' benevolent paternalism and her obligation to acknowledge their generosity. Having broken the delicate mask of race and class through her resistance, Olivia became the problem.[40] Mrs. Smith's comment taught Olivia that successful passing requires embracing the new identity—if she expects access to elite privileges.

Quality and *quantity* are common terms used in describing working parents' time spent with their children. For Olivia, the issue of time spent with her mother was most prevalent when she described her relationship with her mother as a teenager. Olivia found neither quality nor quantity time with her mother when she was younger, but the situation worsened as she got older. The only assurance that Olivia had that her mom, as a live-in maid, could be with her as family rather than at work was to physically remove her from the presence of employers.[41] Consequently, Olivia constantly pressured her mother to take time off at the end of the day, instead of cleaning up after the Smiths in the evenings, and to leave Liberty Place on her days off. Olivia became increasingly frustrated at the little time she got to spend with her mother.[42] Olivia felt that mother-daughter time was only available after employers had consumed all her mother's energy. However, she also knew that her mother never seemed to be too tired to work for employers on Sundays and would challenge her need to rest instead of going out for dinner or visiting friends. A theme that emerges throughout Olivia's narrative is her mother's accusation that Olivia was ashamed of her and really wanted to be one of the Smiths' daughters.[43] At the same time, Olivia resented competing with employers for Carmen's time. She felt that her mother was pushing her aside and onto the Smith family in order to spend more time and become further involved in the lives of her other employers.

> I hated to be at the Smiths' on Sundays. I didn't want my mom to go to work and return to the Smiths tired at the end of the day, just to sit in her little room and watch TV. I hated being in that house when it was our time. I wanted us to go do things. Before she started working on Sundays, we did get out and do things together. When my mother first started working on Sundays, I made a big issue of it.
>
> My mom bought me things out of guilt because she didn't spend any time with me. Some of it I wore. Some of it I didn't. I knew this is how people expressed their affection or their guilt. This was how people got things off their chest. They went out and spent money on me. So I had to let them do it.
>
> I always forced her to go to the movies with me even if I hated the film. I forced her to go do things with me. I knew my mother hated it. She was always so tired

or not interested in going anywhere. When we went to the movies, she fell asleep. That really pissed me off. I told her, "You know, if we were at the Joneses, you wouldn't fall asleep. If you were at somebody's party, you wouldn't fall asleep."

"Yeah, well, I'm working then."

"That's bullshit. You like to work. You like to be around them. You like to be with them."

I really resented that.

Since she wasn't around much on Sundays, Mrs. Smith started to include me in family activities or invited me to go places with her. Sometimes she asked my mother if we had plans.

My mother didn't ask me what I wanted to do on holidays. Where I had Christmas or Thanksgiving dinner depended on whether my mother was working or not. First my mother discussed with Mrs. Smith if she was going to have a party or not. She would find out if Mrs. Smith needed my mother. Mrs. Smith had first priority on my mom. If Mrs. Smith didn't need her, then—and only then—did she go work for others. But she never asked me, "What do you want to do for Christmas?"

One Easter, Mrs. Smith asked my mother if I could go with them to dinner at the country club. "Ted and David everybody is going to come home this weekend, and we're going go to the country club. I'd like Olivia to go with us if you guys aren't going to do anything together."

Then my mother would say, "No. We're not going anywhere."

Afterwards my mother was resentful and hurt. When I came home, she would tell me, "You were gone so long. You didn't even worry about me."

I said, "Look, you're the one who discussed with Mrs. Smith and made plans for me. If I want to stay home all day long and watch TV, I want to be able to do that. I don't want you to find little activities and compromise me and commit me to going with them without even asking me if I want to go." (Interviews, January 1988 and June 1990)

Major incidents between mother and daughter occurred when one of them accused the other of wanting to belong to the employers. The first time this accusation was voiced was when the Smiths moved Olivia out of the maid's room and into a bedroom upstairs alongside them. The second major eruption occurred when Olivia confronted her mother with the accusation that she was actually the one that wanted to be part of the employers' families and community.

At one time our relationship was real bad. I don't know if it is normal for that age. I was a teenager. I remember it being horrible, and my mom crying all the time. And she said, "You wouldn't treat Mrs. Smith this way. You wouldn't talk to Mrs. Smith this way. You would never say no to Mrs. Smith. I'm going to tell Mrs. Smith how bad you treat me."

I didn't understand it until I was about eighteen. I just said, "It is your fault! If I treat the Smiths differently, it is your fault. You chose to have me live in this situation. You chose! It was your decision to let me have two parents and for me to balance things off. So you can't tell me that I said this. You are the one who wanted me to treat them like this."

My mother just worked all the time! I don't think she worked because of the money that she made; but it was having control of how things were going to be done and when they were going to be done. I think that part of it was that she wanted to have power and control over this community. She decided who to place [as new employees] in these jobs because she knew everybody trusted Carmen. Once again, like in Juárez, it was *"lo que diga Carmen"* [whatever Carmen says]. It was just a different context. (Interview, November 1992)

This argument addressed several aspects of Olivia and her mother's relationship that were difficult to overcome. As employers, Mr. and Mrs. Smith exerted enormous power over the relationship between Olivia and her mother. First, Olivia and Carmen had to negotiate their relationship within the context of blurred boundaries of work and home. While they referred to the Smiths' house as their home, the space never exempted Carmen from her role as a domestic and a nanny. Second, as a live-in employee, Carmen had no formal work contract, which left work expectations and hours unclear. Consequently, Olivia could not assume that her mother was "home" or "off work" at any time in Liberty Place. Third, living in the employers' house placed Mr. and Mrs. Smith in a position to assume decision-making over Olivia's education and activities. While Carmen wanted her daughter to have elite opportunities that she could not offer, she feared that the Smiths could buy Olivia's love. Carmen was employed in an occupation in which improving working conditions, pay, and benefits relied on the manipulation of personal relationships with employers. Carmen obviously tried to take advantage of her relationship with the Smiths to provide the best for her daughter. This included demanding that Olivia spend time with the Smiths and accept their embrace as family. Olivia was also caught in the payment of the "gift" and felt the burden of the debt.

SCRIPTING AN IDENTITY

Throughout Olivia's narrative, I found that her social-class status remained ambiguous. Economically, her mother was clearly working class, engaged in an occupation in which there is little job security, benefits are rare, if not nonexistent, and working conditions are completely left to interpersonal negotiations between worker and employee.[44] At the same time, Carmen owned property in Mexico and financially supported her family. Unrelated to Carmen's investments, her personal relationship with employers gave Olivia access to the best private schools in the area, material objects signifying membership in the middle class (e.g., brand-name clothes, shoes, handbags), and social opportunities to acquire cultural capital. However, as an adolescent, Olivia was not exactly middle class. She only owned the signs or symbols of class (speech, clothing, and educational aspirations), yet she did not have an economic foothold in the middle or upper class. Her ethnic identity was similarly class based; she lacked access to learning about Mexican "high culture." Her ties to the Mexican American and Mexican-immigrant community in the United States were only working class. Access to the U.S. upper-class Hispanic community was entirely linked to her mother's white employers. Olivia used her ambiguous class position as a strategy of empowerment. I recognize that racial ethnics attempting to enter the white upper class do not need to have the physical ability to pass for white (although it helps). However, to pass for upper class requires shedding evidence of poverty or working-class background.

Positioned as an insider and an outsider, Olivia developed a double consciousness that enabled her to see through the eyes of the employers her own "otherness" and the "otherness" of Blacks and other Mexicans. As W. E. B. Du Bois wrote, "It is a peculiar sensation, this double-consciousness, this sense of always looking through the eyes of others, of measuring one's soul by the tape of a world that looks on in amused contempt and pity."[45] Although silenced by passing, Olivia mentally documented every ethnocentric or racist comment made by the employers and their children. Her memory recorded the locking of car doors in Black and Latino neighborhoods, the turning of diamond rings to conceal their presence from men of color walking down the street, the body language used at the country club to make the valets, maids, gardeners, and other service workers invisible, and the Smiths' complaint about Spanish-language forms at the post office. She also engaged in intentional acts of resistance by violating norms. These are the ways that Olivia attempted to create her own identity.

The politics of passing are based on the ways in which censoring structures are organized throughout society and culture, from entrance to private schools and private clubs to the social poise required to be successful in a job interview. Passing becomes so much a part of everyday life, not to draw attention to one's difference—a difference that is socially constructed as inferior, dangerous, impure. Individuals are forced to engage in various and subtle forms of self-restraint to gain access to opportunities. Having served as an assistant dean at Yale College, I am aware that learning to fit in involves knowing what not to talk about, what emotions not to express, what language not to speak, what colors not to wear, what jewelry or hairdo can expose an ethnic identity. Passing to avoid racist, sexist, or classist verbal or physical assaults becomes a form of self-censorship, not a journey of self-examination or self-disclosure. Racial and class passing morphs into a form of censorship, forcing one into silence, a state of denial. In an era of identity politics and binary conceptualizations of gender, race, and ethnicity, many people fear to claim an authentic self that is multicultural and expands these limitations of class and gender. The act of passing engenders the denial of identity's contingency. In Olivia's case, she is silenced by her mother's employers, who speak only English, who live in a world in which being white and upper class is the norm, and who allude, conversely, to Latinos as high school dropouts, teenage mothers, and welfare cases, as poor, lazy, and hypersexed, and as potential criminals or sexual threats.[46]

The rigidity of the cultural script for social mobility in the United States involves assimilating into the mainstream—white, upper-class, heterosexual, and gender-specific norms. The script demands following a desperate path: passing to be white, passing as upper class, and passing as a heterosexual male or female. Modifications of the script are considered inferior and a problem. The Smiths' acceptance of Olivia and Carmen as part of the family was framed by the mother and daughter's ability to be cast as "good" immigrants or Mexicans. The cultural script fixes in place social and racial roles. People are typecast and are to stay in these roles to maintain proper class distinctions—"do not flirt with waiters or chit-chat with the maid"—and to stay in the appropriate racial and class positions.[47] At the same time that Olivia claims to feel loyalty to "*la gente*" and works hard to hold on to her social niche within Chicano working-class society, contradictions in her behavior reveal that here also she is passing, by masking the class remnants of her life with the Smiths.

5

Leaving "Home"

A crucial event in Olivia's life was when she moved into her first apartment, because she then had a place to call home outside of the Smith's house and located in an urban space absent of residents employing maids and nannies. Getting a first apartment as a young adult is always a rite of passage in establishing one's own space away from home. However, Olivia's case was unusual in that she saw moving to an apartment as a way of uniting with her mom and separating the boundaries of home and work. The apartment was intended to be a place to spend holidays with her mother rather than being apart from her and forced to attend activities with the Smiths. She assumed that her mother would also see the apartment as their home, rather than seeing the Smiths' house or any employers' house as home.[1] After a battle of wills, her mother accepted that Olivia was not returning to occupy her bedroom upstairs in the Smiths' house and eventually accepted her invitation to visit her in the apartment.

> When I first moved to this apartment, my mother kind of boycotted me. She didn't call me. She was mad because she wanted me to move home.
>
> I told her, "I don't want to live at somebody else's house. There is not enough room here for the both of us. I don't want to live in Liberty Place. I don't want to come home from college and go to Liberty Place."
>
> "Well, why?"
>
> "I hate it there."
>
> "Why? Because you just don't want to admit you're the maid's daughter?"
>
> "No. I'm sick and tired of these people in my life. There's just no peace. I'll never have a life of my own and be able to do anything."

So she was real mad. She never called me at home. I had to call her.

I don't remember what happened, but my mother came over, and she spent a weekend there with me, like a Saturday night and the next Sunday. She really liked it! Then she invited her friends over, and we cooked *menudo* at my house. María Rosa came over and cooked. She was a good cook. She was the one who had the restaurant in Juárez. It was really weird for my mother to feel like a guest in my apartment. Then when I went to Seattle, she spent more time in my apartment. That was the summer my cousin Miguel came to visit with his kids. They stayed together in my apartment.

Meeting at my apartment was real fun. I made them [women employed in Liberty Place] margaritas. I bought beer. We had a party at my house. My mom invited Ofelia and her friends. Everybody came over, and we had this big party at my house. I liked this because for once my mother did whatever she wanted to do, and there wasn't anyone in the next room yelling, "Carmen, do you know where my shoes are?" We had a sense of our own identity for once. (Interview, July 1997)

Establishing a family space for mother and daughter outside Liberty Place was a slow process. Olivia first had to convince her mother that renting an apartment and spending time with her had nothing to do with being ashamed to be the maid's daughter. She wanted her mother to be part of another community and embrace life outside work. Employers' requests, framed as paternalistic debts that could never be paid, enslaved both mother and daughter into fulfilling employers' needs rather than their own.

I said, "You know I'm just so sick of the Smiths invading my life. I'm so sick of me not being able to have my own life. I can't even go to college without all these little families everywhere."

Then she'd say, "Well you're just embarrassed because I'm a maid."

"No, you don't understand. It's that these people have invaded my life. They want to follow me around everywhere, and I have no peace of mind." (Interview, June 1990)

Olivia had no problem with being identified as the maid's daughter among her working-class Chicana friends, many of whom had relatives employed as domestics and nannies. However, the identification among the children of employers placed her in a subservient position, and their expression of familiarity with her mother as "the maid" rather than as an equal was offensive to Olivia. Comments from the employers' children, such as "she was like a mother to me," were not endearing to Olivia but a reminder that she did not receive the same attention and that their demands on her mother's time and energy resulted in less time for her.

Nonetheless Carmen refused to allow Olivia to make a complete break from Liberty Place. While Olivia stood her ground on the issue of not moving back into the Smiths' home, Carmen took a firm stand on Olivia's presence at social events with the other maids. Olivia was comfortable with these terms and used the visits as an opportunity to update her mother and the other immigrant women about immigration policies debated nationally:

> When I was in college, my mother sometimes insisted that I have dinner at Ofelia's on Fridays. Her friend Ofelia, who my mother had known for twelve years or more, lived down the street from where the Jimenezes [employer] used to live—in the house that had a maid's quarters above the garage with a little kitchenette. On Sundays, I came home and took all the maids grocery shopping. They bought whatever they were going to buy, and I took them to Ofelia's house. Ofelia cooked for my mother and all the other maids in the neighborhood. They all went and had dinner together. Friday was like a briefing session. I went, and we watched the news. They listened to the news in Spanish, and then I filled them in on the issues, and we sat and talked. I was doing a lot of immigration stuff at the time. My mother was very proud of this. When I had boyfriends, I took them over there. It was like a community thing. Everybody went and had dinner. (Interview, June 1990)

Instead of separating social worlds, Olivia brought her boyfriends and her expanding activism in Latino justice issues into the maids' social world in Liberty Place. Since the maids' social gatherings in Liberty Place were dominated by Mexican-immigrant women speaking Spanish, eating Mexican cuisine, and surrounded by Spanish-language music and television, the space did not force Olivia to interact with her boyfriends in the presence of the employers and avoided blending the different social worlds.

Olivia was delighted when her mother finally agreed to spend time with her in the apartment and cherished the experience of relating as mother and daughter away from Liberty Place. Years passed before

Olivia fully recognized the way that work shaped their relationship or the way aspects of domestic work were imprinted on their lives. Since Olivia perceived the other live-in maids as a community away from employers, she did not recognize that Carmen only traveled outside Liberty Place accompanied by fellow employees. This practice was adopted for almost every occasion when Carmen accepted her daughter's invitation. When Olivia insisted that Carmen attend an event at the university or in the community, Carmen always brought at least one of her colleagues employed as a live-in maid. Only in Mexico did Carmen venture outside the world of maids and mistresses.

Olivia soon found herself pulled back into Liberty Place and assumed the familiar role of child-care worker. Carmen worked full-time for a dual-career couple who were both extremely ambitious and wanted children. Dr. Jimenez was the first and only of Carmen's employers who was from a poor, working-class, Mexican American family; his wife was from a white, middle-class, southern family. Mrs. Jimenez hired Carmen and others to clean the house, do laundry, manage the house, cook meals, care for the children, garden, and do errands, such as grocery shopping and picking up the dry cleaning. Given Carmen's long work days and unwillingness to take days off work, Olivia took over child care for Mrs. Jimenez while attending college. Unlike her mother, Olivia was able to add errands to her list and assure that the children were engaged in a wide range of planned activities offering concerted cultivation. More important for Olivia, this job kept her in close touch with her mother and yet did not require daily face-to-face interaction with the Smiths.

> When I was in college the first year, I continued to work for Mrs. Jimenez. I came home and worked on certain days of the week. It was partly so that I could be with my mother. She felt like I was in school all the time. Mrs. Jimenez had hired a nanny, but she was never happy. They had hired someone to do the accounting, the shopping, and errands. But it never really worked out, because the nanny wasn't really comfortable doing such a wide range of things. So I did it. I ran errands. I picked up the girls at school. I babysat Nancy since she was three months old and Judy since she was a newborn.
>
> They ended up going to the same school I had gone to. Nancy learned French when she was real little. They began teaching her French in kindergarten. She

took piano. She was always exhausted, that poor child. On the weekends when the Jimenezes went out of town, I took them to the movies or to the zoo, so they wouldn't be lonely.

Mrs. Jimenez started relying on my mother more and more. I had a discussion with Mrs. Jimenez, because she was expecting too much from her and wanted her there all the time for her. I said, "You know, Mrs. Jimenez, my mother needs some free time. She needs a little control of her life. All you have to do is call on her, and she is there. You have to understand that she enjoys what she does, and she loves your kids. She wants to be with them, but don't take advantage of that."

She said, "Well, I pay your mother a lot of money."

She just saw her as labor. I said, "My mother needs control of her life. She needs to be able to say no. But you are not letting her say no. You think that by just giving her a raise and paying more money that is going to do it. My mother is fifty-five years old. She doesn't have to deal with this anymore. She loves your kids, and she is with them because she loves them. There is no price you can pay to substitute for that. There is never going to be enough. You don't know how lucky you are to have somebody who loves your children, who really cares about them and is interested in their well-being. There is no amount for you to pay for all the time that you can go off on vacation and know that your kids are safe and know that your kids are being taken care of. It has nothing to do with how much you pay her."

My mother was resentful that I came out and told Mrs. Jimenez this. She didn't like me speaking for her. She felt like I had intervened and I shouldn't have done it. Shortly afterwards, my mother started to get really ill. She started to have a lot of heart palpitations. (Interview, July 1997)

Concerned about her mother's health, Olivia recognized the vulnerable position a maid is placed in when she is emotionally attached to the employers' children. Because Carmen had spent more time with the employers' children than their parents did, the children developed extremely close relations with her.[2] Olivia placed her mother's safety and health over reproducing privilege in the upper classes, and she observed the extra strain placed on her mother by waiting hand and foot on the children.[3] Mrs. Jimenez was well aware of her position as the "greedy employer" but rationalized the situation as not being exploitative because Carmen was well paid for her services. Carmen was an extremely responsible employee and had gained a reputation throughout Liberty Place as the "perfect maid."[4] Her life was the job, and any personal or family conflict came second to fulfilling her employment obligations. However, as Carmen reached her fifties, health concerns became one thing that Olivia was not willing to negotiate. Consequently, Olivia felt compelled to plead with the employer to acknowledge that the issue was not simply monetary. Her mother's health needed to be taken into consideration. No longer living with the Smiths, Olivia became more assertive in addressing employers, but in doing so, she reduced her mother to a victim who was unable to negotiate with the employers herself.

Having learned lessons of control and domination from upper-class white employers, Olivia was not cognizant of the subversive ways that the underclass or subordinates manipulate relationships and situations to gain some leverage in negotiations.[5] At fifty, Carmen had observed the upper class long enough to know their dependency on others for the mundane, everyday tasks of maintaining a family household and reproducing their privileged lifestyle. She knew how to reverse circumstances on a daily basis to maintain some control over the situation.

UNMASKING ECONOMIC REALITIES

The limits of the Smiths' "generosity" and real acceptance of Olivia as "one of the family" were starkly drawn when it came to Olivia's needs for the same benefits as their own children—college tuition, down payment on a house, or other privileges granted to upper-class children. Although Olivia and her mother never expected such inclusion, the Smiths had difficulty acknowledging the enormous difference in their "real" economic circumstances. There were two particular incidents that highlight these differences and the Smiths' inability to comprehend or recognize the significance of Carmen's low-wage work with no benefits. The first incident involved Mrs. Smith's assisting Olivia in filling out financial-aid forms for college and the humor the Smiths found in the questions asked to determine financial need. The second incident occurred after Olivia had left for college, and Mrs. Smith and Carmen got into a major argument, resulting in Carmen's moving to another employer's residence.

Olivia's inconsistent grades in high school placed her in a weak position to compete for a place at Yale or Harvard, but she did have a strong enough academic record to be considered at one of the state universities. Wanting to stay near her mother, she decided to apply to the University of California.

I remember when I was applying to college; Mrs. Smith was real involved in helping me fill out my financial-aid application. She'd ask if I finished filling out the forms. I said, "You know, the only question I couldn't answer on this form is 'Do you live in a barrio?'"

The form asked all these questions about being disadvantaged. I answered every single one of them, but not the one "Do you live in a barrio?" They had this questionnaire that asked, "Is Spanish your first language at home? Are you the first in your family to go to college?" I really didn't know how to answer these questions. Mrs. Smith helped me fill out the forms.

Later, Mrs. Smith laughed about the questions to her husband. Mr. Smith made this big joke out of it. Mr. Smith laughed with his friends about my situation.

His friends asked me, "Well, where are you going to college?"

"I'm going to UCLA."

Then Mr. Smith said, "Yeah, Olivia is the only one who got financial aid living in Liberty Place."

When his friends came over, he told them, "Oh, yeah, Olivia got a full ride to UCLA, a grant for the whole thing. When she was filling out her forms, the only question she couldn't answer was that she didn't live in a barrio."

They all stood around and laughed. It was like this big joke. I didn't think it was very funny. I got full financial aid because of my mother's income. They had never paid my mom Social Security or any other benefits. Mrs. Jimenez was the first to raise the issue of Social Security and health insurance with my mom. Based on my mother's income, I qualified for all these things. (Interview, November 1992)

While the Smiths and their friends recognized that Carmen was in no position to pay for her daughter's tuition to UCLA, they still found humor in the fact that she grew up in one of the wealthiest areas of Los Angeles and was going to receive financial aid. Certainly, Olivia was the only student receiving financial aid to enter UCLA from an address in Liberty Place, but this phenomenon was due to her residence as the maid's daughter—not as an employer's daughter.[6] The Smiths did not recognize their own contribution to her economic circumstances. Employed by the Smiths for several decades, Carmen never received the benefits that Mr. Smith took for granted, such as health care, Social Security, and paid vacations.

The second incident was one that Olivia reflected on many times over the years as she struggled to understand the meaning of her relationship with the Smiths. This particular episode was frequently recounted as evidence revealing the true nature of her relationship with the Smiths:

> Tension started building between my mother and Mrs. Smith. She wanted my mom to help her with her grandchildren and spend less time taking care of the Jimenezes' kids. Mrs. Smith gave my mother an ultimatum: spend more time helping her or vacate her room so Mrs. Smith could hire another maid. My mother needed the job with Mrs. Jimenez and told Mrs. Smith she would leave.
>
> When my mom told me about this big fight with Mrs. Smith, I said, "The bottom line is that Mrs. Smith thinks that you are her servant."
>
> My mother said, "Oh, no! They don't. They love us."
>
> She even tried to separate us and said, "They may not love me as much as they love you. Oh, Mrs. Smith really cares about you."
>
> I said, "That's irrelevant. She cares about me because she failed as a mother. All her kids aren't doing shit, so she's got to have pride in someone. So it doesn't have anything to do with me—my personality or who I am. It has to do with her inability to be a good parent. So she's got to take credit for something. So she might as well take credit for me."
>
> I discussed the racist comments the Smiths made with her and said, "They don't love me. This is what they really think. They think they are always doing me a big goddamn favor, and they are not doing me any favors. You have earned everything that I am. They haven't given me an education. They haven't given me shit. You got cheated for it."
>
> When I told my mother that, she started crying. She felt that I was the big bad guy: I was insensitive and that I didn't realize that she was doing this all for me. She felt I should have realized that.
>
> I got so pissed off when my mother told me she had this fight with Mrs. Smith. I rushed home and took everything out of the closet. I helped my mother move. David was so upset that he was crying. Jane was there, and she was crying the whole time. She said, "Olivia, you are like my sister. I don't want you to move out.

Don't be mad at them. You have to understand that this is just between my mom and your mom."

I couldn't even deal with Jane because, to me, she was the whole cause of the problem. She didn't take responsibility for her own life and was screwing everybody else's life up. I was crying and real upset. I said, "We are just going to move out. I can't believe your parents. I am so disappointed after living here for so many years, and in the end, it is just exploitation. I just really feel like I hate your parents for them pretending all these years that they loved me and they cared about me and pretending they really cared about my mother. And in the end they are just interested in her labor. I don't want to have anything to do with them."

I remember Jane told me, "Olivia, don't cut them off. Don't be stupid. There are things that they can help you with. You need things that they can do. Don't cut them off."

I said, "Jane, there is nothing that I can't do for myself. I don't want to deal with them. It is just exploitation, and this is happening because you are not taking care of Skip [her son], and they [Mr. and Mrs. Smith] have to take care of Skip."

She said, "It is not fair to blame me."

I said, "Yes, it is. Jane, you are twenty-seven years old. Goddamn it! Grow up! If you are not going to take care of your children, don't have them. Don't expect everybody else to be helping you grow up. You are too old."

When we were leaving and putting things in my car, Mr. Smith came home, and I refused to speak to him. I didn't even look at him. I remember the disgust I felt towards him.

My mother decided to stay at the Jimenezes', which really made things worse. My mother had been independent all this time and had control. Now she was being pushed into a dependent position where she didn't have a place to live. She moved to the Jimenezes, and she had her room, but she had no one place to keep all her things. She felt so uprooted. She didn't want to be at the Jimenezes because she didn't want to be dependent on them.

They said, "Oh, Carmen, don't worry about it. Eventually we are going to build an apartment for you above the garage."

They proposed to my mother that she be full-time there. She really already was. When they went away for the weekend, my mother stayed there the whole time. She took care of both of the little kids, and it took up a lot of her time.

For about four months, Mrs. Smith and my mom hardly spoke to each other. They lived in the same neighborhood. The whole neighborhood knew what was going on, but no one talked about it. When I came home, I didn't go to the Smiths. They saw my car at the Jimenezes and knew I was there. But I did not go home.

Then my mom talked to Mrs. Stein. Mrs. Stein had a little guest house in the back of her house. Mrs. Stein and my mother made an agreement that she could live in the little house in exchange for some work each week. Now my mom had a refrigerator and a little hot plate, so she could do some things by herself. That was probably the most independence she has ever had in term of her living situation. (Interviews, November 1992 and October 1997)

Olivia framed the incident as revealing class issues that could not be resolved by maintaining the illusion that Olivia and her mother were part of the family. When the employers attempted to continue their fictitious familial relationship with the maid's daughter in the absence of her mother's employment, the ambiguous and blurred boundaries between family and worker became sharply and clearly defined. The incident unleashed concealed feelings and attitudes about the paternalistic nature of the mistress-maid relationship, particularly the Smiths' expectation of gratitude and Olivia's accusations of exploitation. The fight became a significant point in Olivia's relationship with the Smiths when she questioned the realities of family belonging represented in the adage "just like one of the family." She recalled her meeting with Mr. Smith, expressing feelings of revulsion at his arrogance:

I went home, and Mrs. Smith drove by and saw my car parked at the Steins. I didn't go home. I didn't go home or talk to anybody. I didn't call, and Mrs. Smith didn't call me. Then one day after about six or seven months, Mr. Smith called me and said he wanted to take me to lunch. He called because Mrs. Smith was really upset because I hadn't come home and didn't call. She saw my car in Liberty Place. She knew I was coming home, but I didn't go to her house.

Mr. Smith picked me up in his fucking Mercedes. Here I was involved in MEChA [Movimiento Estudiantil Chicano de Aztlán][7] at the university and involved in all this political activity, and I think, "Oh, my god, get out of my life." We went to the Bel Air Country Club for lunch, and he explained how Mrs. Smith was really sorry. He told me that I was like his daughter, and I was never to feel that I didn't have a home, that I had grown up there all my life, and that was my home.

He said, "Mrs. Smith and your mother are good friends, and they really care about each other. They are just having a disagreement. It is just a disagreement, and you have to let them work it out. Mrs. Smith is very upset that you don't come home. She is very upset that you don't call. We want you to come home and not to go to somebody else's house. This is your home."

I remember being really frank and saying, "I can't believe that after all these years, you tell somebody to leave."

"Oh! Mrs. Smith didn't tell her to leave. They just had a disagreement. I understand about Jane and Skip, all of them." He treated her as if she was going senile or something, like she is just going through this stage, and this is just her little problem. "They will work it out. It will work itself out."

I just sat there thinking, "Look at what you are doing. You pick me up in a limousine. You are trying to, like, buy me out!" I was just really disgusted that he had this illusion that I needed him or I needed the status or there was something in this relationship that I wanted. He thought I was not going to take sides and be neutral.

I got into it with him and told him I didn't give a shit. I said, "Well, I don't think it's some little argument! And it affects me! You guys are all a bunch of liars. You tell me that this is my home and that you love me very much. But then I'm away at college, where I'm supposed to be doing well, and I turn around and hear this is happening. I have to come home and move my mother out."

He said, "You have to understand that they are going to get into arguments. It was just a matter of business, and you have to separate the business from the emotion."

I said, "She is my mother, and nobody's going to take that away from me."

He told me, "I understand that your mother wants to make money. But you need to understand that Mrs. Smith felt really abandoned."

I said, "Wait a minute. My mother is like below the poverty line. And you're trying to tell me that my mother, who is over fifty, should not be interested in making money? Is that what you're saying to me?"

He was just taken aback. We always had one-sentence conversations. He never heard me put together more than one or two sentences. So it was really devastating for him to see me be articulate. He was just really surprised.

I remember him just being more shocked and saying, "Well, what does your mother need the money for?"

I said, "What do you need your money for? My mother has just as much right as you do to provide for the future for herself and for retirement. She's never had Social Security."

That was the issue. They didn't feel she needed it. What was the purpose? She could always retire with them—like that's what she really wanted. Mr. and Mrs. Smith were pathetic. "Oh, yes, Carmen and you are just going to get old and live out your life in this house with us." They made it seem as if this was a lifelong affair. I really resented that they had made a decision about what my relationship was going to be with them. I had no intention of it being that way.

I was really pissed off that my mother humored them that way. My mother never gave them any sense of having another life: "No. I'm going to have a life for myself, and I'm going to retire with my sisters in Mexico." I think she put too much emphasis on the differences between her and her sisters and how accustomed she was to life in LA. This only set her up to be exploited even more, because the threat of her leaving was not prevalent. I mean, it was just nonexistent. She always encouraged them to think that she would be with them forever: "Oh, yeah, we'll stay together and drink wine till we're eighty, sit in the Jacuzzi in the evenings."

The thing that really upset me was that they had always talked about how "Olivia was going to move away from home. Mr. Smith, I, and your mom are just going to always live here and grow old together." Yeah, right! As if it was all equal.

I just knew that my life was always going to change. I ended up having to deal with a more adversarial situation. Eventually the situation was going to have to change, and it was going to be because of me. I have different values and different ideas. I was *not* going to be what they expected me to be. I was not going to be the one that made everything better. Their kids had fucked up and amounted to nothing. They expected me to fulfill their dreams and go off to Harvard and meet the right guy and do the right things. I was never going to do that.

What happened eventually is that my mother and Mrs. Smith started talking again. I don't know why. Maybe it was just the tension of living in the same place. They just started to talk again. They invited her over. I guess it didn't really happen until I had really moved away from home. I remember coming home from college and finding out that my mother was going over there, drinking wine, and having dinner with them on Sunday nights. I guess I realized that I didn't get rid of them. No matter what I wanted, my mom was going to continue to have a relationship with them. I was really angry at my mother because she had befriended them. She had kissed and made up.

I came home and was really resentful of the Smiths and really bitter. I didn't want to see them. My mother said, "Oh, *mija,* you should go down and see the

Smiths. The other day I ran into Mrs. Smith, and she asked me about you to see how you are doing. *Mija,* you should go see them."

"How dare you? They hurt you, and they humiliate you, and they exploit you, and then you are telling me to go back?" I just didn't understand it. I just didn't understand why my mother became friends with them and reconciled. Maybe my mother was very grateful to them because she wondered as a mother, "What would my child have turned out to be, had I not been with them?" But to me it was only an economic situation, and it was only exploitative. (Interview, November 1992)

For Olivia, the argument between Mrs. Smith and Carmen stripped away the facade of familial relationships and placed class issues at the center. Carmen's position as the domestic precipitated the move out of the Smith house. The family analogy was completely disassembled in Carmen's decision to move out of the maid's quarters so Mrs. Smith could hire another live-in worker. A family member cannot simply be replaced by another individual, but workers are routinely replaced; in this case, one domestic was replaced by another Latina immigrant woman. Mr. Smith's representation of the conflict between Mrs. Smith and Carmen as an argument between friends indicates the degree to which the economic realities of domestic service are denied.[8] Mrs. Smith did not consider the option of offering Carmen additional pay for additional hours, because the familial characterization of their relationship erased the labor involved in child care and housework.[9] As in many employment situations that are characterized in familial terms, Carmen found herself faced with an employer's request that blurred her job description, and she confused paid labor done as an employee with unpaid labor done as a friend. The informality of the terms of employment were further aggravated when familial terms clouded the boundaries of time on and time off work, as well as confounded labors of love with wage labor. In the process of redefining Carmen's work from wage labor to labor of love, her manual labor became invisible. The personalism embedded in the work relationship assured that the labor remained not only shadow work but also unpaid labor. "Personalism camouflages work conditions which become distorted and unintelligible within the context of the interpersonal relationships between domestics and employers." Employers' refusal to relate to domestics' concerns "as workers' rights distorts the real conditions of their interaction."[10] Carmen's labor was also interpreted through a sexist lens that challenges whether housework is "real" work.

The invisibility of Carmen's paid labor was further demonstrated in Mr. Smith's question about Carmen's financial needs. The question captures a popular gendered narrative of immigration that denies the presence of Mexican women as immigrants and as workers. Mr. Smith's question appears absurd because Carmen is an immigrant woman in her fifties with no Social Security benefits. He knows she is a single mother with a daughter in college who supports her relatives in Mexico. However, Mr. Smith does not perceive Carmen as an employee selling her wage labor but rather as a servant under his care.[11] His promise to care for Carmen after retirement is consistent with the reported behavior of employers of domestic service throughout history and fits into the larger practice of characterizing domestics as family. There is a legacy of images of master-servant and mistress-maid depicting the faithful old servant taken care of in old age or the young, single, attractive domestic marrying into the employer's family.[12] Employers' promises of economic security and advancement are so common that the "rags-to-riches" stories are part of the folklore in domestic service. Although Mr. Smith's promise to care for Carmen in old age appears unrealistic, Olivia concludes that he actually does believe that Carmen will be with the Smith family for the rest of her life, retiring with him and his wife. But this is a fantasy. As I argued in *Maid in the U.S.A.*, the United States is not a feudalistic society but a capitalistic one. Employers are not masters responsible for their serfs and servants in their old age. As a wage laborer, Carmen is responsible for her own livelihood. "Under capitalism, employers' gifts or promises of a reward for employees' loyalty are not the same as the obligation a master had to care for his servants. The employee's involvement in the interpersonal relationships is a gamble."[13] Olivia not only challenged Mr. Smith's "promise" to care for Carmen in her old age but also pointed out that he was not demonstrating good faith because at the time he did not even pay Social Security or provide health benefits.

However, Olivia was also pulled into promises of social mobility through her pseudo-family relationships with Mr. and Mrs. Smith.

Allowed to follow the same rituals as the other children, she came to expect inclusion—for example, in going to cotillion—but she found out that she was not included. She waited to get braces like the other children but never got them. When she asked her mother about getting them, she faced the reality that they could not afford them. At the same time, Mrs. Smith was promising her that Mr. Smith had included her in his will: "Oh, when Mr. Smith dies, you'll get the same as everyone else."

Although Olivia was away at college and was not living with the Smiths at the time, she refused to separate herself from her mother's plight and became involved in moving her mother out of the Smiths' house. Mr. Smith claimed that the fight had nothing to do with Olivia; however, she not only was implicated in the system of gifts and obligations but was expected to participate in it. Past arrangements for the Smiths to pay Olivia's grade-school tuition in lieu of paying Carmen a salary created an appearance of familial exchange. Olivia was expected to assume some of the debt of obligation and loyalty, not by doing manual labor but by doing emotional labor. The pressure on Olivia to do emotional labor is obvious in her mother's comment, "Mrs. Smith really cares for you." Olivia also felt direct pressure from the employers; Mr. Smith's advice that Olivia not get involved in the fight between Mrs. Smith and Carmen is a call for her loyalty to the Smiths. His request that she separate the emotional component from business required Olivia to manipulate her personal feelings in order to make Mrs. Smith feel good about herself and her relationship with the former employee's daughter.[14]

Under enormous pressure from her mother, Olivia reconciled with Mrs. Smith and resumed a relationship. Not knowing any other kind of interaction with the Smiths, Olivia easily fell into old habits of passive resistance that she engaged in as an adolescent. Consequently, Olivia did not vocalize her opinions or attitudes toward racial segregation, inequality, or difference but rather restricted herself to symbolic messages, such as speaking to the valet in Spanish or hugging the service workers at the country club. She continued this type of interaction when she went to college:

At one point I started working for the first Chicana elected to the State Assembly. I really pissed the Smiths off when I wore this shirt, "Democrat for Assembly." They were all big Republicans. Mr. Smith was really disgusted with the fact that I was a Democrat. But Jane was doing worse things to him at that time. Jane wanted to go off and work in Nicaragua. She really harassed him. I thought that was really entertaining. She got into arguments with him about his conservative views. I wore my little MEChA tee-shirts at home, and they took note of it. Mrs. Smith really didn't say anything to me. Jane tried really hard to identify with me, because she was trying to be so damn progressive.

I was telling him [Mr. Smith] about my job—what I was doing. He said, "How much—what do you think your education cost? You got a twenty-, thirty-thousand-dollar education"—he could put a price on it—"a twenty-, thirty-thousand-dollar education, and now you've got this civil service job, and you've got it all guaranteed for yourself." I was just offended that he acted like I ripped him off, or this was welfare fraud—I had gotten something for nothing, that I was a farce, and I didn't deserve it, or I didn't achieve it. He always talked about how he was so offended of me getting this so-called free ride. I just ignored him because there was no point.

I remember Mr. Smith saying, "You know, it is so ironic. You have a like a hundred-thousand-dollar education, and you are using it against us." I laughed it off. I am not going to be the Republican that they want me to be. I don't have their values. (Interview, July 1997)

Olivia's friends challenged her decision not to change her interaction with the Smiths. One such encounter involved her college classmate Dolores, a Chicana from a working-class background. When Olivia invited Dolores to spend the weekend with her in Malibu at the Smiths' summer rental, Dolores observed firsthand the interaction between the maid's daughter and the employers. Not knowing any other set of practices or ways of interaction with the Smiths, Olivia immediately conformed to her expected role and engaged in emotional labor and deferential behavior.

In my first year of college, a good friend of mine, Dolores, went with me to Malibu for the weekend to stay at the Smiths. She pointed out how patronizing they were towards me and my life. She saw the glaring racism and said to me, "Olivia, these people are so fucking racist! Can't you see? Can't you see the way they treat you? Can't you see all these things?"

I really did stop and listen. I don't think I ever really heard it before, or maybe I just blocked it out of my mind. They were patronizing. I remember feeling so humiliated that Dolores pointed out how racist they were, and I hadn't seen it myself. I hadn't noticed it all this time. I thought that I had escaped it. I thought, "Okay, I made it out of Liberty Place. I didn't have to deal with their comments about Ernie [former boyfriend] anymore, and I wasn't seeing him anymore." But when my friend Dolores went with me to Malibu and pointed out the comments and behavior of the Smiths and their friends, I did see the racism. She was really disgusted with it.

I told her, "I see it, but I don't deal with it. I don't deal with it because I recognize that is how they are, and they are just fucked up, and that is how they are going to think. I am not going to change them, but I am not going to listen to them. It doesn't do me any good to sit there and confront them, because they're never going to change. It's not like—"

She said, "Olivia, that is not your perspective. Why don't you try to educate them?"

This really kind of identified something in me—I really did care for them, and it is just not worth it to be that upset over it. I was never going to change them, and I have to recognize that they are never going to accept certain parts of me. I am not going to pretend that they are. (Interview, July 1997)

Dolores exposed Olivia to the fact that she did have a relationship with the Smiths and that her attempts to just play along or to engage in this passive resistance were not a solution. Dolores reprimanded Olivia for not taking the time to educate the Smiths about the issues that were important to her, rather than just writing them off as racist and turning away completely. Having grown accustomed to taking on a different form of behavior and attitude within the gates of Liberty Place, Olivia set aside her critical class and race perspectives and assumed her accustomed place.

MERGING WORLDS IN COLLEGE

For Olivia, leaving Liberty Place to attend college was a rite of passage that symbolized living like other children of Mexican-immigrant workers in Los Angeles. However, the move was not the utopia that Olivia had imagined. First, interaction with employers' children did not cease. Many of them attended the same university, making encounters more difficult and complicated. She was unprepared to interact with employers' sons and daughters in the same time and space as she interacted with other Mexican American students. Moreover, Olivia (re)discovered that she was quite different from other first-generation Mexican American students from working-class backgrounds. Although she shared the ability to speak Spanish, experience with a transnational family, and familiarity with Mexican culture, she did not blend in easily because of the social networks and cultural capital she accumulated during her years living in Liberty Place.

Olivia believed that her final experience of passing would occur on the day she left the gated community to attend the university. Instead, college politics posed a new set of challenges for Olivia. As she became more involved in working closely with Mexican American students from working-class and immigrant backgrounds and white student leaders from the upper middle and upper class, she found managing the presentation of herself challenging. Unlike other first-generation Mexican American college students, she had attended some of the best private schools Los Angeles. Along with strong academic skills, she was articulate and assertive and demonstrated confidence in her interaction with university administrators and faculty and with state politicians. She had no trouble engaging in bureaucratic-speak and knew how to push agendas through student government. For the first time in her life, Olivia became aware of the vast cultural capital she had acquired from both her experiences of growing up in Liberty Place and her summers in Mexico. Her attendance at numerous social events involving politicians, entertainers, and producers at the Smith home and at the Los Angeles Country Club had required her to learn how to comfortably converse with a range of people that most working-class children did not encounter. She was caught off guard when her unexamined cultural capital provided her powerful advantages in advocating for more inclusive educational practices, for recruiting more students from urban public schools, for hiring more faculty of color, and for addressing the hostile learning environment created by racist acts on campus.[15] All her anger about growing up in Liberty Place was built on the foundation that she was denied her culture and living a "normal" Mexican American life. Having focused entirely on the negative aspects of the upper-class lifestyle, particularly the racial and class exclusivity, she now experienced her acquired social skills as powerful instruments to gain a seat at the table to push political agendas.[16] For the first decade of my interviews with Olivia, her narrative contained incidents and reflections of grappling with the significance of her inherent cultural capital and figuring out how to manage her obvious differences in working with other Latinos.

Arriving to the university and becoming involved with the student organization MEChA, she found that the other Mexican American student officers were surprised at her knowledge of the bureaucracy and her self-confidence in interactions with all levels of administration and faculty. The flexibility of linguistic skills to speak middle-class English with bureaucrats, to engage in code-switching with Chicano classmates, and to speak Spanish with janitors and grounds workers was an extremely rare set of skills not found among upper-class or first-generation Mexican American college students.[17] Her repertoire of skills raised questions: How did she know how the university and legislative system worked? How did she have the resources and social networks to get things done? Where did this odd combination of cultural capital come from? She had connections to gain access to high-level administrators and the board of regents and the experience to maneuver in the social milieu of MEChA and student government to stand out as a spokesperson and a leader.

In a political environment that emphasized identity politics and required a litmus test for racial-ethnic identity defined in terms of "authenticity," both lived experiences and ancestry were scrutinized.[18] Olivia did not fit this essentialist definition of Chicana identity and knew that to admit to growing up in an all-white, upper-middle-class neighborhood raised questions of her "authenticity" as a Chicana. Mechistas (members of MEChA) would not allow her to pass back and forth between the Smiths and Chicano politics. The identity politics framing Chicano student activism assumed a world of fixed identities and similar experiences and left few options for plural identities that crossed class and ethnic boundaries. The essentialism underscoring the identity politics of MEChA and the struggle for Latino representation made full disclosure of Olivia's experiences as the maid's daughter difficult, if not impossible.[19]

I remember one Chicano, who was involved in the administration, saw my permanent address listed. He said, "Since when do you live in Liberty Place?" I basically
just ignored him. I was embarrassed about having lived with them. I didn't see it
as a plus in my life. Some people now say, "You know, Olivia, you are real polished,
and you really gained from that experience. You are a different kind of Chicana.
You are very different." But I didn't see it as something that was positive. Being put
into the situation that forced me to deal with things that I didn't want to. I felt it
was unfair.

I felt that culturally I was really deprived. If it wasn't for me going to Juárez every summer, I don't know what I would have turned out like. Maybe I would have
been a big "sellout" and thought that I was so much better than everybody else
because I had the benefits of a good education. (Interview, July 1997)

At times, Olivia's experienced denial of her background as a betrayal
to her friends. Only after she had gained the trust and loyalty of a friend
did she reveal parts of her life growing up in Liberty Place. In an effort
to maintain constant contact with her mother, she was unable to erase
this part of her life and introduced her best friends to life in the gated
community. She was quite comfortable in sharing her relationships with
the maids in the area but was more guarded about placing her friends
in a position of dealing with the Smiths or other employers. Recalling
the Smiths' attitudes toward her working-class Mexican boyfriends in
high school, she did not want her college friends subjected to questions
about their family background, their parents' employment, or their future goals. Friends and mentors did not question the authenticity of her
Chicana identity and supported her use of upper-class skills to advance
social justice causes. Part of this acceptance was the recognition that her
identity developed from sitting around the kitchen table talking with
the maids, spending her summers in Mexico, and sharing meals with
friends in Pico Union, as well as living in the Smith household. They
also observed firsthand her commitment to working with other student
leaders on diversity issues on campus, participating in community activism against anti-immigration legislation, and campaigning for political
representation.

Employers' adult children who accepted their "differences" and lack of
commonality to first-generation Mexican Americans assisted Olivia by

participating in her avoidance behavior.[20] She had no interest in fraternity or sorority life and kept her involvement in student life focused on political activities. Lack of interest in these social organizations by the sons and daughters of employers limited Olivia's encounters with them, those children who called her mother by her first name and referred to her as being "like their own mother." Instead of assisting Olivia's efforts to avoid such encounters, her mother informed employers about Olivia's attendance at the university and encouraged their sons and daughters to get in touch.

> I was real involved with student government. I got appointed to this position in student government. Everybody in student government was like frat boys. I knew half of them from elementary school. Here I was in MEChA and involved in all these Chicano things. I would run into them in class or see them, and they would pretend they didn't know me. I would pretend I didn't know them. My mother knew the Goldbergs, this one Jewish family. She was a big Democrat running for city council. Her daughter, Marjorie, and I had been friends. I used to go over there and swim. My mother saw Mrs. Goldberg, who said, "Oh, Marjorie is going to the same university now." Marjorie actually went to look me up. Marjorie found me one day and asked me if I would go have lunch with her. I didn't say no. I went and had a sandwich with her. I asked her about her school. I just avoided the whole topic of my political activity. It was horrible. I had nothing to talk to her about. I barely made it through lunch. I told my mother, "Don't encourage these people to go find me."
>
> I babysat for the Wright girls, and they went to Santa Clara and were in sororities. I made a conscious decision that they were no longer kids, and I didn't have to maintain a relationship with them. But they always tried to maintain a relationship with me and asked my mom about me. "When's Olivia coming home? Tell Olivia I really want to see her." After a while she [Carmen] stopped because she realized I didn't want to hear it. (Interview, July 1997)

Olivia's being engaged in different campus activities than the employers' children were and her political organizing around social justice issues, particularly issues addressing race and gender inequality and immigration reform, placed her apart from the employers' children, who were pursuing high-paying careers.[21] Class, racial, ethnic, and citizenship distinctions that had been easily ignored when they were all children now took on significant social meanings, and crossing social boundaries became more deliberate and difficult.[22] To encounter employers' adult children who wished to continue a relationship with the maid's daughter who babysat them was appalling to Olivia. She no longer wanted to engage in rituals of deference or to pretend they had common interests and beliefs. Her continuing to interact as the maid's daughter with former acquaintances would have retained the expectation that she would engage in emotional labor and place their needs and interests at the center of the relationship. But her encountering the employers' sons and daughters as fellow students at the university removed her from the assumed position of inequality, and she could limit and shape face-to-face interaction.[23]

However, Olivia's serving in student government brought her into direct face-to face interactions that were difficult to control. In these encounters, she wanted everyone from the employers' network to participate in concealing their past shared social spaces at private schools, dinner parties, and the country club. However, she was not always able to keep encounters with employers' college-age children on the basis of one student to another but found herself being (re)positioned as the maid's daughter.[24]

Steve was in student government. He had inherited all this money from his grandfather. He was always a mess. He went to school looking like he just pulled his clothes out of the dryer. He was a chain smoker. We became real good friends. I was always giving him a ride home because he didn't have a car.

We were sitting somewhere having lunch. He said, "God, you know, you look so familiar. I feel like I've met you somewhere before."

I had never put it together. Then I remembered that this guy was the one who followed me around at the party with the judge in Malibu. I couldn't get rid of him. I didn't talk to him. I went into one room, and he followed me into another room.

Steve says, "God, you seem really familiar."

He clearly knew, but he just didn't know how to approach me about it because I was really involved in MEChA. He asked me if I knew the Facios. I said, "Yeah."

It took him like a whole week to finally broach the issue with me. He said, "You know, I think I remember you. Weren't you at this party that they had this Fourth of July out in Malibu? I remember I thought you were really cute."

I said, "Oh, come on."

He said, "No, I remember you. I remember you because you were the only Mexican girl there. I don't remember who you were with or what you were doing, but you were there." He was so uncomfortable telling me this. He said, "I was there with my grandfather. I couldn't figure it out why you were there. I just thought there were so many people there."

I said, "Well, who the hell was your grandfather?"

"Oh, you probably don't remember him."

I said, "I'm sure I don't."

"My grandfather is the judge."

I said, "So, it was your grandfather, the judge, who helped me get into school."

He goes, "No. I just remember you being there and not wanting to be around anybody."

I said, "You're damn right. I didn't want to be around anybody. I didn't want to be there."

"Do you remember me?"

I said, "No. I remember some little blond kid that kept following me around the kitchen and following me all over the place."

He goes, "Yeah, remember I followed you out to the beach and you ditched me?"

I said, "You're right. I remember now."

He said, "I thought you were so cute. I asked my grandfather who you were. He told me, 'That's the Smith maid's daughter.'"

I didn't want him to talk about it anymore. (Interview, July 1997)

Olivia's ability to successfully manage her identity in college allowed her to be Carmen's daughter for the first time. This identity was distinctively different from being "the Smith maid's daughter," which linked ownership to the employer and her inferior class status in their social world. Even though Steve ignored Olivia's insinuation that he wanted gratitude—"So, it was your grandfather, the judge, who helped me get into school"—when he expressed his physical attraction toward her, Olivia was not ready to accept his friendship, knowing his family's social networks.

An incident that brought Olivia in direct confrontation with the employers' sons involved a MEChA protest against one of the fraternities for using a demeaning "Mexican theme" at a party, which established a hostile environment on campus and reinforced racial stereotypes.[25] Olivia challenged their assumptions that she was "different" from other Mexican American students and that she was ever one of them.[26]

I protested an incident involving the fraternities with these guys that I had been in elementary school with. They had this Mexican party called a Viva Zapata party. They put up this fence, and in order to get into the party you had to crawl under the fence. There were mock border-patrol agents there. They had these piñatas butt-fucking. Everybody just got drunk and got laid.

MEChA already had a ban on these fraternities, because one of them had this incident. One fraternity tried to violate the ban by not telling anybody that they were having another party. We got to school, and there were mariachis—so it was very clear that they were having a party. We organized and monitored this party and took pictures. We ended up having this five-day massive protest and a sit-in outside the frat house. It became a real confrontation. I was real involved in the sit-in.

All the frat rats were in classes and approaching all the Chicanos asking, "Why do you think we're all racist?"

Two of the guys in the fraternity worked for me on staff [of the student government]. I was their boss in terms of the student government. Another guy had been in elementary school with me. They all knew me from school, and they told me, "Olivia, you've known me for years. You know that I'm not a racist."

They came up to me and said, "Olivia, what are you doing? Why are you involved in this stuff? We've been friends forever."

I told them, "We're not friends. We went to the same school, and that has nothing to do with it."

They felt like the rest of the Chicanos were just barbarians. They were just from the barrio. They understood why they were angry because of the economic inequities. But they didn't understand why I sided with them, because after all, I had been part of their very social structure.

I sat down with them and said, "I'm not part of your social structure. I'm not involved with you. My mother was the maid at your house. So don't try to claim I am in the same place."

"Yeah, but, you know—the proms, and this and that. We were in CCD [Confraternity of Christian Doctrine] class together."

"No. We don't have anything in common."

They kept saying that we were at the same intellectual level.

I said, "You guys just don't understand." (Interview, July 1997)

The worldview of the employers' sons disconnected Olivia from poor Mexican migrants crossing the border under the surveillance of the INS and from the pornographic piñatas. Being accustomed to treating border towns and Cabo San Lucas as U.S. playgrounds, they were completely caught off guard to find other students seeing the derogatory images of Mexican culture and the mocking of immigrants crossing a militarized border as having anything to do with U.S. race relations.[27] Rather than accepting that their actions were racist, they only heard the complaints as an attack of their "attitudes" and argued that they were not racist people.[28]

As proof of not having racist attitudes toward Mexicans, they asked Olivia to note the times she was allowed to participate in their social world as evidence that they did not consider her any different from them. Similarly, they denied being racist because of their inclusion of Blacks and Latinos in their fraternities and sororities. Olivia began by correcting their perception that she was ever an equal in their social network. Attending the same schools or CCD classes did not mean that their lives were not different. They denied their own class, racial, and gender privileges—privileges that she did not have. She was an oddity because she had the same cultural capital but had no connection to their families' money or inheritance.[29] Instead, Olivia shared the same economic circumstances as the other Chicano students from working-class backgrounds. She was familiar with the practice of supporting an extended family in Mexico and learning English as a second language, and she shared many of the same cultural traditions and politics. Olivia rejected the fraternity students' argument that she had anything in common with them by refusing to accept their definition of her as different from the other Mexican American students.[30]

Although Olivia's eclectic social skills gained her access to a wide range of social spaces in which she appeared culturally competent, her lack of everyday experience as a racial minority in the United States did not inform her choices and actions, which were based on privileges learned in Liberty Place. Olivia was overly confident in her ability to move back and forth easily between the two social worlds and was un-aware of the invisible privileges she took for granted. An incident that challenged her assumptions and actions is highlighted in the story about Dolores's joining her on a Saturday night to go to Latino dance clubs in the barrio. The story illustrates how oblivious Olivia was to the white, middle-class privilege she automatically assumed when borrowing Mrs. Jimenez's Mercedes to drive to the dance club. The incident points to young adults' lack of street smarts when they grow up in a "bubble" of the upper class.[31] The risk involved in her action of driving the Mercedes was recognized by Dolores and by Olivia's mother.

> My friend Dolores and I wanted to go out dancing, and we didn't have a car. I tried to find anyone else's car before I resorted to using one of the expensive cars, like Mrs. Jimenez's Mercedes. We thought we were real cool while riding this huge, brand-new, four-door, smoke-colored, diesel Mercedes.
>
> Dolores and I had gone out dancing and stayed out all night. I was taking Dolores back to the university, cruising through town, and we ran out of gas near Beverly Hills.
>
> This tow truck drove up and said, "Do you have a credit card? Or a AAA card? Or something else?"
>
> "Nothing." We had nothing.
>
> So they said, "Well, we can't help you."
>
> So they left us there for about an hour. By then Dolores is freaking out. She said, "Some cop is going to come and think we stole this car. The registration is going to say Vanna Jimenez on it, and we are not going to have anything to prove we borrowed the car."
>
> "Calm down. It is all right. Relax."
>
> "No! No!"
>
> She is getting more and more hysterical: "We are going to be taken away. We are going to get into trouble. They are probably going to take a blood-alcohol level, and they are going to find that we have too much alcohol in our blood, and we are going to get taken away."
>
> "No. No. Calm down."
>
> Practically crying, Dolores screamed, "I'm never going out with you in this stupid car. You thought this was such a hot idea. We're never going to be so desperate to go out to take this stupid car."

We figured that after a while the highway patrol would come. We stayed there for like an hour and ten minutes. We couldn't figure out what was wrong with the car. We thought someone might have done something to the car when we were partying all night, because we had gone to bars in the barrio. We couldn't figure out what was wrong it. The car didn't start, and it looked like it had a quarter of a tank of gas. Finally, the tow truck felt sorry for us, and the guy from the truck came. They saw that no one had picked us up.

"Look, it probably doesn't have any gas in it."

"No. No. Look, it has a quarter tank of gas in it."

"If you take it in, it is probably going to cost you lots of money, and you will have to have something to pay for the tow truck."

Finally this young guy, who had no teeth in his mouth, says, "Okay, we will give you a ride to the gas station."

By now we have been there for two hours. We are still in our clothes from the night before—these little miniskirt outfits, our hose and our pumps on, our makeup smeared. I am sure that my mother was freaked out, because I was supposed to just take Dolores home.

They towed us with the Mercedes. We went to a gas station owned by an Armenian, who explained to me for about twenty minutes that, "When you drive a diesel Mercedes, you have to understand, that diesel runs out, and you can't tell—it's heavier. It looks like a quarter tank of gas, but there is not really a quarter tank of gas."

Together, Dolores and I had twenty dollars. We had barely enough money to buy gas and give this guy at least a tip. We gave him ten bucks for bringing us in the gas station and bought ten bucks of diesel. It barely got me to Dolores's house and back.

Then my mother screamed and yelled at me. My mother was afraid that I had wrecked the Mercedes—not that the Jimenezes gave a shit. I am sure that she had so much insurance on it that she'd go and buy a new one, a better one, a newer one.

We swore never again to be so cool or so desperate to want to take out the Jimenezes' Mercedes. I filled the tank of gas all up and took it back to the Jimenezes, put it back in there garage, and never touched it. No more rich people's car out on the town in the barrio. (Interview, November 1992)

Olivia's frame of reference in this incident was likely no different from that of one of the Smiths' children, who wrecked their parents' cars on a regular basis. However, unlike them, she did not have this privilege. She did not even have a credit card to deal with emergencies. As a working-class Chicana in Los Angeles, Dolores knew that a Mexican American driving a Mercedes in the city raised suspicion that might result in a police stop. Without proof of ownership, Dolores knew that they would be arrested until the matter was resolved. The fact that Olivia had been drinking made the situation even worse.[32] Having regularly borrowed Mrs. Jimenez's Mercedes, Olivia failed to understand the difference her actions made in a different urban space dominated by working-poor residents of color. Because Olivia knew that Mrs. Jimenez's insurance covered her use of the vehicle, she was not concerned about damage to it. Olivia grew up observing employers replace cars with insurance as a normal occurrence, and she certainly did not see it as a reason for much concern. However, Dolores recognized the danger involved in being arrested and how easily young lives can be ruined by one mistake.

REFLECTIONS ON DIRECTIONS AFTER COLLEGE

As Olivia reflected on the experiences of sons and daughters who gain social mobility and the continued relationships and identity with their parents, siblings, extended family, or community, she considered the choices that one of her mother's employers made. As a Chicano from a poor, working-class background in Texas who was married to a white, southern woman he met in medical school, Mr. Jimenez adjusted to an upper-class lifestyle and interaction with his family. Having babysat for the Jimenezes' children for a few years, she also wondered what identity paths and choices they would take.

> I wonder sometimes how the Jimenezes' kids are going to turn out. Dr. Jimenez is from Corpus Christi, and his parents are very poor. He came from low income and went to the University of Texas as an undergraduate and then went to the University of California to medical school. They [the Jimenez family] sit at the dinner table, and the kids have a silver rattle, and they all have silverware, special baby ware, and utensils.
>
> His mother comes to visit and feels so uncomfortable because "*es la casa de mi hijo*" [it is my son's house], but she can't touch anything. He is really

horrible. He is really stingy. He doesn't want to spend any money on anything, and she [Mrs. Jimenez] is very different. When Dr. Jimenez's mother is in town, Mrs. Jimenez [the wife] tells my mom, "Make a list for me of the things that she wants that we don't have at the house—tortillas or anything that you two can make food." My mom and Dr. Jimenez's mom have become real good friends. When they are there, they talk in Spanish. She spent her whole day with my mom. Mrs. Jimenez [wife] would even tell my mom not to work or to take the day off and to spend it with her so that she was comfortable. My mom said that they would have coffee, and my mom would ask her if she wanted more. She'd say, "Oh, no, that's okay." And then my mom would say, "No, let's make a whole new pot of coffee." And they would make more coffee. They had a really strong bond.

My mom says that Dr. Jimenez's mom is really afraid to ask for things and to use things, because she might break them. She's never had these luxuries. Initially both of the parents came. But then soon after her husband passed away, she would come. And that was worse, because she didn't have the ability to say, "Well, your father wants . . ." or anything like that. She really felt more vulnerable. She felt real uncomfortable and felt that she would go and open the refrigerator, and there wasn't anything that was appetizing to her or that she wanted.

She tells my mom, "*Mijo, es tan mal.*" [My son is bad.] My mom was real surprised that Mrs. Jimenez, his mom, would talk about how poor they were and that he put himself through school. She sees how her son has changed.

I remember my mom telling her, "Well, when Olivia gets married, I'm not going to feel uncomfortable at all about telling her, "Well, buy me this," or telling her husband, "Buy me that" or "Take me here" or "Do this," because she is my daughter."

My mom would always talk about him coming home starving, and the only thing he'd make himself was a tortilla with chili. So she saw that kind of self-identifying icon that he was working class and just grab sometimes a tortilla or a tortilla with chili to hold him. It wasn't as though he came home and had an apple. So my mom always kind of saw him as a big hypocrite.

He [Dr. Jimenez] is so out of touch with himself. He would tell me how, even though he didn't have much money, he was in a fraternity when he went to UT, and his first car was a Mercedes 450 SL, just like Richard Rodriguez. (Interview, July 1997)

As the only Mexican American employer Olivia's mother worked for, Mr. Jimenez became a study in examining the choices made in conflating social mobility with assimilation and acquiring the material objects of an upper-middle-class lifestyle. He clearly embraced whiteness. Olivia compared him to the writer Richard Rodriguez, who became a symbol of a "sell-out" or "*tío taco*" (Uncle Tom) after writing *Hunger of Memory* and criticizing bilingual education and affirmative action. Olivia noted Dr. Jimenez's early choices in college that distanced himself from his family and community, as well as his acquisition of symbols of the privileged class—joining a fraternity and purchasing a Mercedes. As Dr. Jimenez acquired a new house in a gated community and surrounded himself with objects of luxury, Olivia observed his use of class privilege to separate himself from his family and his community of origin. Yet, when he was in the isolation of his own home, Carmen observed him eating a simple Mexican, working-class snack and conversing with her in Spanish. Carmen interpreted these actions as his trying to pass for white when he still had not been able to shed all his cultural traits as a Mexican. Rather than demonstrating his status by spending money on his children or parents, he excluded others from his wealth.

Olivia's consideration of career paths brought her closer to acknowledging the shared values among both the Liberty Place employers and her Latina/o friends and faculty at the university. Academic success and the pursuit of professional careers are valued in each community. As future lawyers or doctors, they might not choose the same areas of expertise or the same environments in which to practice their profession, but their dreams and hopes are not entirely distinct from each other.[33] At the same time, she knew that home ownership and driving a dependable car require financial success and that without inheritance, a career that pays well is necessary.[34] Access to a comfortable middle-class lifestyle was not incompatible with her goals. But she felt a sense of cognitive dissonance to discover that she had worked so hard to rid her life of the same wants, needs, and values as her mother's employers, only to find out that she too wanted status and success.

There was a lot of pressure on me to do it the right way. Go off and acquire status—to me that was really giving up everything that I was and embracing their values, their culture, and what their dreams, their idea of success.

My whole life had turned into a circle. And these were the values of American society, and these are the things that made somebody successful. These were the things that are valued in this country as a success. It was a disgusting realization that the things that are valued so much are so meaningless. You can end up being as unhappy as they are. In the end you can lose a lot, and it was really not worth it to me.

I am really afraid to value the things that I have benefited from. I am at a real point where it's real confusing. I don't know where I'm going to go. It is my whole perception of myself—how my community is going to deal with it at a critical time. I think that my best way of dealing with it is living in Texas—just moving on from it and not trying to reconcile the whole thing and just realizing that there are certain things that I have acquired that are going to be beneficial for my own community. There are also things that aren't, but I'm going to have to be focused on those particular things that I can do, do them well, and not worry about all the other things that can be—not damaging but just unhealthy in some ways. I think the hardest thing is just generally feeling really unacceptable in my family.

There is a lot of things that I am finding out about myself on a daily basis: different attitudes and habits that I have that I didn't know, like things that I've grown up with, mannerisms, values that I've learned, WASP values of how to eat—the dinner plate has to look pretty—things that are really meaningless I find myself doing. It is real frightening sometimes to hear something that I'll say or something that I think or some way that I'll do certain things that demonstrates how much I have already internalized—unconsciously—and how it comes out in different things. I just think that I am always going to be that way. (Interview, September 1997)

Employers and extended family members were quick to attribute Olivia's success in school and careers to assimilation. She learned to competently interact in a wide range of English-speaking, upper-middle- and upper-class white settings. However, Olivia rejected the notion that to do so involves assimilation but aimed to maintain bilingual and bicultural skills and to embrace social issues significant to Mexican American and Mexican immigrants.[35] She was determined to demonstrate her ability to succeed without embracing elements of the "American Dream" that erase the hard work of immigrants, daily discrimination, and barriers faced by lacking the privileges of race, class, and citizenship.[36] She was certainly not willing to say that assimilation and breaking away from her culture of origin was the path to her success.[37] However, she soon realized that many working people believe in the American Dream and embrace politics that are not in their class interest.[38] Having viewed upper-class families and the working poor, Olivia observed false assumptions embedded in the ideology of meritocracy and the lifestyle choices individuals make.[39] Observing the daily work of maids, nannies, cooks, and landscapers involved in sustaining a life of privilege for the upper class, she linked that privilege directly to the working class's low wages, long hours, and absence of benefits.[40] This class consciousness distinguished her from the employers' children but also from upwardly mobile Chicana/os who embraced elements of the American Dream she knew to be false. Still, moments of difficult interaction challenged her assumption that she could competently move in and out of different class and ethnic social spaces. Social interactions in spaces involving persons from different class, racial, and ethnic backgrounds set her apart from other Latinos. Olivia slowly became aware that she had internalized aspects of both cultures and that she was unable to separate behavioral characteristics ingrained in her in the Smith household when interacting with Latinos, and vice versa. Her identity was a compilation of all her experiences, but she most desired to belong in the world of Latinos in the United States.

6

Making a Home

Olivia began to consider the possibility of a career in politics. She had already been involved in several local, state, and national Democratic campaign efforts, which made the pursuit of a career in politics a distinct possibility. Recognizing her potential in politics, Mr. Smith's brother offered to help her raise money for a campaign if she decided to pursue political office. Her experiences at the university had given her a taste for this type of work, but she wondered how she could possibly reconcile receiving support from a Republican base in an upper-middle-class, white district and represent a low-income, nonwhite Democratic base. The contradiction of gaining the skills to successfully compete in a rich, white man's world and lacking the connections and experiences of the community she wants to work with became a difficult problem to tackle in Los Angeles. Establishing her own place and identity outside the "bubble" of the Smiths and other employers, Olivia's journey involved exploring ways to use her social networks and cultural capital to work and live among Mexican Americans.[1]

> I began to realize a disadvantage that I can't run for office, which had always been one of my aspirations, in that community. Who am I going to represent? I felt that there were advantages and disadvantages of growing up there. Yes, in certain ways, I am polished, and I have gained some skills, but in other ways, I really can't represent their interests. And even though they can look at me, somehow palatable, I am still not them, and they are never going to be able to accept me. I felt that I didn't belong in any particular place. Liberty Place is not my home, and it is not what represents who I am. I was able to somehow gain from two different cultures and in my own way put them together, but they were forced upon me. I had

to reconcile being a Mexicana and dealing with being a first-generation Chicana. Then I had to deal with all of these issues imposed on me from my mother's work situation. I still saw growing up here as something that was very demeaning—not demeaning in the way that I was treated, but bitter and resentful that it was imposed on me and I had no choice. I had to reconcile those choices from taking a little bit here and taking a little bit there and saying "this is good" and "this is not good," deciding this is something that I am going to do and not do. I felt like I wanted to get out of LA, because these people were infiltrating my life. Everywhere I turned around it was somebody I knew. (Interview, November 1992)

No longer wanting to be treated as a community charity case, Olivia decided to move out of Los Angeles. As she met other first-generation Mexican American college graduates, she began to look at other border states as a possible new home. Because she had spent a great deal of time in El Paso visiting relatives, Texas became a new but familiar place to relocate. Soon after graduating from college, Olivia moved to Texas in another effort to establish herself away from the shadow of the Smiths and other employers. However, feelings of love, respect, disrespect, intense self-interest, intimacy without genuine knowledge of one another remain part of her complex relationship with the Smiths. The snarled set of arrangements developed between worker and employer also complicated the mother-daughter relationship.

MERGING A PROFESSIONAL AND ETHNIC RACIAL IDENTITY

My first interview with Olivia occurred when she was working with a civil rights organization in Texas, the Mexican American Legal Defense and Educational Fund (MALDEF).[2] Her work at MALDEF was an important connection point in our lives. Although I had not been employed by the organization, I knew many of the lawyers and staff in the late '80s. In 1990, I volunteered with the San Francisco MALDEF office in the "¡Hagase Contar! Make Yourself Count!" campaign, which aimed to get a complete count of Latinos in the 1990 census. I worked closely with their team traveling to nearby communities to present demographic data and to discuss the significance of a complete count for Latinos in the United States. Our knowing the same people and identifying with specific political issues and politicians opened an important path to our establishing trust, as well as discussing shared interests.

MALDEF was Olivia's first job after college and provided her the means to work on the ground level in Texas. This was Olivia's opportunity to learn the issues and become a part of a political community away from her mother's employers. She was not granted access through her connections at Liberty Place but rather established her own identity outside the social world of mistresses and maids. Her emerging identity was not constructed to confront the everyday racism that attributes fixed sets of meanings to Mexican bodies but rather placed her in a position to employ the wide variety of her life experiences. Rather than having her conversational abilities interpreted as different from other bilingual Mexican Americans, Olivia could focus on using her verbal skills as a source of power to level the playing field in a political arena. Meeting politicized Latinos who had been educated alongside the elite in the Ivy League provided Olivia with a point of comparison to her own experiences and a framework to find meaning in her experiences. She could savor the multifarious sets of lives, lifestyles, and identities in the Latino community. Living in Texas fulfilled Olivia's desire to reconnect with those features of contemporary multiethnic and immigrant societies that she once gained by switching to Catholic school and later encountered at UCLA. She understood that "cultural identity is neither one thing nor static, it is a key focus of cultural political struggle: it is constantly produced and reproduced in practices of everyday life."[3] Her first emergence in political advocacy work with Mexican American organizations in Texas was difficult because she found that her older co-workers from working-class backgrounds interpreted her confidence and assertive behavior as arrogant, pompous, and overbearing:

> I am younger than most people I work with. I put on this conference, and all the women that I was organizing are at least thirty-five years older. They are women who have been in professional areas for a long time, and they have really paid their dues in San Antonio. The women were really resentful—"Who is this nineteen year old?" I am twenty-four. It is amazing to them that I've been able to pull off a conference on the telephone with ten different cities and in one particular place that I am working. To this day, some of them won't deal with me because they are

very, very threatened. In some ways, in my own community, I am unacceptable. I am just starting to realize that it is always going to be that way. It is really unfortunate and sad. I have to find my own strength and recognize that it [having skills] is okay. I think that I am constantly reevaluating and trying to feel good about myself and trying to feel accepted. (Interview, November 1992)

Even when her differences were accepted by her friends, she was pained that they were so obvious to others, while she experienced them as so natural. Her mannerisms, speech, and clothing style were all influenced by growing up among elite professionals:

I have adopted some of their social values, some of their ideas. I finally have come to the realization from my friends. They really joke with me. When I was working at the capital they used to call me "Suzy Sorority" because of the way I dressed. I don't think they understand what statements like that mean to me, but it forced me to see the fact that I have picked up things from them [the Smiths]. Whether I want to negate it or not, they exist—certain ways of thinking, certain ways of feeling about things. They had an impact on my life and have influenced me. (Interview, July 1997)

Olivia began to understand that intimidation is a result of insecurity, and many times her colleagues automatically placed their relationship on a level of competition rather than one of collaboration. After a series of unsatisfying work situations, Olivia moved toward consulting and self-employment:

People assume that I want something, that I am really driven, and that I want their job. I feel like I'm very misunderstood and that fifty percent of my experience, if not eighty percent of my experience, is based on people's inability to deal with me. I really shift their paradigm, whether they're white or Latino. Whatever the circumstance, I have to manage their reaction to me. That's really annoying to me because it really isn't deliberate—with intent. I feel like I need a whole new set of skills that really help me deal with that. I don't feel like I should go into a circumstance that really saddles me with a lot of baggage. Being on my own the last year makes me realize that you're either going to be intimidated by me or you're going to find me completely entertaining. (Interview, November 1992)

As Olivia encountered more Mexican American and Latina/o professionals from working-class origins, she reflected on the significance of her experiences as class issues. The growing number of upper-middle-class Mexican Americans who speak Spanish and retain their cultural practices allowed her to be more comfortable with her own mixture of cultural skills and diverse experiences. Yet most upwardly mobile Latinas and Latinos she encountered did not have an upper-class community pulling to remain in their life, as she did. She experienced that community's interest as a demand for gratitude. As she tried to grapple with negotiating a relationship with her mother's employers while still maintaining her own chosen identity, she reflected on how life in Liberty Place impacted her real family relations:

> They need to realize—not just the Smiths but the Joneses and the McDermotts, everybody—that a dynamic relationship occurs by bringing somebody into your home. There is vulnerability associated with being in somebody else's home and having somebody in your home—what they feel like being in somebody else's home. That experience has the potential of having so many far-reaching implications than a labor issue. It has life-determining factors. (Interview, July 1997)

VISITING LIBERTY PLACE

Trying to renegotiate patterns of interaction with the Smiths was an ongoing process for Olivia. When she returned to Los Angeles for business meetings or to visit her mother, Carmen insisted that Olivia stay with the Smiths. She did not have the option to avoid the Smiths, if she did not want to disrupt her relationship with her mother. In addition, Olivia's mixed feelings about Mr. and Mrs. Smith did not allow her to completely ignore the reality of her deep connection with them. Although she tried to gain personal satisfaction in reflecting on her history of passive resistance, the reality of her deferential and demeaning interaction with them remained present.[4] Just as Delores had pointed to the Smiths' racist behavior when Olivia was in college, Olivia was again reminded by another friend that Mr. and Mrs. Smith's interaction with her was demeaning. After she finished college and was living in Texas, her friend Donald was extremely uncomfortable observing their behavior:

> I had this white friend Donald, and I used to tell him all the time he was my only white friend—a good friend of mine. He always picked me up at the airport and

then takes me to the Smiths'. On one occasion, they had some people in the back-yard and were so excited to see me. Donald was horrified at the way that they treated me. He didn't like it because it was something that he could not identify as a part of me. He saw it as so classist. He hated to be the one to pick me up and finally talked to me and said, "I just can't do it." I think it's an issue [her relation-ship with the Smiths] I'm always going to need to deal with. (Interview, November 1992)

Rather than Olivia's being greeted as a family member or friend return-ing for a visit, Donald witnessed Mr. and Mrs. Smith showing off the maid's daughter to their guests as their successful charity case. Donald was unable to stand seeing a friend he respected transformed into an ob-ject of entertainment.

Donald's observations haunted Olivia. She became determined to move beyond superficial conversations and allow them to understand her values, politics, and dreams. During the years she worked for MAL-DEF in Texas, she frequently went to Los Angeles to attend conferences and various events. In previous business trips, Mrs. Smith avoided con-versations about her civil rights work:

Mrs. Smith's way of dealing with me is to take me shopping. She bought me an outfit that I was going to wear at MALDEF [at an annual fund-raiser]. She didn't want to know the details, just the kind of event—should we look for cocktail dresses or what? She really didn't want to know anything about it. (Interview, No-vember 1992)

During one of Olivia's early trips, she decided to talk to the Smiths about her job. Mr. Smith had accused her of using her expensive educa-tion to work against his economic and political interests. In addition, her mother told her that Mr. Smith refused to give their new Mexican-im-migrant maid the letter she needed to file for the immigration amnesty.[5] Olivia knew that he did not support amnesty efforts for immigrants, al-though he clearly knew that a number of maids and gardeners working in Liberty Place were undocumented. Olivia decided to try to open a door of communication with Mrs. Smith:

I realized that I had to sit down and explain to them what I was doing. What does it mean to work for this civil rights organization? One night I sat down with Mrs. Smith when we were alone and she had been drinking. I started to talk to her about my new job and how important it was to me and how I have always wanted to work for a civil rights organization.

And she started—she said, "Yeah, Olivia, but you can do other things."

I said, "You know, I am really upset that I am having to now sit down with you and tell you, when I am twenty-four years old, what I am doing with my life. This is who I am, and these are the things that are important to me. This is how I look at myself, and I value these things. I am really excited to have the opportunity to work for MALDEF. These are the people that I've always wanted to work for. I am excited. I am intimidated. I didn't expect to be able to do this until later in life, and I am doing it now. I am really having an impact on how things are going in my life. I am really having an impact on Texas politics—how attitudes are being shaped. It is important to me."

I said, "You know, being in Texas is really difficult for me, but I feel that I can't live in California."

She said, "Olivia, I think you can be anything that you want to be."

"I did always know that I can do anything that I want, and as a result I can choose not to be what you want me to be. I don't have to do any one particular thing, and I am not limited to anything. But whatever it is, I am going to do it because I want to do it."

She said, "Olivia, you belong back here in California. This is what you should be doing. You need to be here. This is your community."

I said, "*No*. What community is my community? Living at Liberty Place is not my community. It says nothing about me. I have nothing . . . done anything. . . . There is nothing here that I can do for you, and there is nothing that I can gain from this community."

She said, "What do you mean?"

I said, "Well, you know, I don't have anything in common with anybody that lives here, other than I know their kids and I know where they went to school. We don't have the same values. I am not a Republican; I am not ever going to be a Republican. I don't have these values."

"Well, still, there are other things for you to do. I am sure that you can work for the people you worked for before. You should be governor of California. That is where you belong. This is the only place where you can succeed. You can't succeed in Texas because those people are different than us. Those people are racist; those people are, you know—they don't have the same image of you that we have here."

I said, "What are you talking about? It is no different here than it is there—except there I feel like I have my own community. I can start from new and do things for somebody and be able to have a role. I have skills that I can give to people that have contributed in some way to me. What do I have to give to your community that I've gained from it? Are you going to sit there and tell me what it is like to deal with the Mexican community?"

"No. But Olivia, see, you have these two perspectives of what is going on, and that makes you electable. That is what is going to make you succeed."

I told her how resentful I was that she had told Mrs. Stein that I graduated from high school and that the Smiths went to my high school graduation and I didn't thank them. I explained to Mrs. Smith how I thought they really had exploited my mother. My mother could have been earning more money that they never paid her. My tuition of three thousand a year at this Catholic school was an insult—to just think that's all my mother was worth. I didn't see it that they had helped me. I feel that they had distracted my mother from the exploitive issues of pay and what she was worth. I told her that my mother had earned it, and that just took her completely by surprise.

I started to cry, and she started to cry and said, "Olivia, but you don't understand how much better you are because you've gone through that. And what is wrong with being different?"

I said, "There is nothing wrong with it. I am not angry at myself. I am not hating myself. I am just not the same. I have to deal with the fact that, no, I didn't grow up underprivileged, but I recognize the hardships that my community goes through—because it is a part of me. I recognize from being in Juárez and in El Paso, and I know. But it's not an easy thing to reconcile. It is not something that is going to be easily understood. It's not been easy for me. "

"What better thing to know," Mrs. Smith said, "but bilingual education and to be able to learn both Spanish and English? They are both valued, and they are both important."

"I went to Juárez and spoke in Spanish and then came here and had to relearn English. Sometimes I didn't understand when I could use one and when I couldn't use another," I said. "Remember that time that you went to the post office and came back so mad because all there were bilingual ballots. 'And goddamn it! This is America, and they ran out of English registration forms?' You think I don't remember that? Did you tell me how important it was to be bilingual? Sure, you sent me to Prep High, and I took Spanish, and I did it. And yeah, maybe one day I can sit and have a conversation with Spanish royalty, but what does that mean? I feel that you made some critical decisions in my life without my consent or involvement in any of those decisions. You decided when I was going to take Spanish instead of French. You decided. I am not going to tell myself that I wasn't successful just because I didn't do it your way. You have to look at what I am doing."

She basically said, "Everybody is fucked up. Everybody has a hard life. Look at Jane, and look at how fucked up she is and how irresponsible she is."

Mrs. Smith does not say to herself, "I had something to do with that."

She said, "Everybody has it hard, Olivia. What makes you any better? And so it was hard, so what?"

I said, "Well, at least you got to choose your choices. You naturally just assume that your culture was better and that I would naturally want to be a Republican and I would naturally want to be in a sorority and all these things." (Interview, November 1992)

Olivia's conversation with Mrs. Smith represented an attempt to become both a subject and an agent in their interaction. As Olivia recalled the times that she was not allowed to make her own decisions, Mrs. Smith refuses to acknowledge that Olivia was denied choices about her future. Olivia was unable to break the wall of privilege. Mrs. Smith could not see the contradiction in denying the existence of structural constraints in any choice that Olivia wanted to make. She failed to understand that the tensions in their relationship were related to objectifying Olivia and treating her as a community project. Olivia did not want to be representative of the Smiths' parenting abilities, and she did not want their narrative of her success to erase her mother's hard work. The importance of "talking back" was her "movement from object to subject—the liberated voice."[6] Olivia no longer wanted to carry the burden of proof or representation in an environment that normalized whiteness and ignored the multiracial landscape of the country.[7]

In Olivia's narrative of her unsuccessful attempt to establish a more equitable and meaningful relationship with Mrs. Smith, Olivia countered Mrs. Smith's disapproval of her working for civil rights organizations. Rather than seeing Olivia's work as contributing to immigration and justice advocacy groups, Mrs. Smith evaluated Olivia's work as underachieving, when she had the experience and connections to run for a political office. Olivia acknowledged that she had no real claim to politically represent the citizens of Liberty Place any more than those of Pico Union.[8] Mrs. Smith argued that Olivia would bring a unique perspective to the political arena because she had the ability to mediate between the white upper class and the growing Latino population in Los Angeles. Mrs. Smith's description of Olivia's bilingual and bicultural life as easy and as providing future opportunities erased Olivia's struggle to maintain her "Mexicanness" against pressure to assimilate. Olivia was shocked by Mrs. Smith's turning this experience into positive characteristics and responded by pointing out contradictions. Olivia was not encouraged to establish ethnic solidarity with Mexican Americans but rather was pushed toward dating white males. She recalled her Mexican Spanish being defined as insufficient and too working class, and instead she was forced to study Castilian Spanish in school. Olivia also recalled Mrs. Smith's anger at finding only Spanish ballots at the post office, and her comment at the time did not suggest that she thought Spanish-speaking citizens belonged in the political process. These memories highlighted a long list of demeaning and degrading actions that were the foundation of the inequities in their interactions.

Many years later, when Olivia began to work with numerous corporations, she opened the doors of communication with Mr. Smith by asking advice about negotiating job contracts and other dealings with corporations. This strategy was extremely successful because Mr. Smith was interested and curious about Olivia's career experiences and was intrigued by her ability to find a niche in the corporate world to utilize her skills within a Hispanic market and to focus on social issues. At the same time, Olivia recognized that Mr. Smith's experience as an agent in the entertainment business crossed over into the corporate world, and he was able to play a mentoring role. She acquiesced to this relationship and called on him prior to making decisions. Although she frequently had consulted others before calling him, she knew this was a way for them to develop a meaningful relationship:

> Mr. Smith asked, "What are the corporations that you have interaction with?"
> I went through this litany of them.
> He said, "God, that's really great."

I never really had a lot of conversations with him. I never went to him for advice until I already had the job. I remember having an entire conversation with him after I had the job and he taking a real interest at my succeeding at this venture.

"How did you get this job? Who do you know?" He tried really hard to translate relevance to me, as if it was going to do any good at all. I always thought he was really patronizing. I didn't begin to find value in the relationship until the New York deal. Rosalyn really convinced me that I might find some value in her father's advice. I knew that, by then, he was really sick and wasn't going to last too long. So what harm would it actually be for me to humor him and let him believe that he had influence? By then, I knew that they didn't have any money and that they didn't have much influence. The sphere of influence that he did have was really in entertainment, and I was far from that. Before I went to go see him, I told them that I had gotten this job, that I had been offered this job.

"Well, bring your offer letter." He then took a look at it. We had a moment by ourselves. He looked at the letter and said, "First of all, it's telling you you can't quit in a year. How do you know in the first year they won't change management and bring in somebody that doesn't like you and will want to get rid of you? What kinds of protections do you have? Do you have a lawyer? Have you had somebody look at this?"

I thought it interesting that he immediately picked this out: "What if they don't like me and some second person comes in?" Everything was exactly the way he said.

I remember him telling me, "Olivia, nobody is really going to understand you, because you are not really like any of them. And you are going to do really well with your clients, because you are committed and passionate. They are going to see that, but you should probably have a discussion with your boss." He always focused on preparing me for being accepted by his own [other white, middle-class businessmen], but he knew it was going to be a really difficult thing. (Interview, March 1998)

Olivia began again to reinterpret her past relationship with Mr. Smith, giving more weight to Mr. Smith's socializing her to be a competent actor in a white man's world. While she disliked the competitive and patronizing nature of the game, she realized she needed to enhance these skills in order to be effective in the corporate world. While accepting each other's polar-opposite position on political issues, Olivia and Mr. Smith did find a way to establish a relationship that eased further interaction.

Olivia's visits to her mother after moving to Texas also gave her a new relationship with her mother. She began to have moments with her mother that pointed to how little she really knew about her mother:

My mother said something that really had a major impact on me. This past October, we were in bed talking, and it was the weirdest thing. When I came home this time, we were having like a slumber party or something. We just wanted to stay the whole night and talk and talk and talk. She asked me questions about this, and "What about this?" I was just really exhausted, because my mother had never been like that! We had just talked about school. I think that maybe she was trying to make the relationship different again. I was talking about Gerardo [current boyfriend] and telling my mom that I really loved him very much but that I just felt that some things are not worth it to me. I am not willing to give everything up just to be with him.

My mother turns around and says, "You know, I've really never been in love with anybody. I mean, I never really loved anybody to the point that I would do anything for them."

It was just a shock to me! I always thought that my mother must have really been in love with my father. But then I thought, "Well, maybe it was like a one-night stand. Maybe my mom just wanted to get pregnant and wanted to have a child on her own." I don't know. I don't know that I am really ever going to ask her. I think she was being very sincere with me. I think that I got really afraid that I feel the same way. It really kind of shakes me up thinking, "Well, maybe I don't have to do anything. I could do it just like my mom." I don't know why she was telling me though. I kind of thought, "Well, maybe my mom did have more control and wasn't as vulnerable as maybe I would think that she was at that particular time." She never talks about it really. She only tells me that one time she went to look for my father. She went to look that Sunday that he didn't come home. She went on the next weekend to go talk to his sister to go see where he was. She didn't have any idea where he was. My mother never went back. But I just thought it was so weird that here I thought that maybe that means that my mom just had a lot more control over her relationship than she was ready to admit. It was not really that important to her.

Like sometimes she tells the Jimenezes, "No! I'm not going to do that." It is weird because she does that. I don't remember what it was, but she told Dr. Jimenez she didn't like something. They don't say anything to my mother. (Interview, November 1992)

For Olivia, knowing her mother became an evolving process. Her mother had always been the Rock of Gibraltar—never bending to the wind or waves. As she gradually learned more about her mother, she could never make a final decision to pigeonhole her as a victim, as a survivor, or as being in complete control of the situation:

I said, "Mother, you have no idea of what is happening in my life—no idea! Raul is telling me that I am fucked up because my father is not around. I don't know shit about my father. I have no idea about him because you never wanted to take time to talk to me about it.

She said was, "Okay, let's talk about your father."

Then I said, "No. No. You know what? It is really not that important. If I am twenty-one years old now and knowing about my father hasn't made a big difference, why is it going to matter now?"

I just closed it off, and I just said, "No. I am not going to accept the fact that my father has or hasn't been significant, because how is he going to be significant if he hasn't even been there at all? How can I now deduce that he somehow affected me, if he wasn't here? There is nothing wrong with the way I feel, and there is nothing wrong with the way I think. If I think it is fine to be a child of a single mother, then fine, it worked for me. It worked for my aunt, and it worked for my other aunt. So who says that we have to have two parents? And who says that is the way things are? And who is to say that just because I didn't grow up with a father that I am fucked up? I am not even going to deal with it."

Then she blurted out to me—it was horrible—she just blurted out to me, "What is there to talk about? I didn't know anything about this man. Why do you want to have so many discussions about this man I knew nothing about?" She had dated him a couple times and gone to the movies. Then she got into the car to go with him to get some cigarettes, and he raped her! She said she was so naive. "Oh, yeah, let's go for a ride in the car to go get cigarettes." Then he took her someplace really far away. Back then there were a lot of ranches and open space in San Fernando. He took her to some deserted place and raped her. He told her, "Oh, come on, you liked it. You didn't even say no or move."

"What else do you want to know, huh, huh, huh?!!"

I was just shocked. Then I cried. Then I really just got pissed. I got angry at my mother because she would hide this from me. She is so open about everybody else's goddamn business. She never talked about how she feels about anything.

In my mind I had thought my mother made a conscious decision to have sex. And maybe she even had a conscious decision to have unprotected sex and to get pregnant. I mean, she was thirty-six years old. That's what I would have done and not told him a word. I really thought it was my mother's conscious choice to be a single mother. It wouldn't be unlike her.

My father knows I exist; my mom said that he once saw me. When I was about two or three, one of dad's cousins saw me in a restaurant. So his family has not tried to contact me either. Part of me really wants to contact them, but I'm afraid that once I would start contacting them, it would become an obsession for me. What do I have to say to him? "You raped my mom." (Interview, October 1997)

As painful for Olivia as was her mother's admission that her daughter had been the product of rape, the most shocking aspect for Olivia was how little she actually knew about her mother. Obviously, the topic of Olivia's father was an extremely painful one, particularly since Carmen claimed responsibility for having been so easily tricked into an unsafe environment. Olivia was shocked because this image of "rape" was irreconcilable with her image of her mother as this incredibly independent matriarch. She had always assumed that her mother decided to have a child but not a husband, because she did not see her mother in a "traditional" patriarchal relationship. Instead, she knew her mother as this incredibly strong business woman who brokered all the live-in positions in Liberty Place and organized the maids to agree on pay and working conditions; in this image of her mom, Carmen was not a woman who was a victim of rape and did not consider the option of an abortion. With Olivia's not knowing the details of her mother's pregnancy but only the way that she managed to support her extended family in Mexico and to be a financially responsible mother, she had imagined her mother to have decided to have a child and to have gotten pregnant on purpose. Part of that scenario was her mother's choice not to have a husband. After all, her mother had frequently called unacceptable her relatives' and other maids' signs of weakness in putting up with worthless, lazy, and irresponsible men. Olivia was shocked at the thought that her mother could be vulnerable, because Carmen's relatives, the employers, and her daughter had always perceived her as strong and independent: "*¡Que dice Carmen!*"

When Carmen heard her daughter interpret her actions as a mother's lack of interest in her daughter's life, she attempted to engage in the mode of mother-child conversation that she heard Olivia yearning for. The news of Carmen's rape shocked Olivia into the realization that she really did not know her mother. Prior to this argument, Carmen told Olivia about a friend's granddaughter who was pregnant, and she expressed dismay that the granddaughter did not consider having an abortion. Over the years, Olivia reflected on that conversation and thought it odd that Carmen herself had not had an abortion. She assumed that her mother had decided to be a single mom and was ready to make things work out. She had no idea that her mother simply accepted fate and did the best she could.

> I don't understand where my mother stands in a lot of these issues: what she would do if I got pregnant and decided to be a single mother. She kept me, and I turned out okay. It is weird not to know how my mom stands. For the first time, when I went home in October and I left, my mother cried at the airport. My mother never really shows any emotions at all for me, and now I started to tell my mother how much I loved her when I talk in the phone. I say, "You know, mom, *te quiero mucho* [I really love you]" and "How are things going" and all that. She started to say it—but never before would she ever tell me how much she loved me or how important I was or anything. She just always had to be strong and never show an emotion or anything! I don't know what she thinks now, what she thinks I'm doing with my life. But I think she just trusts that I'm going to do the right thing. She doesn't really understand me, and she is not going to try. She is just going to accept it for what it is. (Interview, October 1997)

NEGOTIATING THE MAID'S RETIREMENT

Olivia continued to discourage her mother from hoping that she would eventually move back to Los Angeles. At the same time, her mother declined offers to move to Texas and live with her daughter. Given her mother's insistence that Olivia be independent and self-sufficient, Olivia developed a growing network in Texas that further connected her to the area. She remained strongly attached to family obligations involving her extended family and made frequent visits to assist her mother in El Paso and Juárez. Concerned about her mother's health, Olivia tried to open the door to discuss plans for her retirement. However, Olivia discovered that, rather than making plans to retire, her mother had expanded her workload to include catering parties. Carmen showed no signs of slowing down, but Olivia knew about her past health problems with heart seizures and urged her to think about retiring.

For more than three decades, Carmen's life had been structured around the families of Liberty Place. Olivia had not really given a great deal of attention either to the impact that live-in work had on Carmen or to the degree to which her mother's identity was based on playing a meaningful role in employers' families. Over the past two decades, she had become a respected member of the community, now in her early fifties.

She lives at the Steins' old house and in her room. The Steins moved in June, and they sold the house to a Chinese couple. They made this contract. Mrs. Stein told them about my mom and that she cleans one day a week but that she wanted to keep living in that little house and everything. So that was, like, part of the agreement—my mom would live in that part of the house. Even though they own the property and everything, my mother lives there. "She is an important member of our community" kind of thing. "You can't get rid of her. So you have to just accept the fact that is where she lives. This is your house and everything, but she is going to live there. You could decide not to, but people would be really upset with you."

They are really nice to my mother. She cleans for a couple hours, and then Mr. Woo says, "Oh, Carmen, sit down." They'll take her to lunch, and they treat her in a way that employers never treated her. They bought her a refrigerator, and they bought her a bed, and they never went into her apartment. They really respect her privacy and don't go in. They bought her this massage thing to put on her back. They understand that is labor; it is not a favor. And they are really good. They don't pay her, but the cleaning is exchange for her rent. But at the same time, they don't exploit her. They don't expect that because they take her out to dinner or buy her something that it means she has to do more or that is going to mean something.

My uncle told me something incredibly disturbing. He has never said anything negative about my mother. He finally had the nerve to tell me, "Look, your mother is enslaved literally to these people. She does not owe them anything. She does not have to take care of their children. She does not have to feel responsible for their children or what mistakes their children are going to make. Your mother needs to get out of there immediately, because she has convinced herself that they need her, and that is a crock of shit. Your mother is dependent. She has somehow convinced herself of that in order to rationalize her presence there. We can't nag her and tell her to move. You have to do something about it." (Interviews, November 1992 and July 1997)

Olivia was confronted by employers about her mother's health and was urged to make retirement plans for her. Recognizing Carmen's place in their lives, they recommended that Olivia return to Los Angeles to care for her mother. However, Olivia was already committed to living in Texas and had no intention of returning to Los Angeles.

Mrs. Smith sat in the waiting room, and Dr. Jones asked that I go with my mother. Dr. Jones said that her heart and blood pressure were not regular. My mother cried the whole time.

Dr. Jones came in and says, "You know, Olivia, your mom has had a few heart seizures over the last six months. She has had three, and that is a lot. I really think that it is because you are not home, and she really misses you. She gets worried. I think that she should go back. Maybe she wants to go back [to Mexico] and be with her sisters. Maybe she just works too much."

My mom starts crying and saying, "It's not that I'm working too much! Who is going to give me money if I don't work? Who is going to support me if I don't work?"

I said, "Well, Mom, you don't have to work as hard. You don't have all these expenses." She recently bought other property in Juárez. She could live there, but she cannot go back and live with her sisters. She wants to be able to just do things, have influence, talk to people, and help other people get jobs and work. Having access to that network is continuing to work, and that is what she does best.

I asked, "Mom, do you want to go back?"

"No. I don't want to go back." She has grown accustomed to a certain lifestyle, which is not hers.

She tells me, "Aren't you going to come back to California? When you come back, then we can get a house, and things will be fine."

I said, "No, Mom—maybe I won't come back to California. You know, I have a good job. I like Texas. Maybe it [returning to California] is not good for me."

She says, "Well, I don't want to go back to El Paso."

I said, "Dr. Jones said you are going to retire. You are fifty-eight turning fifty-nine, and you are going to retire two years to three years." (Interview, July 1997)

Growing up, Olivia had always heard her mother tell her family that she was going to return to Mexico and live in one of the houses she owned. Olivia began to see that her mother's retiring in Mexico was highly unlikely and that her mother did not fit there anymore than she herself did. She also heard Mrs. Smith talk about Mrs. Smith and her mother retiring together in Arizona and confronted her mother about playing along with this fantasy.

I've been real distraught about her need to plan on retiring. She visited me one summer. We went to the Social Security office, and something was wrong. Half the money wasn't reported to her right Social Security number. Her payments are really ridiculously low. My mother conned me into thinking she wouldn't need to move to Texas, and she wouldn't live with me. She said the cost of living is higher and you get higher payments, and she has no intention to stop working.

I asked my mom, "You're really thinking about going to live with these people?"

She said, "I don't know, Arizona seems like a nice place to live. That's where everybody else is going and retiring, and who's cleaning all these old people's house?"

Maybe my mom thinks it would open up a whole bunch of new work. (Interview, July 1997)

Carmen's visits to Texas became more frequent after Olivia married a bilingual Latino from a working-class background. Since his first language is Spanish, he and Carmen became close, and he accepted her management of their home. Carmen finally moved in with Olivia and her husband when her first grandchild, a boy, was born. During this period, Olivia moved to Washington, DC, and later to New York City. As she moved toward public relations and consulting work in the public and private sectors, she appreciated her mother's assistance with her children but was constantly finding that she needed to tell her to relax and not to work so much.

Accepting that her mother had an ongoing relationship with Mrs. and Mr. Smith, Olivia maintained contact with them through infrequent phone calls and visits when she was in Los Angeles. She had a few exchanges with Rosalyn, who had opened a Mexican-import shop in Arizona and displayed some of her own art. Rosalyn became involved in a committed relationship with a female partner, and they had one son, whom Olivia knew. Jane had numerous jobs but tried to hold on to her connections in the entertainment business, which were dwindling. Ted and David were never completely financially independent from their parents. Both married but clearly had fallen from the class status they had in Liberty Place. Olivia rarely interacted with them. Olivia continued to maintain separation between families and did not invite the Smiths to her wedding, but later she did introduce them to her husband and later to her two children. Carmen continued visiting her former employers. However, she now took her young grandchildren when she visited the Smiths. For a time, Carmen's grandson called Mr. Smith "Grandfather," but Olivia continued to call him "Mr. Smith" and maintained a cordial distance, with infrequent phone calls about her work projects.

> My son has always kind of known the Smiths. When he was three months old, they were moving from Liberty Place to Arizona. I had to go back to work, and my mom was going to help them [the Smiths] pack. She actually took my son for a week when he was three months old. I remember they were all so fascinated: "Look! This is a Latino baby!" My son's perception is that it's a family connection that's very strong from his grandmother's side. There's always been this presence, and so there's no question that he's really had to examine.
>
> My daughter, on the other hand, pays a lot more attention to those things. "How come I call her Grandma Smith, and you call her Mrs. Smith?" They know there is a connection. I don't think that it's really ever dawned on them they're not Mexican, but these folks are Anglo. All those kind of class or social barriers have really changed because they don't live in this gated community. Things are really different from their vantage point than they were from mine. They don't have the money and influence that they once did.
>
> My son was sitting on the couch watching TV, and my mom was talking to Mrs. Smith on the phone. As soon as my mom hung up, he turned around and said, "Grandma, I didn't know that you knew how to speak English!" It was the first time

Olivia was aware that the Smiths had been living beyond their means for the past two decades, and as an agent, Mr. Smith did not have new clients. There was little if any difference between the neighborhoods that she and the Smiths lived in that would suggest class distinctions. The Smiths had experienced a major economic decline and change in lifestyle. The context in which Olivia's children interacted with the Smiths was completely different from the one their mother had experienced. They were not identified as the grandchildren of the Smiths' maid. There was no room in the Smith house that was designated as the maid's room. The only significant distinction that the children were aware of was language. Their grandmother always spoke Spanish to them, and Olivia and her husband spoke Spanish with Carmen as well. Although Olivia's children were too young to figure out the relationships, they were aware that Olivia did not embrace the Smiths as family, as their grandmother did.

Olivia's relationship with her mother matured, and Olivia gained an appreciation for Carmen's accomplishments, which she increasingly recognized as managing an enormous political and influential network. She came to understand why so many employers had always told her that her mother was smarter than all of them. As Olivia and her husband became involved in politics that overlapped with the entertainment business, Carmen was able to plan and cater important business-meeting luncheons and became a family member who was recognized in their business dealings. This collaboration brought Carmen and Olivia closer and eliminated the doubts about their family allegiance to each other. Olivia no longer doubted her mother's ability to step in and provide important insight into her business with the corporate world.

During this time, Olivia became aware of her and her mother's shared interests and her mother's abilities to comprehend her daughter's work on political campaigns, administrative government jobs, public-relations work, and consulting work.

I remember when Bush gave his State of the Nation address. My mother watched it in Spanish in its entirety. Then we talked about it afterwards. She called me and asked me what I thought. We have foreign-policy discussions, which was really bizarre.

She is very comfortable going toe to toe with me on anything, and she did not at all ever feel that, oh, well, I have more education, therefore she's going to bow down. My mother went toe to toe with me on every single issue that I discussed. (Interview, January 2003)

This transformation in their relationship was significant in pushing away the doubts of each one's commitment to the other. Instead, Olivia had confirmation that her mother supported her career choices and shared her politics. Furthermore, she appreciated the fact that she had more to learn from and about her mother.

There she is, as a domestic—it doesn't matter if she's twelve hundred miles away— and the point is my mother has access to information from her employer. She called me like as if it was real hush-hush—the same conversation that I would have with a politically conscious, politically astute, and college-educated friend.

"Well, I just wanted to tell you, don't worry. I heard your boss is going to get something, so don't be that concerned."

I'm just completely overwhelmed that I can think I'm so self-important and that I have achieved all this much and that I know so-and-so and so-and-so, but it doesn't matter. My mom will always be able to come in, over the top of anything, any network that I've got. My mother always has a more powerful connection. (Interview, January 2003)

An incident that Olivia found particularly amusing involved her consulting project to provide health information to a Spanish-speaking community. As she laughed retelling the story of her encounter with the daughter of her mother's former employer, I also marveled at the distance covered by Carmen's Liberty Place network.

In May, it was time for me to launch this program in LA. My client said, "The other people that you have to talk to, Olivia, are at Hope Care Hospital. They have a VP who's very influential. She sits on their board. We've never had much interaction with her, but her name is Linda Olsen. She's the one who really handles the hospitals. We first have to talk to this woman Linda, and then she will put you in touch with the PR agency. Linda does the newsletter for the hospital—so you should take a look at it, because when we do this launch, we'll probably want to include it in this newsletter. I'll fax you the newsletter.

I get this newsletter, and I look at it, and I see this white woman, and somehow this flash comes. This face looks really familiar. Her name is Linda D. Olsen. I read on, "D" spelled out. It's Linda Dillard Olsen. I think the blood drops from my face, and I realize, "Oh, my God, Linda Dillard is the daughter in the house that my mom first worked at!" Now me sitting in New York—as far as I can from Liberty Place—the furthest point that I could ever be, and I'm right smack back.

I asked my mom, "Look at this. Who is it?"

"That's Linda Dillard. She looks just like her mother."

"Come look at this website at the hospital. There's Mr. Dillard."

Then my mom starts to relate to me that this Hope Care Hospital is really the place that I was born. Hope Care was bought and changed, but it was St. Ann's Hospital. It was a teen-mom home, and the only reason I was born there was because Mrs. Dillard arranged for my mom to qualify for the program, because her husband, who is a lawyer, sits on the board of the hospital. I'm having this entire event at the place that I was born! All because of this family.

I have to call Linda, because I don't want to have this all unravel in front of my client. This is not an opera. So I call Linda Dillard, and I get her voice message. I say, "Linda, this is Olivia Salazar. You may not remember my name, but I'm sure you remember Carmen Sanchez. I am Carmen's daughter. It turns out that we may be working together on a project with X. Please give me a call. I'd love to connect and chat with you before we have the opportunity to meet."

A day or two goes by, and she calls me. I'm really caught off guard because I'm in the middle of doing something else and I've completely forgotten. I don't really know her family. I don't really know her brothers and sisters or any of them. I just have, like, horror stories and feelings of remembering falling down the stairs and living in the back house. Probably my worst experience of culture shock is associated with her and her family.

"I remember you as a child, and I probably hadn't seen you since I was five years old."

Here I'm trying to, like, clear the air so that when I'm with my client, we don't have to deal with any of this.

So we go to meet for the first time, and Linda sees me, and there's like this dramatic moment.

"So, Olivia, they want to have the event at this hospital, and it's right next to this teen-mother thing. Do you think it's a problem?"

And I'm like, "No, I don't think it's a problem. I was born there."

"What! You were, like, born ... ?"

I said, "Yes, I was born there."

Now they're [the clients] thinking, "Okay, we thought she was this pretentious name dropper who politically had all these connections, and in the end, we're getting to know that she's an illegitimate child who has these incredible power connection."

So they said, "Linda is really important. We don't know how she's connected."

"Well, here's the deal in a nutshell. Linda was a banker, and when she had children, she wanted a different job. Her father is the founder of the hospital and this whole operation. He is on the board. Linda is on the board. This is a part-time gig for her. She only really works there two and a half days a week."

I said, "Her father, who was the lawyer, created the hospital. When the tenant bought the hospital, he did all the paperwork and negotiation. They were a nonprofit hospital. They have this huge foundation, because that's the way they wanted it. I actually know all of Linda's family. One of her brothers is a judge ..."

They're like, "Oh, my God, Olivia not only knows this woman Linda but knows the color of underwear all her family wears, where they went to school and everything—but she's the illegitimate child, born at the teen unit."

I mentioned that it's my mom that Linda remembers, not me. She hadn't seen me since I was five years old. So they're all just fascinated with why I'm sitting in New York but have, like, these huge extensions. (Interview, January 2003)

Throughout the years, Olivia found that most people were so overwhelmed or confused about her connections that crossed such enormous class divides that they did not pursue an investigation into her background. And if they did, her educational and employment history offered few details in explaining these connections. Inquiries about family backgrounds, particularly class backgrounds, do not emerge in "polite" conversation.

AN EPIPHANY FOR ONE OF THE FAMILY

Mr. Smith died in the late summer of 2002. Shortly after attending Mr. Smith's funeral, Olivia called me and asked to meet, because she knew I would be interested in recording her experiences. Since she wanted to get away from home and collect her thoughts, we spent several days together at my home. As she recounted the funeral and wake with the Smith family, Olivia expressed a wide range of emotions. She was completely unprepared for the funeral and had never considered going. She understood why Mrs. Smith wanted her mother to attend but did not understand why their family considered her presence so crucial. Acquiescing to her mother's pleas, Olivia agreed to accompany her mother. In recounting the funeral, she laughed at revisiting sibling feuds. She cried in anger at revisiting painful childhood memories. Her emotions were completely jolted by new revelations. She was shocked at being treated as Mr. Smith's daughter and at sharing a place alongside his wife and daughters.

> I assumed that the sitting arrangements would be like a wedding: his family and her [Mrs. Smith's] family. But the setting was kind of interesting to me. We got there early, and we [Olivia and Carmen] both sat together. Then Rosalyn came and said to me, "Let's go. Stand up. We're moving to the back party room." It was really strange to me that they had orchestrated my part to be locked arms coming in with the so-called procession. (Interview, October 2002)

Carmen sat further removed from the family, whereas Olivia was placed next to the widow and her biological daughters. Not only was she being claimed by the Smith family at the funeral, but her place among his children was to be engraved on a tombstone.

> According to Jane, the tombstone will say, "Ronald David Smith, loved by five children." It will not name my husband or my kids, but it would have their four kids, my name, and then, "loving friend, family friend of 30 years, Carmen." They wanted my mom's name on the tombstone. I thought it was interesting that they claimed an adoption of me as one of their children, as family. And how do you reconcile that? Whose cross are we carrying? Whose guilt are we dealing with? (Interview, October 2002)

Olivia expected her mother's role in the Smith family to be publicly acknowledged, but she was shaken by being named as a family member and placed in prominence above her mother. Her name was even published in the obituary. She had not kept in touch with the family on a regular basis since leaving college and had never joined them in a family reunion, weddings, or holidays. Her infrequent calls to Mr. and Mrs.

Smith were usually yearly, and she never felt like she had siblings. She was curious that they still perceived her as a family member after all these years.

Olivia was completely unprepared for Mr. Smith's clients in the entertainment business to acknowledge her by name, approaching her in a familiar manner and expressing their condolence to her—many of them did not extend that same recognition to his children. Even now she reflected back on her interaction with them as being demeaning:

> I thought it was like going to the zoo. It was like letting an animal out: "Oh, oh, let me see how you will react! Are you a closet racist? Are you going to be entertained because you didn't know I could be articulate? What kind of—what will be your reactions? Will you really engage me and ask me what I think about?" (Interview, October 2002)

The memorial service was held at a nightclub, and entertainers were invited to perform. Olivia perceived that renting a club and inviting entertainers for this memorial was a status symbol for the family more than a celebration of their father's life. Olivia was amused at Rosalyn's reaction to her father's clients and friends espousing attitudes that were politically incorrect.

> "God, I think that guy was outlandish, and it was inappropriate" and yadda, yadda. I thought, "Oh, come on, who did you think he was?" I knew that it was the whole Hollywood environment. I never purported to think that Hollywood represented me, so there's no sense—I didn't lose anything. These are not my institutions. These are not my ideals. (Interview, October 2002)

In the tradition of the Hollywood that Olivia knew, she was not the least bit surprised to hear racist humor. Having heard racist attitudes and words while growing up in Liberty Place, she did not expect these people to consider their comments as directed at her. However, the distance from childhood made the youngest daughter, Rosalyn, embarrassed that these jokes were being told in front of Olivia and her mother. However, the contradictions of Mr. Smith's having racist colleagues and a treasured relationship with a Mexican-immigrant woman's daughter made Olivia recognize that he must have struggled with the contradictions:

In fact, there's a sense of acknowledgment that he struggled with it. Obviously I impacted his life much more than I ever anticipated and ever thought of. I was dying to have the opportunity—and I had to really struggle with myself and not go up to that mike—to say, "Well, I'm just pleased to say, I was his fuckin' pride and joy." I resisted. I was the gracious person that he would have wanted me to be. I still had dignity to know that I was there as the conscientious objector. I had paved my own way, and I didn't pretend to be closer in his final days than I ever was. It was always just who I was. And now I'm more and more comfortable that it is their relationship with my mom. It's not so much my relationship with them, as they really understand their relationship with my mom. My mom was still being there and affecting their lives and still so closely connected. (Interview, October 2002)

Olivia observed the familiar family drama of siblings arguing over responsibilities and the distribution of their father's valuable possessions. Rather than comforting their mother or each other over the loss of their father, they took the time to rehash childhood jealousies and evaluate each other's economic success or failures. As Olivia said,

Again, trivialities—it doesn't matter. (Interview, October 2002)

The sibling interaction took Olivia back to her childhood watching the Smith children compete for the most money from their grandparents and parents. Although Jane was financially the most successful, she wanted no responsibility, just as she acted as a young mother. David and Ted still relied on their male privilege in the family and assumed that they would be pampered. Olivia's observation of the contradictions and conflicts highlighted all the ways that she never wanted to be "one of the family."

Incorporated into the funeral events was a taco night. While growing up, David's favorite treat was tacos that Carmen made. Wanting to relive old memories, he requested that this be incorporated into the time they spent together. They decided that taco night would be the night after the funeral, to bring everybody together again. It was the one commonality, the one thing that everybody remembered as being awesome. David had insisted as one of the conditions for coming down for his father's funeral was they had to have taco night. So it was my job to go and find someplace where we were going to get tortillas, another place where they were going to get the rest of the stuff. They realized that my mom is not going to be making tacos for fifty people.

"You had to get other food," I said.

"Well, I know where they sell enchiladas and chile rellenos."

But nobody wanted that. We went and bought them, but they wanted tacos! It turns out that the youngest cousin had a restaurant, and they all worked in restaurants. They all know how to speak Spanish from talking to the kitchen help. Everybody had a job. It's Skip's job to make this killer salsa and guacamole, which I have to say was awesome. I remember asking him, "Where did you learn this?"

"This is from the cooks."

He had this awesome recipe. Everybody had to do something, so that it was less work for my mom, but there weren't enough tacos. The vegetarian psychos had to have turkey tacos. And so my mom ended up having to do twice as much work, because you had to have meat tacos and turkey tacos. And they wanted corn tortillas from Whole Foods. I finally said, "Look, is this fuckin' taco night, or is it politically correct night?! You can't have both. You can either have Mexican food, or you can get Whole Foods food!" My mom cannot cook when she had [ingredients] from Whole Foods. (Interview, October 2002)

Encounters throughout the funeral and memorial service offered Olivia glimpses into the ways that she and her mother became incorporated in the Smith family's stories and the ways that their cultural identities had been appropriated. Olivia was confronted with a wide range of stories constructed by the Smiths to claim Carmen and Olivia's Mexican culture and identity. First, Olivia heard from David, who was obsessing over a co-worker's grievance that had happened five years earlier. Both Mrs. Smith and David recounted the incident of a Latina employee's accusing David of being racist. As he told his story, Olivia listened to his claim of innocence, which was based on his relationship to the live-in maid and her daughter:

"I have my second mother who is Mexican, and I have a sister who is Mexican. They lived in my house, and I grew up with them. I went to school with them. I've had friends."

I always felt that I was somehow supposed to validate this employment conflict by my eventually saying, "Oh, okay, it's not really David; it's her."

Olivia found herself again placed in a position of doing emotional labor to validate David's perception of himself and of having to go along with the "second mother and sister" classification, rather than the maid and her daughter who never had the same privileges or claims to the privilege of being a family member.

Olivia recalled that this was not the first time that she had heard David identify himself as having some kind of affiliation with Mexicans. In a family effort to teach David a work ethic, he worked for a time at his grandfather's ranch. Instead of working with other whites on the ranch, he was sent to work side by side with the farm workers. He returned and shared his experience with Carmen, proudly demonstrating the Spanish words he had learned and announcing, "I am Mexican too, you know." However, Olivia had no idea that he seriously believed that these events made him nearly Mexican or that he was unaware that he had not lost his white privilege. His appropriation of her ethnic identity was so bold that she felt it was a sign of desperation, since he had clearly wasted all the opportunities his family's class and status provided over the years. Therefore, rather than claiming his current class status among the white service class, he was able to ignore his loss of class by embracing a Mexican identity, which he assumed was always working class and, thus, without class stigma.

The changing construction of identity that surprised Olivia the most was that of Jane's eldest son, Skip. As a teenager, Olivia babysat him when Jane returned from Portugal, divorced, and became a single mother. Rather than settling down and caring for her child, Jane left Olivia in charge, sometimes not returning for days. Recalling her difficulties with Jane as an adolescent, Olivia remembered Jane treating her like a nanny and expecting Olivia to be her own personal maid. Consequently, when Olivia did care for Skip, she always made a point not to do any housework, not even to wash a dish. Olivia had not seen him for many years but was aware that he was a high school dropout and had spent time in jail for a drug conviction.

When I saw him as an adult, he had wonderful loving memory and feeling of me, really embracing and coming out with this incredible Spanish.

"Where did you learn to speak Spanish?"

He said, "*Mi connecta,* you know, my drug connection was from Mexico, and I had to speak Spanish."

He had this beautiful Spanish, not just Chicano Spanish. He has like a Chicano slang Spanish, but it had to be Mexican, you know—immigrant enough, because his vocabulary would never have been as extensive as it is.

He, my mom, and I had entire conversations in Spanish in front of everyone.

So even his two uncles wanted to be really Mexican. The one who really has the closest tie and the closest relationship was the jailbird grandson. It is really interesting to me the way Skip is very smart and sophisticated and knows that he has something over on everyone else, a sense of Mexicanness. His language—the terminology that he uses—he had to have really immersed himself at one point with Chicanos to know the nuance and as a culture and Chicanismo. He plays one of us and talks about racial circumstances. (Interview, October 2002)

Olivia's hearing Skip acknowledge the cherished memories of Olivia's care work was gratifying to her. At the same time, she was reminded of the way Jane exploited her by not returning home when she had promised and causing problems between her mother and Mrs. Smith because she refused to be a responsible mother. Although Jane attempted to embrace Olivia as a sister, she reminded Olivia of the times Jane treated her poorly and stole her makeup and shoes. Like Mrs. Smith, Jane denied any possible grounds of inequities between them, because they were all family. She expected Olivia to listen to her complaints about having to financially care for her mother and the grievances she had toward her brothers. Along with Jane's claim of Olivia as family were the expectations of her emotional labor and any denial that their lives were different.

If Olivia felt similarities to any of the Smiths, it was to Skip. He resembled her, with a similarly unusual repertoire of class and cultural skills. While she was Mexican American and the maid's daughter, Skip was white and the son of a producer. No one expected her to be competent to interact among corporate executives, and no one would expect him to be able to interact so easily among Mexican immigrants. Like Olivia, Skip's level of competency involved complete submergence into a community. His drug dealings with the Mexican mafia and the time he spent in jail enabled him to learn the wide range of Spanish spoken by Mexican immigrants in the United States. He clearly did not share the same values of whiteness or class consciousness that his mother did. Instead, he ignored his actual place in the Smith family and claimed Carmen and Olivia as his real family. It never occurred to Olivia that one of Smiths would actually assimilate to the Mexican-immigrant world and engage in passing.

Whereas Rosalyn was embarrassed by a racist joke told in Olivia's presence, her mother was blinded to the fact that Carmen and Olivia might consider the word "wetback" to be offensive. Just as the frat students Olivia encountered in college had done, Mrs. Smith was able to separate attitudes of white supremacy from her embrace of individual persons of color as best friends or even as "one of the family." Having lost that battle as an adolescent in the Smith household, Olivia was not surprised that Mrs. Smith had not changed the way she talked about Mexican immigrants. However, if Skip was going to appropriate a Mexican identity, he needed to confront his own family members rather than expect to be consoled by Olivia and her mother.

Olivia's experience attending the funeral and spending time with the Smiths stirred up emotions and issues she thought she had laid to rest years before. The family gathering and interaction completely shattered her self-image as being a powerless actor in the Smith household who was dominated by their whiteness and class privilege:

> In some ways, I felt like my mom gave them status in Liberty Place. A lot of people didn't know who they were, other than the Smith kids who got—they're constantly expelled and in trouble and at the bottom of everything. "Oh, but that's okay. That's where Carmen works." My mother achieved some acceptance or acknowledgment from them. I remember the very first time that Mrs. Smith ever met the Steins, a family that Rosalyn knew from school. My mom needed to go over to their house to bring somebody new over for them to clean their house, and that was the first time they ever met. I remember being really fascinated with that. "Well, you [Mrs. Smith] never would have come here. They never would have known, and then you never would have become friends with them or anything—never would have crossed paths, if the maid didn't bring you here." I remember conversations in the car with Mrs. Adams and my mom, that she was constantly milking my mom for information as to who is doing what, who's significant, how

much money do they have, how much is that house's value: "Carmen, do you know how much their house is worth?" It's constant social information, gathering that would take place. And I thought, "I guess she's not in the in crowd. Why the fuck would she be asking my mom all this shit if she's so pretentious and knows everything?" (Interview, October 2002)

Olivia's impact on the Smiths' lives was not something that she had previously ever considered. The way that Mr. Smith's former clients acknowledged her at his funeral as the grieving child and hugged her instead of his biological children made her realize that she had deeply touched his life. She began reflecting back on her experience with him and his attempt to mentor her.

He'd [Mr. Smith would] leave the room, and Jane would say, "God, my dad was full of shit, him and his white-boy thing." There wasn't a lot of quiet time for me to make my own analysis. A lot of it was somehow dictated and labeled by Jane as it being white-boy privilege. I didn't feel like they applied to me because I wasn't playing in those circles and didn't want to. Therefore, I always felt like Mr. Smith wanted to tell me the rules of the game, because he naturally just assumed that I would select his same playing field and playing circumstances. I really believe that he thought that I would be in those circles, and he wanted to prepare me, and he generally wanted me to succeed, because his success was tied to mine. But I always kept trying to draw this distinction, but I'm not in the circle. (Interview, October 2002)

Mr. Smith must have spoken about Olivia's career trajectory with pride to his friends in order for them to remember her and to express such heartfelt condolences to her rather than to his own children. She had no idea that she had been Mr. Smith's pride and joy.

That whole funeral experience made me realize that I have all the power. I have absolutely nothing to lose. I have all the power and control. Mr. Smith couldn't have portrayed me in any way other than what would really benefit me, because it had to make him look good. They [his children] could have done all of these things, had all the money, all they power, but ultimately [they] are fucked up. They don't have good parental relationships, their marriages failed. His kids were not the most successful, but he had this one that really capitalized on the entire experience and did something with herself. However, it is how he painted it: I was the success story. So how can this be damaging in whatever way? It had to empower me in the end. (Interview, October 2002)

Watching the wake in the night club, Olivia saw all the trophy brides, and since she had gone to school with so many of their children, including the Smiths, she knew that making a marriage work was not one of their talents, nor was successful parenting. Many of their children relied solely on inheritance to replicate their class status or focused on marriages as a path to class comforts. Olivia had not arrived to the funeral thinking of herself as Mr. Smith's success story—but here she was, the Mexican-immigrant maid's daughter playing alongside his business peers and moving further into the corporate world. She had always wanted to deny the Smiths any credit because she wanted her mother's hard work to be acknowledged. Now, she saw that there was nothing to lose in letting them feel like "one" had been successful. She had nothing to lose in letting them claim her.

Mr. Smith's funeral had no impact on Olivia's construction of her family, but now she knew that she had impacted and influenced the Smiths' own family relationships. When she was growing up, she worried about losing her mother, as the boundaries of work and family were blurred, yet the Smith family boundaries were the ones dissolving along with their class status.

I walked away from that funeral and that weekend feeling like I really affected their lives much more than they affected mine. I really walked away with a real sense of control over the relationship and control over how I defined it. So that was kind of the big surprise to me. Wow, you guys were really affected by me! (Interview, October 2002)

BEYOND LIBERTY PLACE

Some readers may argue that Olivia's life is a freak accident, and living a life between the social worlds of employers and domestics is certainly not a common Chicano experience for children. I counter that her story represents a microcosm of power relationships in the larger society. After several decades of my deep and often emotional conversations with Olivia, and collecting, rereading, and analyzing transcripts, I am still captivated by her descriptive accounts of negotiating boundaries in employers' homes and the gated community—and the similarities to society's boundary work in establishing social policies that maintain class and race divisions.[9] From Olivia's detailed and reflective accounts of the daily lives of mistresses and maids and their families emerges a microcosm of social relations that reproduce both social inequality and forms of resistance.[10] The fluidity and complexity of social exclusion and inclusion are threads throughout her life story. Olivia's life as the maid's daughter in an upper-middle-class neighborhood exemplifies many aspects of the Mexican American experience as a racial/ethnic group in the United States. The setting facilitates a microanalysis of issues that occur nationally at a macrostructural level, including tensions involved in people's maintaining ideas of family/peoplehood while socially located in different positions of privilege and power. Olivia's counternarrative challenges the master narrative's persistent emphasis on assimilation rather than "integration," "incorporation," or "inclusiveness" in political, economic, and social life in the United States. As the maid's daughter moves between social worlds rather than rejecting her Mexicanness and becoming assimilated, she links privileges and oppression in the same neighborhood and society. The ideology that shaped Mr. and Mrs. Smith's relationship with their Mexican-immigrant household worker and her daughter is the same one that informs popular opinion: if immigrants will just give up their old ways and culture, they can become "just like one of the American family." The unspoken or sometimes outspoken expectation of gratitude highlights important social distinctions of rights and privilege. Olivia's story is symbolic of the way that racial/ethnic groups participate in a racist, sexist, and class-structured society.

Juxtaposing Olivia's narrative with the master narrative of immigration/assimilation identifies important conceptual issues that appear in the national dialogue on race. As Olivia describes the events and circumstances determining her inclusion or exclusion in the employers' family and community activities, the similarities to racial discourse surrounding racial minorities and immigrants in the United States become evident. Strategies for complying with fictitious membership as "one of the family" reflect the contradictions of assimilation in a society that defines citizenship on the basis of "whiteness." The level of paternalism that shaped

Olivia's interactions with employers and served to place both mother and daughter in constant debt embraces the mainstream's expectation that immigrants of color and their descendants show ongoing gratitude to work under any conditions in the United States. These expectations are not much different from the public discourse that demands citizens of color be grateful for being American or that reminds immigrants of color that whatever hardship and discrimination they face in the United States, their condition is better than in their homeland.[11] Olivia negotiates interactions marked by race, class, gender, and citizenship privileges and subordination by pointing to the practices that society tends to keep invisible.

Epilogue

Before I completed this project, I felt a strong need to spend time with Olivia again. Since I had not interviewed her since she visited me after Mr. Smith's funeral, I needed to inquire about her current circumstances and wanted to get her reflection on the project. I wanted to know whether her opinions and feelings about the Smiths, Liberty Place, and social mobility had changed or remained the same. Now, as she is the mother of two children almost entering their teens, I was curious about her parenting and the choices she makes as a mother. Having a point of comparison, as a working mom, I wondered if her view of her mother's absence while working had changed. As she has had her mother live with her for the past seventeen years, I was curious about their relationship and how it had changed, since they now are a family living in the same household. Fortunately, she agreed to take time from her busy schedule to spend with me. She invited me to stay with her family and rearranged her schedule for further interviews.

As I entered Olivia's house, I immediately saw Carmen, and we hugged. As always, everyone who enters the home greets Carmen with open arms and receives her wide smile. I was surprised to see how much she had aged over the years. Working as a live-in maid for fifty years or more has left an indelible mark on Carmen. At eighty years old, she is in good health except for arthritis in her ankles and hands. She moves quite slowly, dragging her feet around the kitchen as she leans on the counters to maneuver around to clean and cook. Olivia always makes sure that she continues to wear high-quality walking shoes. She still prefers to be comfortably dressed in jogging suits. She still is the first one up in the morning and greets the family in the kitchen with coffee and is prepared

221

to make breakfast. Although her room is larger than her grandchildren's rooms and is upstairs with the entire family, she spends most of her time sitting in the kitchen reading the Spanish newspaper or watching the *novelas* on the television mounted in a corner of the kitchen. I could not help but notice the way that she assumes the position of a maid on her own. I watched her collect the family laundry and proceed to wash, fold, and put away clothes. During my visit, she had decided to clean her grandson's closet, repeating the same activity she had done for decades, removing the clothes that are too small or that he no longer wears. Like the housekeeper and nanny she had been for fifty years, Carmen has adapted to the invisibility assumed in her work position as she stands next to the sink and prepares food, listening and watching daily family interaction. Although she rarely comments on arguments between parent and child, she is actively managing the family.

Just as Carmen told Dr. Jimenez's mother, she is not shy about asking her daughter or son-in-law to make arrangements to travel to visit her family or to purchase food or anything else she might want. Carmen frequently travels with Olivia's son, who loves to visit his cousins in El Paso. Olivia never lets her down and goes out of her way to make sure that her mother's wishes are followed. Olivia would move mountains to make sure her mother retains her ability to make things happen in her family. Anyone who does not understand this powerful bond is victim to Olivia's wrath. She is extremely protective of her mother and in maintaining her status among family members. In doing so, she frequently finds herself being called on to help her extended family. Olivia is not actively involved in maintaining any relations with her mother's former employers, including the Smiths, though in the early years of her mother's retirement, she did assist her mother in maintaining any kind of interaction that she wished to continue. Over the years, these interactions have become infrequent. After Mr. Smith's funeral, Mrs. Smith's telephone calls were fewer. Olivia has commented that the declining interaction was likely related to the Smiths' declining social class and status.

After Carmen moved in with Olivia, her behavior as the maid became apparent. Olivia overheard her make an underhanded comment to her husband that before making a final decision on a particular activity, they should first ask *"la señora."* Although it bothered Olivia that her mother said this, she understands that the comment is not about her but rather reflects the only behavior that her mother knows outside her family of origin. She first began to notice her mother reproducing the role of the maid in her house when she spent a year in El Paso. Olivia now lived in a neighborhood that both her mother and her aunts had always hoped to work in. Her mother had sleepovers with Olivia's aunts; her aunts slept in her mother's room—just like the maids would do in Liberty Place. However, in this case, Carmen no longer slept in the maid's quarters, even though the house had such a room. She had a large bedroom alongside the other family members. One of the reasons Olivia's mother and aunts enjoyed sleeping over on Friday night was because Olivia liked to go to garage sales on Saturday morning, and they wanted to accompany her. Olivia felt she was treated as "*la señora*" until Saturday morning, and then once they drove around to the sales, she became one of them. Since moving from El Paso, Olivia continued to observe her mother acting like the maid and recognized that her family was being managed in the same way that she had watched her mother manage the employers' families of Liberty Place. She does not approve of her mother's preferential treatment of her son—engaging in rituals of male privilege toward him. However, having watched the same interaction with the Smiths' sons, she is not surprised. Olivia is a strong feminist and does not advocate gender-specific treatment with her daughter and son. And she is aware of this interaction between Carmen and her son, who is very close to his grandmother. Olivia teases both of them that they have to leave home as a pair when he goes to college because he is unable to do anything for himself and no one but Carmen will tolerate it. Olivia's home has a strong matriarchal presence with two very independent women. While she wishes that her mother would have more substantive relations with family and friends, she recognizes that this role is so structured in her mother's daily routines that there is no need to burden her to change.

Carmen is extremely involved in her grandchildren's lives. She has become an avid spectator at their baseball games. Olivia laughs recalling that her mother yells plays to the coach in Spanish during the games. Although Olivia never reflects on the lack of time her mother spent with her in comparison to how much time Carmen spends with her own children, I do see Carmen enjoying mothering as a grandmother. However,

Olivia has not relinquished decision-making to her mother and remains on top of her son's and daughter's activities and daily experiences.

During my visit, I joined Olivia in picking up her children from the private school they attend. Upon their entering the van, she asked them how their day was and what they learned that day. Her parenting style is a type of "concerted cultivation," with emphasis on outside activities, but she does not buy them the latest brand of clothing and electronics. She is glad to have her children wearing school uniforms and involved in sports. She also incorporates a bit of Carmen's parenting discipline and does not hesitate to ground the children for disobeying or not doing well in school. As she experienced as a child, Olivia tells her children that there are consequences for making choices. If they chose not to do well in class, then they understand that they have given up the use of the phone. Losing the use of their cell phone is high on the list of punishments. Both her children are very outgoing and involved in numerous school activities, in which Olivia and her husband take an active part.

I feel like I got a glimpse of Olivia as a child while watching her daughter, who has developed Olivia's quick wit and humor. Like Olivia as a young adolescent, she is very athletic and attractive. At a young age, she already has a magnetic personality and an expressive communication style that captures your attention. She engages in negotiations with her mother that make it impossible for any adult to keep a straight face. Her ability to create words, phrases, and gestures that mock the "adult world" or the status quo is extremely creative. Before too long she had both Olivia and me using her creations, because they were so useful in our discussions. She is just as stubborn and determined as Olivia described herself being as an adolescent. I get a strong sense that the role of the matriarch will be passed on to this strong young woman.

My visit also gave me an opportunity to observe Olivia in everyday routines. As I prepared for my visit, Olivia strongly urged me to bring workout clothes so I could share her latest passion of zumba and Latin fusion classes at the health club. I am glad I did! As we walked into the exercise studio, I watched her assertively walk in and begin to work the room. Rather than following her, I took a place at the back of the room. Although a few people in the class obviously recognized her from a recent commercial she had appeared in, no one seemed intimidated by her or treated her as an outsider. She seemed to know everyone and brought various people together as she moved around the room. She greeted everyone, crossed the different niches of friends, and frequently reorganized the groups as she brought in others to join the conversation. She spoke Spanish to the Puerto Rican dance instructor and the Mexican-immigrant, male construction worker taking the class. Just as quickly, she switched to English to talk to the African American and white women in the class. The class was populated with the type of diversity she yearned for in grade school. Next to her was a Muslim woman wearing a head scarf and long-sleeve shirt and long pants; several Latina, white, and African American women in their spandex workout clothes; two Mexican men in sweatpants and tee-shirts; and a few Asian American, Latina, white, and Caribbean women in skimpy shorts and bare midriffs. The combination of lively music, Spanish, English, and code-switching men and women of all races laughing as they danced to the rumba and samba seemed like a second home to Olivia. Unlike most persons who experience enormous social mobility within their lifetime, Olivia continues to cross back and forth across racialized class, gender, and citizenship boundaries.

She is still an active observer of the social order and quickly moves to identify the hierarchy present and then acts to work with it in order to achieve her goal. Olivia's relationship to clothing is rooted in her past experiences as the maid's daughter and passing. She is very strategic in using dress as another tool in her profession. Rather than having a particular style, Olivia has a selection of clothing that she treats as costumes to be chosen on the basis of what will gain her entrance into an event or be taken seriously among a certain group of clients. Once she has gained entrance, she begins negotiations, which might involve bringing more Latinos on the board or, as an entrepreneur in a project, pushing for Mexican culture to gain its place in the American mosaic and for acknowledgment of Mexican American history and contribution to the United States, or fighting for Mexican American and Mexican immigrants to be treated equally.

Over the past seventeen years, Olivia has worked in public relations for advocacy organizations, government, and corporations. When her children started school, Olivia decided she wanted to be able to pick them up after school and spend more time in the evenings and weekends with them. She accomplished this by starting her own public-relations firm that includes policy training and communications training for working with corporations, consumers, and the media. She has been quite successful. In addition, her life has indeed blended both of her sources of social networks and cultural capital, and she is fully integrated into the surrounding Latino community and local and state politics. Although she has been financially successful, her major goal in working is to have a meaningful and identifiable end product, which might be a political, health, or consumer campaign, developing programs for corporate responsibility, or increasing numbers of Latinos in corporate boardrooms. Using her bilingual, bicultural, and working and upper-middle-class skills, she crosses various arenas to explore new projects. At forty-seven, Olivia is far from settling into a comfortable life but is always open to challenges presented to her and has not closed the option of running for political office. She continues to mature as a professional and to embrace life around her. To be in her presence takes a lot of energy because she is constantly generating new ideas for a better future and ways to expand social, economic, and political inclusion.

Carmen is an important resource in assisting both her daughter's and her son-in-law's business ventures. Her catering skills are still quite sharp; I watched her prepare a dinner for her son-in-law's colleagues during my visit. Carmen's presence assures that Spanish is the dominant language of the family; although she clearly understands English, she prefers to speak only Spanish. As an avid reader of the Spanish newspaper and the Spanish news shows, Carmen can keep Olivia current on news she might have missed. Her memory is very sharp, and if Olivia encounters a Liberty Place connection, Carmen immediately identifies the family and provides useful background information.

As I listen to Olivia's numerous projects, the link between them and the social capital she gained from her mother is so apparent. The way in which she has taken the social capital she gained from the maid's gatherings, excursions to San Fernando Valley and Pico Union, and her cherished visits to Aguascalientes may only be visible to one who has made her life more than a two-decade study. I certainly do not claim to understand her or to be able to predict her next move, but I feel confident to say I can see how she has woven her unique experiences into a successful profession. Like her mother, Olivia admits to being hyperemployed, in the same way that her mother worked seven days a week in Liberty Place. Much like when Olivia was a child translating for her mother, trying to broker the best working conditions for a new live-in maid or day worker, I see her translating political and health campaigns to best reach the Latino—English and Spanish-speaking—population. She translates educational programs for various exhibits, develops culturally sensitive advertisements, and works as a broker between advocacy organizations and philanthropy organizations. In much the same way that Carmen problem-solved for her employers and their children, Olivia troubleshoots for a variety of organizations in the public and private sectors, engages in crisis communication, and develops strategies for corporations and agencies to meet marketing or campaign goals. Building and maintaining networks, like Carmen did in Liberty Place, is one of Olivia's highly developed skills. She works a room in ways that would make Mr. Smith proud. No event is so insignificant that she does not get to know others present and learn about their interests. As she describes the mentoring she does to help younger Latinos enter the corporate world, she takes me back to her narrative about riding the bus with her mom to San Fernando to visit her godparents. Now, Olivia is the one that does not sit quietly on the bus but reaches out to others and brings them into her networks and recommends strategies to obtain their goals. These connections to the social capital gained by maintaining her "Mexicanness" most likely go unnoticed because, as with the other sons of daughters of domestics I interviewed, the master narrative will be used to interpret her social mobility as successful assimilation.

In reflecting on her life as the maid's daughter, Olivia summed up her current feelings and an evaluation of her life experiences with the comments a friend made to her, "Everything that has happened to you in the past has prepared you to do what you are doing now." During our last visit, Olivia recounted a particular incident that captures her friend's assessment of Olivia's experiences as the maid's daughter and demonstrates the experiences that keep her grounded in immigrant, working-class realities. In addition, she still tells the following great story with lots of expression and humor.

Olivia and Carmen flew to El Paso to be with Olivia's cousin, who had a heart attack and was in critical condition. After renting a car and taking her mother to the hospital, Olivia was told that her uncle was on his way but was going to have difficulty crossing the border because his visa expired when he had been recovering from a heart attack. Olivia went to the border to assist her uncle in obtaining a hardship visa in order to get to the hospital before his nephew died. The crossing became a twenty-four-hour debacle:

> Still today, sheared in my mind are the names of the agents. They figured that I had a BlackBerry, and in their estimation I was a good candidate for paying a high discretionary fee: I fit the profile and [they] figured that I would become exasperated and pay for the hardship visa. I called my friend [in the state government], and I explained the situation.
>
> "No problem. There are hardship visas. You can handle it."
>
> "All right, I can handle it. Hopefully, I will not need to call you back. But if I don't succeed, I will be calling you back."
>
> I made arrangements for my uncle to meet me in an hour. I go to the agent and say, "I need to get a hardship visa and am told, "No problem. Just stand in line." My uncle arrived, and we begin the process.
>
> We are told, "Well, we will do that, but you need to get a letter from the medical director at the hospital."
>
> "I just want you to look me in the eye. I know I might look like a particular image you have in your mind [someone who will be desperate and pay the high fee]. Whatever name or code that relates to all this [high discretionary fees], just erase that. If you tell me that I need X, and I go get it, do not tell me that I need X because I misunderstood you because I need X and Z. I will be back. I just want to make sure we are in agreement. How late are you here? What is your name?
>
> "Agent Lopez."
>
> "Who is your boss?"
>
> "Chief Escobar."
>
> "Okay, Agent Lopez, I will be back."
>
> In an hour I was back with the letter. My uncle is still sitting there after traveling twenty- seven hours on the bus. It is around 11:30 p.m. now. They were shocked that I got X within an hour.
>
> I walked in and said, "Hey, Agent Lopez, I have X."

"Bring it to me." They could not believe it.

"I am going to sit over there, and when you are ready, you call me and my uncle to talk to your supervisor. Where is Chief Escobar?"

"Um . . . he is not on duty right now. He is out in the field but will be returning soon."

I am waiting, and there is a shift change. Around 2:45 a.m., I saw Agent Candelaria had gotten the paperwork and carried it back from Chief Escobar, because I had been observing who was going in and out. They put the paperwork there, and it sat for two hours. Eventually, at 4:00 a.m. they sent a Chicana agent, Agent Keller, to tell me that it had been denied.

"Thank you. Agent Keller. Can you get Chief Escobar?"

She told me again that the visa was denied. I said, "I wish to speak to your supervisor."

She was startled and embarrassed. I am sure this is the first time this ever happened.

I said, "It does say on the poster behind you and the poster over there that if I think I need better service, I can request it. That is my right."

She turned to Agent Candelaria and [*sarcastically*] said, "That is her right!"

I said, "Yes, I am actually as good as you, and I am an American citizen, and I know my constitutional rights. I probably know them better than you do. [*Lowering her voice*] Yes, it is my right."

She turned around from me, livid, and says to Agent Candelaria, "She wants to speak to my supervisor. It is her right."

I am smiling and realize that this is about power.

"Why don't both of you come, and we can make this a teachable moment. First of all, Agent Candelaria, I learned that you like DiGiorno pizza, but your wife is too cheap to buy it. And [*turning to Keller*] I know you go to Coco Cabana for chicken tacos. If I can figure out your eating habits, you can treat me with some dignity. I have been here under duress for four hours, and now you don't have the decency to look me in the eye, and instead you [*turning to Agent Candelaria*] delegate to Agent Keller to tell me the application has been denied. And she is going to be indignant with me when I ask for you to be accountable for your actions. So now that we are all having this moment, please get Chief Escobar, because I am not leaving here until we all have an opportunity to chat."

The blood left their bodies. The whole place came to a screeching halt. They had all written me off. They had all seen me waiting.

"I am going to sit over there, and when Chief Escobar comes, we can all talk. I would like to speak to all of you." Agent Candelaria calls him.

He tried to come to me and my uncle, and I said to my uncle, "*Venga*." [Come.] From watching the scene, he [my uncle] knew it was horrible, and he was sure he would probably be detained. He was scared.

I said, "Chief Escobar, let me introduce myself. I am Olivia Salazar. None of your folks have any idea what my name is. I have been sitting here—actually this is my second tour. Agent Lopez told me to get X. I am sure that I have already surpassed all your expectations for the season if not the whole year, but I got X under the pretense that I could get what I needed. I was assured of that. I have been sitting here for four and half hours. If I find out that my cousin has died while I have been here, you have a lawsuit of unimaginable proportion. You know what your security code is? It is 773148. Do you know how I found that out? I have been here long enough to figure out everyone's eating habits, who talks, who works. I can give you an analysis of your whole staff. I can tell you how many times Agent Candelaria has gone to see you, and you hide behind the curtain and talk. And I can document that at 1:45 a.m. you met, and he came back with the paperwork and put it on his desk until he ordered her to go deny it. So now that we have all become acquainted, and we know what has gone on tonight, you are accountable for your operation. I know how this works, and I am really sorry for you. I have had to shake your shop up. That was never my intention. Unfortunately for Agent Keller and Agent Candelaria and for you, I am independent. I do not have an employer that you can call and put me back into my place. I needed something from you. I am going to have to call my former boss in Congress, who has advocated for people like you. Before I could call him, I needed to relate how I was treated and why I needed to call in a favor to get a service that as a citizen I am entitled to. I want you to explain to Agent Keller why it is my right to engage in this dialogue with you, because she doesn't think I am worthy. You can spend my tax dollars talking about DiGiorno pizza, going to Coco Cabana, talking about what are your favorite baseball teams, and I can figure out your security code. What do you think the director of Homeland Security is going to say about that? I have to call people and tell them about the kind of operation that you run, and there is no homeland security if some idiot like me can come in and figure out what your security code is."

He said, "Well, unfortunately because I have already denied it, I cannot change it unless you pay the fee."

"Surely after all this you are not going to try to bullshit me, are you? You are going to try to tell me that you cannot undo your decisions when every one of your decisions made at your post is discretionary? There is no playbook here. Don't play games with me. I am going to leave here. I know all of your names, and now I am going to have to walk out to my car and call the congressman and tell him what has just transpired. I got X. I followed every one of your arbitrary procedures, and you failed. I don't want you to be surprised or think that we have resolved this. I am going to investigate and examine how many discretionary fees you have authorized and you, Agent Candelaria, and you, Agent Keller. And maybe we need to do an analysis from Tijuana to Brownsville to see what the policy is and investigate how you are using or abusing power in every interaction with U.S. citizens."

I called my friend back and told him, "I don't even want to tell you about the dynamics of what happened, but the names of the individuals are seared in my mind. I need help to get the visa."

"Okay, let me make some calls. You know, you could make these calls."

"Yeah, but I want to make the system work, because I am not calling DC until I have tested the system."

Within an hour, he called the port authority person who is five layers above Chief Escobar and called me and said, "You can come right now. There is a Chief Santiago who is there. Get there in an hour while he is on shift. He is going to authorize the visa now."

I was still wearing the same clothes. When I walked in the door, Agent Candelaria and Agent Keller were still there. They could not look at me. I went in there, and it took fifteen minutes. I said to Agent Keller, "Good morning. I am sure you know why I am here, but I am here to see Chief Santiago. Would you please tell him I am here. You can describe me whatever way you want."

He came out. He did not even make me approach the windows. He came out and said, "Hi," and shook my hand. "Let me see the paperwork. I don't know why this would not have gone through earlier."

All thirty people who had been there earlier were glued to the glass window watching. He looked at the paperwork, so they knew he was going to approve it. Then he said, "Hold on just a second." He walks over to the desk that Agent

Candelaria sits at and goes through the binder, and they had destroyed the paperwork, so there would not be any record that I had been there.

He said, "You have to fill this out."

I said, "I already filled it out."

And he looked at me and said, "You need to fill it out again."

We had to pay seven dollars for the renewal. He said, "I am so sorry." He tried to say as little as possible.

We left, and we had to go through the checkpoint. I was not going to show my passport or any identification. There were new shift guys, and one of them asked me, "Do you have any identification?"

"Did you just get on shift?"

"Yes, I did."

"Well, I spent the night here, but if you want to have an interaction with me . . ." Then I saw an agent that had been there all night at his post. I said, "If I were you, I would ask Agent Gomez, who has been here all night and has seen me, if you should ask me for my documentation." So then Agent Gomez smiles, because he realizes that I am trying to be lighthearted about it. And he said, "I would just let her go."

There is this macho moment, and he says, "No, I want to see it!"

"Oh, you do. Hey, Agent Gomez, you must not have built much trust among these guys if they don't take your word."

I took out my passport, and he scanned it. "Oh, it has never been checked in. You never checked." So now I have evidence!

I said, "Agent Gomez was trying to give you advice that you didn't want to mess with me, but you needed to. What is your first name?"

He said, "Robert."

I said, "Oh, like the chief. I will be talking to you. Now you have put me into the system, and tomorrow when you see Chief Escobar, Agent Candelaria, and Agent Keller and tell them about the woman with the green sweater that you checked in, and Agent Gomez tried to warn you, but you did not take his word, and you put my passport into the system. You should take advice from seniority."

I yelled, "Agent Gomez, how much seniority do you have over Agent Robert Sanchez?"

"Too much for him not to trust me."

I said, "You all have a great day."

By then my uncle is panicked and wants to get out of there, and he is sure he will be detained. But I want to get this on video. I want to create a record. I want Agent Gomez to tell Sanchez when I leave that he has screwed the chief because he had destroyed the record, but now he [Sanchez] created one.

As we walked out, I looked over and saw Chief Escobar standing in the tower. He and Candelaria were there. I waved.

I called DC, and I told my friend, "I have good news, and I have bad news. There is good news for you. Anytime you are going to be in Texas and you want to go to [various events], you have to call me, and I will make sure you have the best time here. I got what I needed, and you were invaluable, and I could not have done it without you. I hope it was not a big political chip you had to cash in with the port authority. It was very meaningful to my family, and I will be forever grateful to you.

"And what is the bad news?"

"The bad news is that at some point I will talk to the congressman, and this will become a big issue, because this is not about me. I know I could get a visa. It's about the thousands of people who have to go through this and don't have you to call and are taken advantage of and have to pay fees. There is no excuse for what happened. And it probably happens often. No one should be treated that way. I will not rest until I deal with this."

My uncle made my mom promise to never let me cross the border with him again. (Interview, December 2009)

While Olivia certainly did not enjoy being belittled by the agents or feeling desperate about getting her uncle to the hospital before her cousin died, she views the incident as an important lesson in reminding her of the everyday struggles of persons without her social capital. This incident demonstrates her motivation to use her skills to address injustices targeting people without race, class, gender, and citizenship privileges. Helping her mother continue to be the problem-solver and to assist in financial emergencies keeps Olivia linked to working-class Mexican Americans and Mexican immigrants. This narrative captures the way that Olivia reflects on her current and past experiences. She has accepted that her past experiences with the Smiths and growing up in Liberty Place, as well as visits to San Fernando and Pico Union and Mexico, have prepared her to meet both the challenges and the opportunities presented to her today.

All the pain and anger she expressed in previous interviews she now interprets differently. She prefaces her new framework for interpreting her experiences by playfully stating, "In my immense maturity," and she identifies the useful lessons that past incidents provide her to engage in the projects that she takes on today. In our most recent interview, Olivia summed up her current state this way:

> I live a charmed existence. I get to negotiate who I play with and who will be in my sandbox. It is very managed and orderly.

NOTES

NOTES TO THE INTRODUCTION

1. The rules of social mobility require persons to move away from their class and ethnic origins, not celebrate them. Allegiance toward extended families is to be transferred to one's nuclear family. Ethnic culture is assumed to be incompatible with an upper-middle-class lifestyle. Consequently, poor and working-class communities are ambivalent toward these members and question their attempts to "pass" for being to the manor born. Most immigrant and minority communities have coined terms for these individuals—"Uncle Tom," "*tío taco*," or "*vendido*" (sell-out). As Iorizzo and Mondello noted in their study of the children of Italian immigrants, "We are becoming Americans by learning how to be ashamed of our parents" (1980: 118).

2. A notable exception, of course, is Rhacel Salazar Parreñas's (2005) study of Filipina children who are left in their homeland when their parents work abroad.

3. See Browne and Mistra 2005: 165–189.

4. This is the pseudonym that she selected for her interview. As we planned for publication, I found myself suggesting that more precautions be taken to conceal identities. At the beginning of the project, Olivia did not want to change names or places. However, these changes seemed more appropriate over time as I saw her life circumstances changing and her relationship with her mother's employers continuing. In the end, we both agreed that pseudonyms would be used.

5. I use pseudonyms for all family members, friends, and employers, as well as for neighborhoods and schools.

6. Several researchers and writers have noted the common practice of employers referring to longtime household employees as being "like one of the family." Author Alice Childress is known for writing short conversations between an African American domestic worker, Mildred Johnson, and her friend Marge. Originally published in Paul Robeson's newspaper *Freedom*, the entire collection was published in 1956 (Childress 1986 [1956]). The adage is used by employers to deny expectations of servitude or subordination in domestics or nannies employed in their home. However, researchers and writers recognize that the phrase is used to blur the boundaries between work and home, which frequently results in household workers being asked to do unpaid work in the form of favors. See my study *Maid in the U.S.A.*: Romero 1992:

123–126. More recently, Patricia Hill Collins (2006) has used the phase to capture the paradox of American identity.

7. The issue of authenticity is summarized in Joanne Nagel's (1997) discussion of Native American ethnic renewal. Along with a person's own view of him- or herself are "the limits on individual ethnic choice that are imposed by outsiders, even in informal situations, and by the structure of imaginable ethnic categories available to individuals and audiences alike. Disputes about ethnic authenticity appear to be part of the ethnic boundary formation, maintenance, and change process" (60). There is an ongoing construction, reconstruction, and deconstruction of identity.

8. In addition to my research on Chicana household workers, I am sure that my own racial ethnic identity helped me gain access to Olivia's willingness to participate in this project. Olivia is also aware of my own biography. As the daughter of a household worker, I knew firsthand the patronizing comments from employers when I worked alongside my mother. However, I was never exposed to life as a live-in maid, except through my observations of colleagues' employees. I experienced the insider and outsider researcher role that Ruth Behar so elegantly presents in her book *The Vulnerable Observer: Anthropology That Breaks Your Heart* (1996).

9. Education researchers identify the different cultural capital that the working class brings to schools and the ways that they are disadvantaged by not having educational systems build on their knowledge and experience. As much as diversity is claimed to be extremely important in higher education, the educational system still remains a foreign environment to working-class sons and daughters. Two excellent works on the topic by Annette Lareau are *Home Advantage: Social Class, and Parental Intervention in Elementary Education* (1989) and "Social Class Differences in Family-School Relationships: The Importance of Cultural Capital" (1987).

10. I interviewed twenty-five adult children of domestic workers over the past two decades. Usually we set up an hour or two interview after our initial conversation or soon afterward. In a few cases, I arranged phone interviews. They all agreed to have the interview recorded.

11. Romero 1992: 64–65.

12. An exception is Ellen Galinsky's *Ask the Children* (1999).

13. Both the El Paso Country Club (Montoya south of Mesa/Country Club Road) and the Coronado Country Club area (top of Thunderbird) are considered two of the wealthiest communities in the city limits.

14. An excellent work documenting and analyzing the race, class, and citizenship relations on the border is Alejandro Lugo's *Fragmented Lives, Assembled Parts: Culture, Capitalism, and Conquest at the U.S.-Mexico Border* (2008).

15. The crossing of Mexican-immigrant domestics from El Paso, Texas, to Ciudad Juárez, Mexico, on Friday evenings or Saturday mornings and then returning on Monday mornings is a common practice. Since Carmen's family was not yet living in Ciudad Juárez, staying with her friends provided a space to remove herself from the employers' household and assure she actually had time off from work.

16. This is prior to the militarized border documented in Timothy J. Dunn's *The Militarization of the U.S.-Mexico Border* (1996) and Joseph Nevins's *Operation*

Gatekeeper and Beyond: The Rise of the "Illegal Alien" and the Making of the U.S.-Mexico Boundary (2002).

17. Evelyn Nakano Glenn (1986) notes that while these networks were useful in finding low-wage temporary employment, they were also limited to the underground economy. Similarly, Sudhir Alladi Venkatesh's study of the urban poor in Chicago found that "their labor takes place with resources amassed in the underground economy" (2006: 20).

18. The first group of Chinese Exclusion Acts was passed in 1882, and the 1923 act stopped all direct immigration into the United States. Since the acts were enforced at major ports, immigrants used smuggling operations through Mexico. Smuggling created a growing Chinese community in Juárez, as immigrants unable to enter the United States through the southern border settled in Mexico. See K.-L. Chin 1999.

19. Highly educated and an extremely confident woman, Olivia set the pace and tone of her narrative. While I did push her at times to explain the significance or interpretation of an action, she never showed signs of resistance or seemed to offer intentionally vague responses to my questions. Our social circles are extremely different, but there are many overlaps among Chicano faculty and politicians. Our current socioeconomic status is quite similar, and both of our mothers were private household workers. Thus, there was very little interviewer-subject power relation.

20. In the early stages of telling her life story, Olivia was involved in analyzing her own stories and in each telling began to make links and identify patterns. Although she never wrote down her stories, she did engage in an autoethnographic reflection and made links to race, class, and citizenship hierarchies shaping her experiences. Arthur Bochner and Carolyn Ellis have described autoethnography as "people in the process of figuring out what to do, how to live, and the meaning of their struggles" (2006: 111). The passage captures Olivia's efforts to understand her feelings about Carmen's employers and moving back and forth across class and racial boundaries and finding a sense of place and belonging.

21. The focus on these crises assisted in my conceptualizing the family as an economic institution. See Langellier and Peterson 1993.

22. In this case, many of these incidents reflected the conditions addressed by Langellier and Peterson's work on "family storytelling." For children residing with their mothers employed as live-in maids, the authors' connection between home and work could not be more accurate: "The ideology of The Family reproduces the asymmetrical division of labor in the workplace and within the home that necessitates the oppression of women" (1993: 52).

23. To a large degree I used standard methods that researchers use in collecting, coding, and analyzing qualitative data. As the project began, I took extensive field notes about our interview sessions and about the periods of transitions from interview mode to other activities. Rather than systematically coding each interview session, I wrote theoretical memos on the themes that emerged and attended to the significance Olivia placed on certain events or practices. See Strauss 1987. In addition, I spent time with Olivia and her mother and family of procreation. We visited Liberty Place together. She also shared photographs for me to analyze.

24. Annette Lareau covers this dilemma quite well in the appendix of *Home Advantage: Social Class and Parental Intervention in Elementary Education* (1989).

25. Romero 1993, 1995, 1999, 2001a.

26. Interpreting Olivia's personal narrative needed to be contextualized in the intersection of race, class, gender, and citizenship that frames globalized care work in the Los Angeles community in which she grew up.

27. Behar 1993; Blackman 1989; Blowsnake 1963; S. Brooks 1987; Buss 1980, 1993; Kekumura 1981; Lightfoot 1988; Skostak 1981; Smith 1985.

28. See, e.g., Rawlings 1942.

29. Although I have not interviewed Carmen directly except for the one time, Olivia frequently asks her to confirm the details of her accounts or to recall missing information. Occasionally, Carmen is in listening distance and will offer additional information about the project, particularly in reference to updates on employers or their children. She has also corrected Olivia when she confuses employers.

30. I have sent Olivia copies of all the articles I wrote based on her narrative.

31. "'Family' is a cultural image constructed out of real individuals, and also, sometimes, mythical ancestry" (Bertaux and Thompson 1993: 2).

NOTES TO CHAPTER 1

1. Anderson 2000; Chang 2000.

2. Without a government child-care program, the range of options available to parents are the following: parents working alternate shifts; parents working part-time during child's school hours; day-care centers, preschools, or nursery schools; licensed and unlicensed family child care by relatives, neighbors, nannies, au pairs, and "babysitters"; out-of-school activities; and children taking care of themselves. See Bloom and Steen 1996: 28–29 (discussion of child-care options by marital status); Helburn and Bergmann 2003: 90 (discussion of care by father's employment status), 30 (discussion of child-care options by mother's employment status), 30–32, 90 (discussion of family options based on income; preferred option of all parents is child-care centers; overview of parents piecing together multiple child-care arrangements), 91 (out-of-school activities, such as sports and clubs, are used more and are more accessible to higher-income families), 90–95 (overview of child-care arrangement by race and ethnicity).

3. See Milkman, Reese, and Roth 1998: 483.

4. Rollins 1985: 198.

5. Romero 1992: 127–129. See also Rollins 1985; Roberts 1997.

6. Romero 1992: 130–135.

7. Hays 1996.

8. Schwartz 1993: 249: "The battles to get children into the 'right' kindergarten, which can involve coaching, bribing, and hard-core résumé-building, have become the stuff of urban lore."

9. Lareau 2000: 5. Also see Lareau 2003.

10. Stearns 2003: 41: "Professionalism replaced sentimentality. Parents continued to be very sentimental about children—this was part of the priceless-child

formula—but experts prided themselves on hardheaded realism, removing the rose-covered glasses."

11. Schwartz 1993: 262. Also see Lareau 2003: 12, which offers the following quotation from one of the interviewed parents: "Sports provide great opportunities to learn how to be competitive. Learn how to accept defeat, you know. Learn how to accept wining, you know, in a gracious way. Also it gives him the opportunity to learn leadership skills and how to be a team player. You know, those, just sports, really provides a lot of really great opportunities."

12. Seiter 1998: 306.

13. Two-career households are more likely than dual-earner households to hire a full-time or live-in domestic caretaker/nanny. As Tronto (2002: 35) points out, the distinction between two-career and dual-earner households is significant because the former describes "professional jobs where the time demands are excessive or unpredictable."

14. Parreñas 2001: 73.

15. See Silbaugh 1997: 112–116 (discusses the applicability of the commodification critique in feminist discourse in addressing paid domestic workers).

16. Colen 1989: 193 (discusses employers' essentialist views of West Indian caregivers in New York City).

17. Momsen 1999: 13.

18. See Wrigley 1996.

19. See Silbaugh 1996. She argues that the language of emotions is used to deny material security to individuals engaged in paid and unpaid domestic labor.

20. See Wong 1994 for a discussion of images of people of color as caretakers.

21. Baquedano-López 2002: 4.

22. Helburn and Bergman 2003: 108.

23. Tronto 2002: 40.

24. Ibid.

25. Ibid., 47.

26. Ibid.

27. Rhacel Salazar Parreñas's (2005) study of Filipina care workers and their children discusses the migration of mothers, with their children remaining behind in their homeland.

28. Hrdy makes the argument that "it is not maternal nature (always contingent on circumstances) that changed through time, but *maternal options*" (2002: 367, emphasis mine). She describes these options as follows: "Dual-career mothers, whether they forage or go to work, have always sought ways to mitigate the costs of infant care. Today, mothers hire nannies, leave children in government-run crèches, *maternales*, or daycare centers; they delegate childcare to kin; or else they continue caring for infants themselves but reduce the amount of care given to each infant" (370); "Of 21 million children under the age of six in the United States in 1995, 12 million were in daycare. Of infants less than one year old, 45 percent were in some kind of daycare. Mothers seek this care in a market where wealthy, nonworking mothers, highly paid professionals, ordinary working women, and mothers pushed off welfare into

the labor market at minimum wages, not to mention government agencies seeking to place foster children, are all competing for all parental care, a commodity not in abundant supple to begin with" (369).

29. Anderson 2000: 118.

30. Lutz 2002: 99.

31. Parreñas 2001.

32. Grace Chang makes this argument in her work. See Chang 2000.

33. Chaudry 2004.

34. Colen 1989: 173.

35. Rothman 1990: 198–202.

36. Susser 1991: 218.

37. Rollins 1985; Romero 1992.

38. In covering the lives of enslaved children, Wilma King (2005) discuses the services children provided slaveholders and the importance in learning the master-slave or mistress-maid relationship. Enslaved Black children were expected to "play" and entertain the young masters and mistresses in a way that is easily constructed as becoming a toy for their pleasure.

39. Rollins 1985: 189–194.

40. The irony of this graduate student's assertions is uncovered in the growing research on the color of wealth—more precisely, the transfer of wealth in the United States. Social scientists' exclusive focus on poverty has generally drawn attention to the actions of the poor rather than the actions of the wealthiest population. For wealthy families, rather than each generation's earning money from hard work, wealth is transferred from generation to generation. See Lui et al. 2006; Oliver and Shapiro 1995; Shapiro 2004.

41. Like the children of Asian entrepreneurs, the successes of the children of domestic workers are in spite of the barriers they faced in the United States and because of the strength and resources from their community, culture, and family. See Park 2005.

42. Stanton-Salazar 2001; Valdés 1996; Valenzuela 1999.

43. Historical research on whiteness points to the racial process that European immigrants undergo that is central to their social mobility. See Ignatiev 1995; Roediger 1994.

44. Mills 1943; Omi and Winant 1987; Steinberg 1981.

45. Annette Lareau's (2003) research on class and race differences in schoolchildren's educational experiences demonstrates the impact that a family's child-rearing practices and opportunities have on developing the skills rewarded in grade school. The impact that social and cultural capital have on college-student retention is also well documented. See, for example, Wells 2008. The rising cost in tuition cannot be ignored in assessing success. Paulsen and St. John 2002.

46. Du Bois 1989 [1903]: 3.

47. Anthropologist Irma McClaurin-Allen (1992) analyzes the complexities of race, class, and gender experienced by the late *Chicago Tribune* journalist Leanita McClain. By acknowledging the distance between McClain's modest childhood and her life

as a middle-class woman, we see the contradictions she faced having a "foot in each world." From her standpoint, she was able to "witness social inequality as it was constituted and practiced" (317).

48. McClaurin-Allen 1992: 217.

49. Omi and Winant 1987; Steinberg 1981.

50. See, for example, Johnson 1999; Obama 1995; Pemberton 1998.

51. Zinn 2005.

52. See Linda Chavez 1991; D'Souza 1991; Herrnstein and Murray 1996.

NOTES TO CHAPTER 2

1. See Romero 2001b: 115. Pei-Chia Lan, in her discussion of boundary work and sociospatial boundaries (2006: 200), captures the work involved in maintaining spatial deference.

2. Traditionally in the United States, the maid's quarters are located next to the kitchen. Since the kitchen is a major work area of the maid, this space is also considered her space, and she is likely to sit in this room rather than in any other room in the house. See Romero 1992: 117–118.

3. This is an example of the way that domestics become invisible. The members of the employers' family make the assumption that the ice maker is not an intrusion on anyone's sleep since all the family members are asleep upstairs. For a detailed discussion of invisibility and domestics, see Rollins 1985.

4. Like other live-in arrangements, the worker becomes quite vulnerable and is placed at a disadvantage in negotiating better working conditions or a raise because keeping the employment is tied to having a residence, as meager as it may be.

5. Judith Rollins's work best describes deference in domestic service (1985: chap. 5). Reference to deference that immigrant Latina women experience can be found in Hondagneu-Sotelo 2001: 144–145.

6. Sharon Hays discusses intensive mothering in *The Cultural Contradictions of Motherhood* (1996).

7. Annette Lareau discusses class differences in childhood socialization in *Unequal Childhoods, Class, Race, and Family Life* (2003). Allison J. Pugh includes class differences in her study on children and consumer culture, *Longing and Belonging: Parents, Children, and Consumer Culture* (2009).

8. Romero 1992: 115–116.

9. From the standpoint of Latinas, and other people of color, the knowledge about the social order is revealed through the everyday struggles against denigration, humiliation, and exploitation. Unlike Euro-American men and women, their cultures and belief systems are not affirmed and enhanced through a wide range of institutional mechanisms, including visibility in powerful positions, positive images in advertising, and having their viewpoints legitimated in news accounts. Although the standpoint of this maid's daughter may not be representative of many other Latinas, her experiences and perspective illustrate the type of knowledge and experiences Latinas learn as ethnic/racial-minority women in the United States.

10. Lareau 2003.

11. See Anderson 2000.

12. For a discussion of the role of domestics as confidents to traditional wives and mothers who are unemployed, see Rollins 1985: 166–167.

13. This is very similar to Bridget Anderson's (2000) discussion of domestics' struggles to exclude their "personhood" from domestic service.

14. Romero 1992: 108.

15. Anderson 2000.

16. Sharon Hays's study of mothering documents the history of child-rearing practices, advice given in how-to manuals on parenting, and mothers' views of child care (1996: 86). Hays identifies the prevailing ideology of motherhood prescribed by child-care experts—and accepted by mothers—as advocating child-centered, emotionally demanding, labor-intensive, and financially draining methods. Although Hays does note class differences in mothering (working-class and poor mothers stress children's formal education, provide rules, and emphasize obedience, whereas middle-class mothers promote their children's self-esteem, provide choices, and negotiate rules), she argues that all mothers "share a set of fundamental assumptions about the importance of putting their children's needs first and dedicating themselves to providing what is best for their kids, as they understand it." Child-care experts who advocate child-care models that involve intensive mothering include T. Berry Brazelton (1990) and Penelope Leach (1997).

17. Lareau 2003: 4.

18. Lareau (2003) defines *concerted cultivation* as parents' concerted efforts at developing their children by structuring their activity and interaction around building skills, learning, and acquiring new experiences.

19. Annette Lareau sums up that working-class parents' focus is to assure the child's natural growth, allowing the children "long stretches of leisure time, child-initiated play, clear boundaries between adults and children, and daily interactions with kin" (2003: 3).

20. Ibid., 32.

21. Carmen's parenting is consistent with Nelson's (2010) description of nonelite parents who make hard choices to secure a good education for their children. They also expect their children to be more responsible and disciplined than wealthier parents do.

22. Ascribing parents' social status to children is a form of social reproduction that links family and work.

23. There is a strong stigma placed on persons relegated to cleaning after others. Historians have documented the distinction housewives made between the domestic work they engaged in and the dirty type of jobs given to domestic workers. In households with more than one servant, the hierarchy among workers placed cleaning and laundry at the bottom, whereas cooks and nannies had much higher positions. See Katzman 1981; and Palmer 1989.

24. Lewis Coser has identified employers' families as a greedy institution, as they "devour the personality of their servant" (1974: 88). Arlie Russell Hochschild (2003) has identified the growing market for family services and comments on the names

selected for their companies; the names suggest that the workers are at the complete service of others.

25. This interpretation of emotional labor is closely related to Judith Rollins's analysis of coping strategies involving a strong sense of self-worth based on morality: "Their intimate knowledge of the realities of employers' lives, their understanding of the meaning of class and race in this country, and their value system, which measures an individual's worth less by material success than by 'the kind of person you are,' by the quality of one's interpersonal relationships and by one's standing in the community" (1985: 212–213).

26. Pierrette Hondagneu-Sotelo found in her study of domestics in Los Angeles (2001: 57) that employers stereotyped Mexican women as naturally suited for the tasks of cleaning and child care.

27. Hochschild's chapter "The Economy of Gratitude" (2003: 104–118) analyzes the obligation and complexity of being in debt to another person.

NOTES TO CHAPTER 3

1. The classic study describing these conditions is Jonathan Kozol's *Savage Inequalities* (1991). A more detailed analysis can be found in Jean Anyon's *Ghetto Schooling* (1997). Nancy Lopez (2003) discusses these conditions in urban education with Latino/a students.

2. More researchers are documenting the ways that immigrant women who are employed as live-in workers are creating spaces to meet and form supportive networks. If state officials discourage the visual presence of immigrant women congregating, then private rather than public space is used. Pei-Chia Lan (2006) has analyzed the public places that immigrant women have privatized in order to have space to visit, such as the train station. She also notes that the use of cell phones is another way that workers keep in touch with each other. Also see Parreñas 2008.

3. Hochschild describes how children learn about care in her chapter "Children as Eavesdropper" (2003: 172–181).

4. The potential for exploitation in live-in positions is an ongoing problem. In the report "Home Is Where the Work Is," Domestic Workers United and DataCenter note, "In most low-wage work, wages are calculated hourly. In domestic work, the standard practice is for employers to pay a flat rate per week for unpredictable and sometimes unlimited hours of work. Live-in workers may be expected to be on call 24 hours per day, 5 to 6 days per week. This practice is a unique feature of the domestic work industry; it is both a manifestation and a cause of exploitation of the workforce. It points to the legacy of servitude from which this sector emerges and a lack of respect for the work itself" (2006: 17).

5. Pierrette Hondagneu-Sotelo also found this to be the case among live-in workers she interviewed in the 1990s (2001: 34).

6. Erving Goffman used domestics as an example of a nonperson, with the expectation that they are invisible while serving others (1959: 151).

7. The materialism of modern childhoods is receiving more research attention than it did twenty years ago. See E. Chin 2001; Cook 2004; Pugh 2009.

8. These myths and biases are strongly interwoven into the Americanization process. For a history of these practices aimed at Mexican Americans, see Sánchez 1993.

9. A cotillion, or débutante ball, in the United States is a formal presentation of young ladies to an exclusive social community.

10. In research on Latina entrepreneurship in the borderlands, Bárbara Robles identifies collective activity as significant in building strong communities.

11. These associations are used by family and friends as a saving strategy. *Tandas* are commonly used by Mexican immigrants in the United States and sometimes include household items, vehicles, or exchange of physical labor, such as babysitting or car repair. See Robles 2006b; Vélez-Ibañez 2004; and Zlolniski 2006, which discusses the significance of *tandas* for immigrants who cannot get bank loans.

12. Informal networks established among the working poor are extremely useful in finding jobs. Evelyn Nakano Glenn (1986) found that most Japanese American women used informal job referrals from relatives, friends, or acquaintances employed as gardeners or domestics. In my own research on domestics, I found that employers frequently asked their employees if they could find someone interested in working for a neighbor or family member (Romero 1992). In a study of Latina domestics in Los Angeles, Hondagneu-Sotelo (2001) discusses the use of social networks in recruiting workers and finding employment.

13. In an essay entitled "Family Legacies," economist Bárbara Robles (2006a: 138–139) reflected on her great-aunt, who worked as a maid for wealthy families in Laredo, Texas, and "knew how to manage and run a household on a shoestring." Although she did not speak English or know how to read, she "ran the only Spanish-language movie theater, located in a bodega [warehouse], Teatro Haydee, in [a] small south Texas town, until 1970." Robles recalls accompanying her on the bus to local grocery and dry-goods stores, "changing money for her and acting as her personal interpreter"; and as an adolescent, Robles "ran the popcorn machine, soda pop stand, and cash register." A leading scholar in the field of Latino wealth and asset building, Robles recognizes that the bartering, gift-giving, and exchanges were a form of "social capital" that "increased the well-being" of the extended family. Among the skills used to create assets were "saving, budgeting, sewing, upholstering, doll making, canning, and gardening: life skills and common-sense financial management practiced at the home level."

14. Park (2005) found this a common experience among the children of Asian-immigrant entrepreneurs.

15. Valdés 2003: 30.

16. Ibid., 77. This counters Zhou's argument that translating "diminished parental authority" (2009: 27).

17. See Buriel et al. 1998.

18. Valdés 2003: 96.

19. Among the practices that illustrate the ways that maids improve their economic situation or provide more for their families is the active participation in the tradition of employers giving old clothes to their workers in domestic service. The ritual maintains the hierarchical status between women of different classes and frequently

different racial and ethnic identities. Gift-giving in this occupation not only occurs in lieu of raises and benefits but most commonly occurs in the form of the employers' discarded clothing (Glenn 1986; Rollins 1985; Romero 1992).

20. Festivities held in Mexico (and Mexican communities) nine days prior to Christmas.

21. A *quinceañera* is a coming-of-age celebration for girls turning fifteen and is held in a church. Godparents present the girl. The church event is followed by a reception or dance.

22. Howes 1996: 9.

23. Both Annette Lareau (2003) and Peter Stearns (2003) have found these conditions to be the consequence of contemporary parenting models.

NOTES TO CHAPTER 4

1. Legal scholar Kevin R. Johnson discusses the issue of class and culture passing in his book *How Did You Get to Be Mexican? A White/Brown Man's Search for Identity* (1999). Johnson's mother and her family stressed assimilation, and he writes about being forced, as a "mixed-race" person, into fixed racial categories that do not capture the complexity of racial ambiguity and racial identity.

2. One can see how under these conditions Olivia constructs identity as binary, with each in opposition to the other. James Baldwin captured the binary racial construction in the U.S. presentation of history in his 1984 essay "On Being White and Other Lies": "America became white—the people who, as they claim 'settled' the country became white—because of the necessity of denying the Black presence and justifying the Black subjugation" (1998: 178). This holds true also for the assumption that Latinos are immigrants and intruders to white America. By classifying discourse on Latinos as immigration, white America erases its history of colonialization and imperialism.

3. Crossing these social boundaries involved "acting" and "wearing masks" because Olivia did not perceive this identity as her real self.

4. I am borrowing this phase from Mary Helen Washington's (1987: 164) discussion of Nella Larsen's (1969) use of passing in her writings.

5. See Prudence Carter's (2005) work for an excellent critique of the "acting white" theory of successful students of color.

6. Nirmal Puwar identities "a burden of doubt" that racialized others experience as a consequence of stereotypes: "In order to combat under-expectations racialised minorities have to prove themselves. As they are not automatically expected to have appropriate competencies, they have to make concerted effort to make themselves visible as proficient and competent" (2004: 59).

7. As Mariam Fraser notes, "Class inequalities, which might be thought of as 'large scale' issues of social and economic justice (or injustice), give rise to 'real' social effects, one of which is classed subjectivities" (1999: 120).

8. Exclusion is significant because the ritual is crucial in reproducing the upper class, it is restricted, and it is an important rite of passage. For more detailed discussion of this subject, see Kendall 2002.

9. See, generally, Berry 2007; Hesse-Biber 2007. Also see Candelario 2007; her ethnographic study of beauty shops illustrates the way that white notions of beauty are reinforced among Dominican women.

10. Cookson and Persell 1985: 22. Also see Stevens 2007.

11. Diana Kendall's book *The Power of Good Deeds* (2002) discusses the significance of these rites of passage in reproducing privilege and the upper class. Membership is exclusive, and one is almost always born into the social network. Very few avenues into the social network are available to others. Although others are allowed to participate in some activities, there are always distinctions made between them and persons who are really members of the elite.

12. Olivia recognized that assuming a role and engaging in performance are not neatly entered into and exited. Engaging in certain behavior over time has consequences. She feared that aspects of the role might actually become her real characteristics, even when the economic means were not entirely owned and at times were even resented by Olivia.

13. Kasinitz et al. (2008: 133–134) argue that many families find parochial schools more attractive than public schools because of the quality of education and the discipline.

14. This choice of schools also offered Olivia an escape from what Puwar has referred to as the "burden of representation" and the "burden of doubt" (2004: 59–60, 62–63).

15. In this case, whiteness is the standpoint that Rosalyn assumed in the presence of riders of color and in her interaction with Olivia. This is related to the second dimension of whiteness that Ruth Frankenberg identifies in her work on women and whiteness: "it is a 'standpoint,' a place from which white people look at ourselves, at others, and at society" (1994: 1).

16. In analyzing the meaning of the interaction, I am aware that the Spanish phrases Rosalyn used were common to her because, rather than Spanish being learned as a way to converse with peers, it was spoken by employers and their children to enable them to give orders to workers.

17. *Zoot Suit* was originally a play written and directed by Luis Valdez. In 1981, a film version of the Broadway play was released. The play and film are based on the Sleepy Lagoon murder trial in the early 1940s and include scenes from the Zoot Suit Riots, which involved the military, police, and white citizens rioting against youth wearing zoot suits.

18. Although Olivia's interpretation may be accurate, Mrs. Smith was also engaged in classic behavior of reproducing social class, which includes teaching children the "appropriate" behavior and beliefs. The arranged party is consistent with practices used to reproduce social class. See Kendall 2002: 83, 90–92. In many ways, Olivia described the social bubble that elite families attempt to maintain in order to protect their children and to assure they have the educational and social skills required to reproduce their class.

19. For a discussion of personalism in domestic service, see Rollins 1985.

20. Romero 1992: 153–156.

21. One important issue was the decision that Olivia should take Spanish classes instead of French classes.

22. Among the elite, cotillion and other formal balls are ways of bringing youth from the same social class together to find suitable partners and, thus, to reproduce the upper class. The history of legal restrictions against miscegenation in the United States is evidence of the fear of racial mixing, as is the social pressure to "stick to your own kind."

23. Here is an example of Puwar's point about the "burden of representation" (2004: 60).

24. See Tatum 1997

25. See Fregoso 1993.

26. See Goffman's (1959) discussion of the "field of public life."

27. Although Philip was from a Catholic family and did not belong to the same country club as the Smiths, he was still considered of the same class—or a good "catch" in the marriage market. Although entry of the Mexican maid's daughter into the upper class is highly unlikely, there are ways that nonwhite women have been accepted. See Diana Kendall's discussion of "worker bees" in *The Power of Good Deeds* (2002).

28. Olivia used her appearance to racially define herself in an attempt to control, influence, and shape her interactions on prom night. Gwendolyn S. O'Neal points out the power of style: "When individuals engage in impression management through dress for the express purpose of controlling interaction, the act is political. In many instances, when the message in the presentation is misunderstood or considered as deviant, the propensity exists to intimidate or dominate (i.e., influence) the interaction. Thus, dress may serve as a political instrument for the purpose of influencing formal and informal relationships. As such, dress is power" (1999: 127). Olivia's makeup in this situation is her "dress" or style.

29. His behavior is a prime example of class, gender, and race privilege. See McKinney 2005.

30. Like the African American community's responses to passing, Olivia knows that her Chicana peers are not likely to call her out and that she will be allowed to pass. However, Olivia knows that if she pretends not to know her Chicana friends in this setting, her social networks will be damaged and severed. Since she does not want this to happen, Olivia crosses the race and class divide in the room to demonstrate that she may be passing this evening but that that certainly is not a life choice.

31. Diana Kendall (2002) found that elite families engage in teaching their children etiquette and the skills required to successfully take their position as adults. "Working a room," particularly the ability to engage in an articulate conversation with adults, is an important part of this socialization. See also Lareau's (1987) comparison of working-class and upper-class "Meet the Teachers Night." Working-class parents sit uncomfortably in the auditorium expecting to be lectured to; Lareau describes the upper-class parents' encounter as a cocktail party without drinks.

32. Olivia's actions disrupt what Goffman (1959) refers to the "interaction order." Performing outside the acceptable class and gender norms, she disrupts an array

NOTES TO CHAPTER 4

247

of evasions, disavowals, and rationalizations that enable whites and the upper-class and elite to obscure their privilege and to deny their active participation in social inequality.

33. Several researchers have documented the normalization of interaction based on social inequalities and the ways that dominant groups ignore and deny their privilege. Barbara Trepagnier's (2006) study of white women examines strategies the women used to classify themselves as "not racist" while being instrumental in the production of institutional racism. Karyn McKinney's (2005) study of white college students demonstrates the practices they used to deny or evade acknowledging their privilege gained by race. Rachel Sherman's (2007) study of luxury hotels describes the type and range of services involved in assuring class privilege, such as making special purchases or doing errands.

34. Employees' dress and manners are geared toward assuring that club members gain a "sense of one's place" and that clubs are sites of "conspicuous consumption" and "conspicuous leisure."

35. For a detailed analysis of the significance of dress and power, see Kim K. P. Johnson and Sharron J. Lennon's edited volume *Appearance and Power* (1999). Also see Diana Crane's book *Fashion and Its Social Agendas: Class, Gender, and Identity in Clothing* (2000), for a historical overview of the use of fashion to construct class identity.

36. In a study of lawyers, Holly English (2003) discusses the slow progress in changing rules about dresses and skirts as the mandatory uniform for women and the caution taken with accessories, such as jewelry and makeup.

37. Speaking Spanish creates discomfort because the act points to the disparity between low-level service workers and club members.

38. As Olivia engages in this performance, she is symbolically telling the Smiths that this is her authentic state of being. As Wendy Doniger points out, "We assume that masquerades lie, and often they do, at least on the surface. But often masquerades tell a deeper truth, that masquerading as ourselves reaffirms an enduring self (or network of selves) inside us, which does not change even if our masquerades, intentional or helpless, make us look different from others" (2005: 203).

39. Olivia's actions were significant in recognizing the workers' personhood and their labor. See Sherman 2007: 187–192.

40. W. E. B. Du Bois described the lingering question ready to be posed to those who conditionally are allowed to pass as "one of the family": "Between me and the other world there is ever an unasked question: unasked by some through feelings of delicacy; by others through the difficulty of rightly framing it. All, nevertheless, flutter round it. They approach me in a half-hesitant sort of way, eye me curiously or compassionately, and then, instead of saying directly, 'How does it feel to be a problem?' they say, 'I know an excellent colored man in my town'; or . . . 'Do not these Southern outrages make your blood boil?'" (1989 [1903]: 1).

41. An aspect of this independence denies Olivia the privilege of having a parent who keeps children entertained. In *Anxious Parents: A History of Modern Childrearing in America*, Peter N. Stearns (2003) discusses the growing parental obligation to keep

children from being bored and engaged in various activities. This is due to numerous factors, including smaller families with fewer children to entertain each other and the growing consumerism in childhood. Lareau (2003) also describes working-class parents as giving their children much more independence and engaging in less supervision. Working-class children are expected to become self-sufficient and responsible at a much younger age than upper-middle-class children are. In describing growing up in upper-class households, people interviewed by Kendall (2002) identify a "bubble" that limited their exposure to the outside world, and maintaining this isolation from other classes and races involved planned and supervised events and activities.

42. These feeling have some overlap with those of the children in transnational families whom Rhacel Salazar Parreñas interviewed in her study published in *Children of Global Migration* (2005). Gifts from their mothers became symbols of their mothers' love, and the children longed for their mothers' return.

43. This is a classic sentiment of working-class parents who have children who experience social mobility that moves them into the upper middle or upper class. The hidden cost of social mobility in the United States is its insistence on assimilation, moving away from one's roots both physically and symbolically. The first interview in Studs Terkel's *Working* (1974) is an excellent example of the pain and loss involved in working-class parents' desire for their children to make it. Mike Lefevre's elegant and powerful interview reveals the rupture created when parent and child experience class difference in the United States. As a steel worker, he wants a better life for his son and expresses the tensions involved in class mobility. The classic work on the topic is Richard Sennett and Jonathan Cobb's *The Hidden Injuries of Class* (1972). Also see Lubrano 2004.

44. See Glenn 1986; Rollins 1985; and Romero 1992.

45. Du Bois 1989 [1903]: 3.

46. Zygmunt Bauman (2004: 39) argues that "the right to claim an identity as distinct from an ascribed and enforced classification" is not an option for marginalized populations.

47. All of these forms of behavior are important for the interaction order and thus maintain the status quo.

NOTES TO CHAPTER 5

1. Traditionally, live-in maids covet having an apartment or place to call home to which they return on their days off. Olivia frequently joined the maids employed in Liberty Place at one of their apartments to share a meal on their days off. She assumed that her apartment would also become her mother's apartment, to be shared with her friends.

2. See Wrigley 1996.

3. See UCLA-LOSH 2002.

4. Idella Parker, the cook and housekeeper for the writer Marjorie Kinnan Rawlings from1940 to 1950, comments on the additional work created by employers' not considering the additional labor in privilege when Idella was expected to work late

into the night to serve at parties, and she resented the notion that she was the "prefect maid." See Parker 1992.

5. Many of the discourses of self and others used by workers employed in luxury hotels to "neutralize their subordinate position," by "establishing a superior ranking on alternative hierarchies," are similar to ones found among domestic workers. See Sherman 2007.

6. Olivia's need for financial aid is not perceived by the Smiths in relation to the unearned inheritance that covers tuition for their own children. This episode exposes the denial to working-class nonwhites of privileges that upper-class whites receive, by government policies benefiting whites and discriminating against nonwhites such as the GI Bill, FHA discrimination in loans, banks' redlining, internment of Japanese Americans, Operation Wetback, and minimum-wage laws. Research on the racial wealth divide has identified a long history of government policies and practices that served as affirmative action for whites. See Katznelson 2005; Lui et al. 2006; and Roediger 1994.

7. Movimiento Estudiantil Chicano de Aztlán (MEChA) is a student organization that began in 1969 to increase the number of Mexican American students and faculty in higher education and to maintain Chicano/a culture and history. The organization is active in social justice issues.

8. Mr. Smith's comments include the classic treatment of domestic labor as non-work and invisible labor.

9. The treatment of women's work in the home is framed as "labor of love" done in the family role of wife, mother, or daughter, rather than as an employee.

10. Romero 1992: 123.

11. The paternalistic attitude calls to mind conditions under feudalism, when masters were responsible for their servants when they got old.

12. See "The Promise and Gift Revisited," in Romero 1992: 150–153.

13. Romero 1992: 122.

14. While Mr. Smith denies the economic realities of the employee-employer relationship between Carmen and Mrs. Smith, he requests Olivia to divide business from the emotional component. However, the "emotional" component of the relationship is actually the one that embraces the illusion of Carmen's being one of the family and that blurs unpaid activities done as a friend and paid activities negotiated between employer and employee.

15. See Bowen and Bok 1998 for data on the increased likelihood of nonwhite students' going into occupations with the intention of making a socially significant difference. In addition, they are more likely to be service oriented. Rather than seeing making money as their sole purpose in obtaining a good education, they are more likely to have a commitment to give back to the community and to improve socio-economic and political conditions for others.

16. See Lareau 2003 for a description of different skills upper-class and middle-class parents emphasize in socializing their children. Also see "Learning the Ropes," chap. 4 in Kendall 2002.

17. Mexican American high school students are overrepresented in public schools,

particularly in cities experiencing white flight to private and charter schools. Access to both private and charter schools is largely an issue of finances, which automatically excludes the children of the working poor and lower-middle-class students.

18. See Alcoff et al. 2006, particularly chapters by Rosura Sanchez, Juan Flores, and Dominick La Capra.

19. Until recently, a particular class identity was assumed in Chicana/o identity. However, now that there is a significant Mexican American middle class, including children who also identify as mixed-race and Central Americans who identify as Chicano/a, the politics take priority over a specific class/culture lived experience.

20. "Avoidance behavior" refers to a strategy of managing interaction that Erving Goffman noted in *The Presentation of Self* (1959). In this particularly case, neither the employers' nor employees' sons or daughters saw value in placing their class status and inequalities out in the open. By not acknowledging their acquaintance with each other, they could limit their interaction, as student strangers on the same campus.

21. See Tatum 1997.

22. See Goffman 1959; and Rollins 1985.

23. Olivia felt a sense of control over the situation if she and the employers' children acknowledged each other only as fellow students and not as acquaintances from Liberty Place, because that would have highlighted the class differences between them. Also, their acknowledging her mother as being like a second mother to them presented a familiarity that Olivia wanted to avoid.

24. Olivia attempted to keep her interaction with the employers' children based on her achieved status as a college student and a member of the student government. However, in the exchange that follows in the text, Steve, part of the employers' social network, imposes an ascribed status on Olivia—not as her mother's daughter but as owned by the Smith family. Although Steve is placing Olivia within his family circle, which includes the Smiths, in doing so, he also points to the social stratification existing at the Malibu party that they are attending.

25. Racial incidents on college campuses across the country are not an exception but occur on a regular basis. Leaving a KKK-style hood in a public place, drawing a noose or a swastika on a bathroom door, and anti-immigrant hate speech create a hostile environment for students. For research on racism and lack of diversity on university campuses, see Davis 1994; Hurtado et al. 1998; Margolis and Romero 1998; and Rankin and Reason 2005.

26. A professor in graduate school made the same claim about me, that I was "different" from the others. This is a common experience for minorities in academia (Romero 2000).

27. See Dunn 1996.

28. Bonilla-Silva 2003.

29. See Lui et al. 2006; and Shapiro 2004.

30. Several studies analyzing race talk note the distinction made between unknown persons of color—a general category—and reference to specific individuals known and considered friends and, thus, different. See Bonilla-Silva 2001, 2003; Bush 2004.

31. Kendall's (2002) notion of the upper-class bubble is applicable in capturing the

assumed privilege Olivia learned while living in Liberty Place. Her experiences in the inner city of Los Angeles had been negotiated by her relatives, her mother, and her boyfriends. She acted on her own much more in Liberty Place.

32. For background on the disparate treatment that Latinos face in the criminal justice system, including police relations, see Bender et al. 2007.

33. In a study of the long-term consequences of considering race in college and university admissions, William G. Bowen and Derek Bok (1998) found that Black students were more likely to be engaged in leading civic activities than whites were. Their findings also suggest that minority students who graduate from top universities are less likely than whites to take their commitment to improving social conditions with them in their careers.

34. The disparities between lifestyles of white professionals and professionals of color contribute to the difference that inheritance makes in the purchase of their first home and the amount they have to make a down payment, which influences their monthly mortgage—as well as where they can afford to buy. Furthermore, the existence or lack of an inheritance places adults in different positions in relation to their parents: whereas whites are more likely to expect an inheritance, adult children of color are more likely to be responsible to care for their elderly parents. See Lui et al. 2006; and Shapiro 1994.

35. Researchers are beginning to identify cultural capital that children of color and immigrant children gain from their families, cultural capital that is significant to their future success. See Park 2005; and Valdés 2003.

36. Stephen Steinberg's classic *The Ethnic Myth* (1981) critiques the American Dream ideology and points to the ways that history has been distorted to support the claim that social mobility is based solely on meritocracy.

37. In the book *We Won't Go Back: Making the Case for Affirmative Action* (1997), Charles R. Lawrence III and Mari J. Matsuda demonstrate the significance of community and families in the economic struggles of working-class people of color.

38. Although it is a much debated concept, Olivia does confront the false consciousness of the working poor and the working class. Instead of acknowledging the barriers faced by the poor and immigrants, persons experiencing some level of economic improvement often embrace the work ethic and ideology of meritocracy that identifies others as lazy and unwilling to defer gratification.

39. See the recent research on affirmative action for whites and on the significance of inheritance: Katznelson 2005; Lawrence and Matsuda 1997; Lui et al. 2006; and Shapiro 1994.

40. The link between class privileges and inequality that the children of factory workers face is not as transparent as that experienced by children of nannies and domestic workers. The link between privilege and subordination is not masked by layers of transactions in relationships between children of domestics and the children of the employers. See Romero 2001b.

1. Olivia had important gaps in her experience of the day-to-day realities of working-class Mexican American youth in the inner city.

2. The Mexican American Legal Defense and Educational Fund is a national nonprofit civil rights organization that protects the rights of Latinos in the United States. MALDEF began in 1968.

3. Weedon 2004: 155.

4. The act of hiring a live-in maid includes purchasing status and deference, of which Olivia was a part. The Smiths' purchase of affirmation of their superior status was disguised by asserting benevolence in calling Carmen and Olivia "one of the family." See Romero 1992: 142–156.

5. This was in the early 1980s, when the Immigration Reform and Control Act (IRCA), also known as Simpson-Mazzoli Act (Pub. L. 99-603, 100 Stat. 3359), was being debated in Congress. Although the act made it illegal to knowingly hire or recruit immigrants without authorization, the act also provided amnesty to immigrants who were able to prove employment and residence in the United States before January 1, 1982. This requirement involved employers' writing letters attesting to the immigrants' employment prior to 1982. The act was signed by President Ronald Reagan on November 6, 1986.

6. hooks 1989: 211.

7. For a discussion on the burden of proof and burden of representation, see Puwar 2004: 59–71.

8. A significant class difference in parenting is teaching children about the world they know. Working-class parents know that the world is hard, but upper-middle- and upper-class parents do not, because that is not their experience. As Valerie Walkerdine and Helen Lucey note, "Successful parenting rests on creating an illusion of autonomy so convincing that the child actually believes herself to be free" (1989: 29).

9. In the same way that Taiwan employers and migrant live-in employees attempt to establish boundaries as described in Pei-Chia Lan's study (2006), nation-states also create boundaries between countries and within each country's borders. These social policies are evident in city and state decisions concerning the location of highways and access to public transportation. See Bullard, Johnson, and Torres 2004. Housing policies are also crucial in keeping populations "in their place." As Patricia Hill Collins writes, "The practice of encouraging families to purchase single-family homes over other housing options works to mask how the property values of the housing occupied by different racial/ethnic groups is central to racial hierarchy" (2006: 43). Also see Lui et al. 1996 for a summary of federal legislation that has maintained segregation between racial/ethnic groups, such as the Dawes Act, the GI Bill, the Bracero Program, and Operation Wetback.

10. Collins 2006: 31: "Within prevailing logic . . . both families and the women associated with them are thought to fall outside the public-sphere activities that legislate racial, ethnic, and citizenship status. . . . [The employer's] perception that [the

employee] was like of one of the family constructed and masked the power dynamics of race and class that shaped their everyday interactions. At the same time, family constitutes a fundamental principle of social organization."

11. Aviva Chomsky addresses this myth in her book *"They Take Our Jobs! And 20 Other Myths about Immigration* (2007). Also see Nevins 2008.

REFERENCES

Alcoff, Linda Martín, Michael Hames-García, Satya P. Mohanty, and Paula M. L. Moya. 2006. *Identity Politics Reconsidered*. New York: Palgrave Macmillan.

Alvarez, Julia. 1997. *¡Yo!* Chapel Hill, NC: Algonquin Books of Chapel Hill.

Anderson, Bridget. 2000. *Doing the Dirty Work? The Global Politics of Domestic Labour*. London: Zed Books.

Anyon, Jean. 1997. *Ghetto Schooling: A Political Economy of Urban Educational Reform*. New York: Teachers College Press.

Baldwin, James. 1998. "On Being White and Other Lies." In David R. Roediger, ed., *Black on White: Black Writers on What It Means to Be White*, pp. 177–180. New York: Schocken Books.

Baquedano-López, Patricia. 2002. "A Stop at the End of the Bus Line: Nannies, Children and the Language of Care." Working Paper 51, Center for Working Families, University of California, Berkeley. Accessed at http://workingfamilies.berkeley.edu/papers.html (last visited 10/10/2002).

Bauman, Zygmunt. 2004. *Identity: Conversations with Benedetto Vecchi*. Malden, MA: Polity.

Behar, Ruth. 1993. *Translated Woman: Crossing the Border with Esperanza's Story*. Boston: Beacon.

———. 1996. *The Vulnerable Observer: Anthropology That Breaks Your Heart*. Boston: Beacon.

Bender, Steven W., Raquel Aldana, Gilbert Paul Carrasco, and Joaquin G. Avila. 2007. *Everyday Law for Latino/as*. Boulder, CO: Paradigm.

Berry, Bonnie. 2007. *Beauty Bias: Discrimination and Social Power*. Westport, CT: Praeger.

Bertaux, Daniel, and Paul Thompson. 1993. Introduction to Bertaux and Thompson, eds., *Between Generations: Family Models, Myths, and Memories*. New Brunswick, NJ: Transaction.

Blackman, Margaret B. 1989. *Sadie Brower Neakok: An Inupiaq Woman*. Seattle: University of Washington Press.

Bloom, David E., and Todd P. Steen. 1996. "Minding the Baby in the United States." In Kim England, ed., *Who Will Mind the Baby? Geographies of Child Care and Working Mothers*, pp. 23–35. London: Routledge.

Blowsnake, Sam. 1963. *The Autobiography of a Winnebago Indian*. New York: Dover.

Bochner, Arthur, and Carolyn Ellis. 2006. "Communication as Autoethnography." In Gregory J. Shepherd, Jeffrey St. John, and Ted Striphas, eds., *Communication as . . . : Perspectives on Theory*, pp. 110–122. Thousand Oaks, CA: Sage.

Bonilla-Silva, Eduardo. 2001. *White Supremacy and Racism in the Post–Civil Rights Era*. Boulder, CO: Lynne Rienner.

———. 2003. *Racism without Racists: Color-Blind Racism and the Persistence of Racial Inequality in the United States*. Lanham, MD: Rowman and Littlefield.

Bowen, William G., and Derek Bok. 1998. *The Shape of the River: Long-Term Consequences of Considering Race in College and University Admissions*. Princeton: Princeton University Press.

Brazelton, T. Berry. 1990. *Families: Crisis and Caring*. Reading, MA: Addison-Wesley.

Brooks, James L., writer and director. 2004. *Spanglish*. Los Angeles: Columbia Pictures. Film.

Brooks, Sara. 1987. *You May Plow Here: The Narrative of Sara Brooks*. Ed. Thordis Simsen. New York: Simon and Schuster.

Browne, Irene, and Joya Mistra. 2005. "Labor-Market Inequality: Intersections of Gender, Race, and Class." In Mary Romero and Eric Margolis, eds., *The Blackwell Companion to Social Inequalities*, pp. 165–189. Malden, MA: Blackwell.

Bullard, Robert, Glenn S. Johnson, and Angel Torres, eds. 2004. *Highway Robbery: Transportation Racism and New Routes to Equity*. Cambridge, MA: South End.

Buriel, R., W. Perez, T. L. De Ment, D. V. Chavez, and V. R. Moran. 1998. "The Relationship of Language Brokering to Academic Performance, Biculturalism, and Self-Efficacy among Latino Adolescents." *Hispanic Journal of Behavioral Science* 20:283–297.

Bush, Melanie E. L. 2004. *Breaking the Code of Good Intentions: Everyday Forms of Whiteness*. Lanham, MD: Rowman and Littlefield.

Buss, Fran Leeper. 1980. *La Partera: Story of a Midwife*. Ann Arbor: University of Michigan Press.

———. 1993. *Forged under the Sun/Forjado bajo el Sol: The Life of Maria Elena Lucas*. Ann Arbor: University of Michigan Press.

Candelario, Ginetta E. B. 2007. *Black behind the Ears: Dominican Racial Identity from Museums to Beauty Shops*. Durham: Duke University Press.

Carter, Prudence. 2005. *Keepin' It Real: School Success beyond Black and White*. Oxford: Oxford University Press.

Chang, Grace. 2000. *Disposable Domestics: Immigrant Women Workers in the Global Economy*. Boston: South End.

Chaudry, Ajay. 2004. *Putting Children First: How Low-Wage Working Mothers Manage Child Care*. New York: Russell Sage Foundation.

Chavez, Linda. 1991. *Out of the Barrio: Toward a New Politics of Hispanic Assimilation*. New York: Basic Books.

Childress, Alice. 1986 [1956]. *Like One of the Family: Conversations from a Domestic's Life*. Boston: Beacon.

Chin, Elizabeth. 2001. *Purchasing Power: Black Kids and American Consumer Culture.* Minneapolis: University of Minnesota Press.

Chin, Ko-Lin. 1999. *Smuggled Chinese: Clandestine Immigration to the United States.* Philadelphia: Temple University Press.

Chomsky, Aviva. 2007. *"They Take Our Jobs!" and 20 Other Myths about Immigration.* Boston: Beacon.

Colen, Shelle. 1989. "'Just a Little Respect': West Indian Domestic Workers in New York City." In Elsa M. Chaney and Mary Garcia Castro, eds., *Muchachas No More: Household Workers in Latin America and the Caribbean,* pp. 171–194. Philadelphia: Temple University Press.

Collins, Patricia Hill. 2006. *From Black Power to Hip Hop: Racism, Nationalism, and Feminism.* Philadelphia: Temple University Press.

Cook, Daniel Thomas. 2004. *The Commodification of Childhood.* Durham: Duke University Press.

Cookson, Peter W., Jr., and Caroline Hodges Persell. 1985. *Preparing for Power: America's Elite Boarding Schools.* New York: Basic Books.

Coser, Lewis A. 1974. *Greedy Institutions: Patterns of Undivided Commitment.* New York: Free Press.

Crane, Diana. 2000. *Fashion and Its Social Agendas: Class, Gender, and Identity in Clothing.* Chicago: University of Chicago Press.

Davis, James Earl. 1994. "College in Black and White: Campus Environment and Academic Achievement of African American Males." *Journal of Negro Education* 63 (4): 620–633.

Domestic Workers United and DataCenter. 2006. "Home Is Where the Work Is: Inside New York's Domestic Work Industry." Accessed at www.domesticworkersunited.org/media/files/215/homeiswheretheworkis.pdf.

Doniger, Wendy. 2005. *The Woman Who Pretended to Be Who She Was: Myths of Self-Imitation.* Oxford: Oxford University Press.

D'Souza, Dinesh. 1991. *Illiberal Education: The Politics of Race and Sex on Campus.* New York: Free Press.

Du Bois, W. E. B. 1989 [1903]. *The Souls of Black Folk.* New York: Bantam Books.

Dunn, Timothy J. 1996. *The Militarization of the U.S.-Mexico Border.* Austin: CMAS Books/University of Texas Press.

English, Holly. 2003. *Gender on Trial: Sexual Stereotypes and Work/Life Balance in the Legal Workplace.* New York: ALM.

Frankenberg, Ruth. 1994. *White Women, Race Matters: The Social Construction of Whiteness.* Minneapolis: University of Minnesota Press.

Fraser, Mariam. 1999. "Classing Queer: Politics in Competition." *Theory, Culture and Society* 16 (2): 107–132.

Fregoso, Rosa Linda. 1993. *The Bronze Screen: Chicano and Chicana Film Culture.* Minneapolis: University of Minnesota Press.

Galinsky, Ellen. 1999. *Ask the Children: The Breakthrough Study That Reveals How to Succeed at Work and Parenting.* New York: Quill.

Glenn, Evelyn Nakano. 1986. *Issei, Nisei, War Bride: Three Generations of Japanese American Women in Domestic Service*. Philadelphia: Temple University Press.

Goffman, Erving. 1959. *The Presentation of Everyday Life*. New York: Doubleday Anchor.

Hays, Sharon. 1996. *The Cultural Contradictions of Motherhood*. New Haven: Yale University Press.

Helburn, Suzanne W., and Barbara R. Bergman. 2003. *America's Childcare Problem: The Way Out*. New York: Palgrave Macmillan.

Herrnstein, Richard J., and Charles Murray. 1996. *The Bell Curve: Intelligence and Class Structure in American Life*. New York: Free Press.

Hesse-Biber, Sharlene Nagy. 2007. *The Cult of Thinness*. New York: Oxford University Press.

Hochschild, Arlie Russell. 2003. *The Commercialization of Intimate Life: Notes from Home and Work*. Berkeley: University of California Press.

Hondagneu-Sotelo, Pierrette. 2001. *Doméstica: Immigrant Workers Cleaning and Caring in the Shadows of Affluence*. Berkeley: University of California Press.

hooks, bell. 1989. *Talking Back: Thinking Feminist, Thinking Black*. Boston: South End.

Howes, David. 1996. Introduction to Howes, ed., *Cross-Cultural Consumption: Global Markets, Local Realities*, pp. 1–16. New York: Routledge.

Hrdy, Sarah Blaffer. 2002. *Mother Nature: Maternal Instincts and How They Shape the Human Species*. New York: Ballantine Books.

Hurtado, Sylvia, Alma R. Clayton-Pedersen, Walter Recharde Allen, and Jeffrey F. Milem. 1998. "Enhancing Campus Climates for Racial/Ethnic Diversity: Educational Policy and Practice." *Review of Higher Education* 21 (4): 279–302.

Ignatiev, Noel. 1995. *How the Irish Became White*. New York: Routledge.

Iorizzo, Luciano J., and Salvatore Mondello. 1980. *The Italian Americans*. Boston: Twayne.

Johnson, Kevin R. 1999. *How Did You Get to Be Mexican? A White/Brown Man's Search for Identity*. Philadelphia: Temple University Press.

Johnson, Kim K. P., and Sharron J. Lennon, eds. 1999. *Appearance and Power*. New York: Berg.

Kasinitz, Philip, John H. Mollenkopf, Mary C. Waters, and Jennifer Holdaway. 2008. *Inheriting the City: The Children of Immigrants Come of Age*. New York: Russell Sage.

Katzman, David. 1981. *Seven Days a Week: Women and Domestic Service in Industrializing America*. Urbana: University of Illinois Press.

Katznelson, Ira. 2005. *When Affirmative Action Was White*. New York: Norton.

Kekumura, Akemi. 1981. *Through Harsh Winters: The Life of a Japanese Immigrant Woman*. Novato, CA: Chandler and Sharp.

Kendall, Diana. 2002. *The Power of Good Deeds: Privileged Women and the Social Reproduction of the Upper Class*. Lanham, MD: Rowman and Littlefield.

King, Wilma. 2005. *African American Childhoods: Historical Perspectives from Slavery to Civil Rights*. New York: Palgrave Macmillan.

Kozol, Jonathan. 1991. *Savage Inequalities: Children in America's Schools.* New York: Crown.

Lan, Pei-Chia. 2006. *Global Cinderellas: Migrant Domestics and Newly Rich Employers in Taiwan.* Durham: Duke University Press.

Langellier, Kristin M., and Eric E. Peterson. 1993. "Family Storytelling as a Strategy of Social Control." In Dennis K. Mumby, ed., *Narrative and Social Control: Critical Perspectives,* pp. 49–76. New York: Sage.

Lareau, Annette. 1987. "Social Class Differences in Family-School Relationships: The Importance of Cultural Capital." *Sociology of Education* 60 (April): 73–85.

———. 1989. *Home Advantage: Social Class and Parental Intervention in Elementary Education.* London: Falmer.

———. 2000. "Contours of Childhood: Social Class Differences in Children's Daily Lives." Working Paper 18, Center for Working Families, University of California, Berkeley. Accessed at http://workingfamilies.berkeley.edu/papers.html (last visited 10/9/2002).

———. 2003. *Unequal Childhoods: Class, Race, and Family Life.* Berkeley: University of California Press.

Larsen, Nella. 1969. *Passing.* New York: Negro Universities Press.

Lawrence, Charles R., III, and Mari J. Matsuda. 1997. *We Won't Go Back: Making the Case for Affirmative Action.* Boston: Houghton Mifflin.

Leach, Penelope. 1997. *Your Baby and Child: From Birth to Age Five.* New York: Knopf.

Lightfoot, Sara Lawrence. 1988. *Balm in Gilead: Journey of a Healer.* New York: Addison Wesley.

Lopez, Nancy. 2003. *Hopeful Girls, Troubled Boys: Race and Gender Disparity in Urban Education.* New York: Routledge.

Lubrano, Alfred. 2004. *Limbo: Blue-Color Roots, White-Collar Dreams.* New York: Wiley.

Lugo, Alejandro. 2008. *Fragmented Lives, Assembled Parts: Culture, Capitalism, and Conquest at the U.S.-Mexico Border.* Austin: University of Texas Press.

Lui, Meizhu, Bárbara Robles, Betsy Leondar-Wright, Rose Brewer, and Rebecca Adamson. 2006. *The Color of Wealth: The Story behind the U.S. Racial Wealth Divide.* New York: New Press.

Lutz, Helma. 2002. "At Your Service Madam! The Globalization of Domestic Service." *Feminist Review* 70:89–104.

Margolis, Eric, and Mary Romero. 1998. "'The Department Is Very Male, Very White, Very Old, and Very Conservative': The Functioning of the Hidden Curriculum in Graduate Sociology Departments." *Harvard Educational Review* 68 (1): 1–21.

McClaurin-Allen, Irma. 1992. "Incongruities: Dissonance and Contradiction in the Life of a Black Middle-Class Woman." In Faye Ginsburg and Anna Lowenhaupt Tsing, eds., *Uncertain Terms: Negotiating Gender in American Culture,* pp. 315–333. Boston: Beacon.

McKinney, Karyn D. 2005. *Being White: Stories of Race and Racism.* New York: Routledge.

Milkman, Ruth, Ellen Reese, and Benita Roth. 1998. "Macrosociology of Paid Domestic Labor." *Work and Occupations* 25 (4): 483–510.

Mills, C. Wright. 1943. "The Professional Ideology of Social Pathologists." *American Journal of Sociology* 49 (2):165–180.

Momsen, Janet Henshall. 1999. "Maids on the Move." In Janet Henshall Momsen, ed., *Gender, Migration and Domestic Service*, pp. 1–20. New York: Routledge.

Nagel, Joanne. 1997. *American Indian Ethnic Renewal.* New York: Oxford University Press.

Nelson, Margaret K. 2010. *Parenting Out of Control: Anxious Parents in Uncertain Times.* New York: NYU Press.

Nevins, Joseph. 2002. *Operation Gatekeeper and Beyond: The Rise of the "Illegal Alien" and the Making of the U.S.-Mexico Boundary.* New York: Routledge.

———. 2008. *Dying to Live: A Story of U.S. Immigration in an Age of Global Apartheid.* San Francisco: City Lights Books.

Obama, Barack. 1995. *Dreams from My Father: A Story of Race and Inheritance.* New York: Times Books.

Oliver, Melvin, and Thomas M. Shapiro. 1995. *Black Wealth/White Wealth.* New York: Routledge.

Omi, Michael, and Howard Winant. 1987. *Racial Formation in the United States: From the 1960s to the 1980s.* New York: Routledge and Kegan Paul.

O'Neal, Gwendolyn S. 1999. "The Power of Style: On Rejection of the Accepted." In Kim K. P. Johnson and Sharron J. Lennon, eds., *Appearance and Power*, pp. 127–139. New York: Berg.

Palmer, Phyllis. 1989. *Domesticity and Dirt: Housewives and Domestic Servants in the United States, 1920–1945.* Philadelphia: Temple University Press.

Park, Lisa Sun-Hee. 2005. *Consuming Citizenship: Children of Asian Immigrant Entrepreneurs.* Stanford: Stanford University Press.

Parker, Idella. 1992. *Idella: Marjorie Rawlings' "Perfect Maid."* Gainesville: University Press of Florida.

Parreñas, Rhacel Salazar. 2001. *Servants of Globalization: Women, Migration, and Domestic Work.* Stanford: Stanford University Press.

———. 2005. *Children of Global Migration: Transnational Families and Gendered Woes.* Stanford: Stanford University Press.

———. 2008. *The Force of Domesticity: Filipina Migrants and Globalization.* New York: NYU Press.

Paulsen, Michael B., and Edward P. St. John. 2002. "Social Class and College Costs: Examining the Financial Nexus between College Choice and Persistence." *Journal of Higher Education* 73 (2): 189–236.

Pemberton, Gayle. 1998. *The Hottest Water in Chicago: Notes of a Native Daughter.* Hanover, NH: Wesleyan University Press.

Pugh, Allison J. 2009. *Longing and Belonging: Parents, Children, and Consumer Culture.* Berkeley: University of California Press.

Puwar, Nirmal. 2004. *Space Invaders: Race, Gender and Bodies Out of Place.* Oxford, UK: Berg.

Rankin, Susan R., and Robert Dean Reason. 2005. "Differing Perceptions: How Students of Color and White Students Perceive Campus Climate for Underrepresented Groups." *Journal of College Student Development* 46 (1): 43–61.

Rawlings, Marjorie Kinnan. 1942. *Cross Creek*. New York: Scribner's.

Roberts, Dorothy E. 1997. "Spiritual and Menial Housework." *Yale Journal of Law and Feminism* 9:51–80.

Robles, Bárbara J. 2006a. "Asset Accumulation and Economic Development in Latino Communities: A National and Border Economy Profile of Latino Families." Pub. 1752-119. Madison, WI: Filene Research Institute.

———. 2006b. "Family Legacies." In Meizhu Lui, Bárbara Robles, Betsy Leondar-Wright, Rose Brewer, and Rebecca Adamson, eds., *The Color of Wealth: The Story behind the U.S. Racial Wealth Divide*. New York: New Press.

Rodriguez, Richard. 1982. *Hunger of Memory: The Education of Richard Rodriguez*. New York: Bantam Books.

Roediger, David. 1994. *Wages of Whiteness: Race and the Making of the Working Class*. New York: Verso.

Rollins, Judith. 1985. *Between Women: Domestics and Their Employers*. Philadelphia: Temple University Press.

Romero, Mary. 1992. *Maid in the U.S.A.* New York: Routledge.

———. 1993. "Cuentos from a Maid's Daughter: Stories of Socialization and Cultural Resistance." *Latino Studies Journal* 4 (3): 7–18.

———. 1995. "Life as the Maid's Daughter: An Exploration of the Everyday Boundaries of Race, Class, and Gender." In Domna C. Stanton and Abigail J. Stewart, eds., *Feminisms in the Academy*, pp. 157–179. Ann Arbor: University of Michigan Press.

———. 1999. "One of the Family or Just the Mexican Maid's Daughter? Belonging, Identity and Social Mobility." In Mary Romero and Abigail J. Stewart, eds., *Women's Untold Stories: Breaking Silence, Talking Back, Voicing Complexity*, pp. 142–158. New York: Routledge.

———. 2000. "Learning to Think and Teach about Race and Gender despite Graduate School: Obstacles Women of Color Graduate Students Face in Sociology." In Social Justice Group at the Center for Advanced Feminist Studies, University of Minnesota, eds., *Is Academic Feminism Dead? Theory in Practice*, pp. 283–310. New York: NYU Press.

———. 2001a. "Passing between the Worlds of Maid and Mistress: The Life of a Mexican Maid's Daughter." In Nancy Marshall and Rosanna Hertz, eds., *Work and Family: Today's Realities, Tomorrow's Visions*, pp. 323–339. Berkeley: University of California Press.

———. 2001b. "Unraveling Privilege: Workers' Children and the Hidden Costs of Paid Child Care." In "Symposium on the Structures of Care Work." *Chicago-Kent Law Review* 76 (3): 101–121.

Rothman, Barbara Katz. 1990. *Recreating Motherhood: Ideology and Technology in a Patriarchal Society*. New York: Norton.

Sánchez, George J. 1993. *Becoming Mexican American: Ethnicity, Culture and Identity in Chicano Los Angeles, 1900–1945*. New York: Oxford University Press.

Schwartz, Judith D. 1993. *The Mother Puzzle*. New York: Simon and Schuster.

Seiter, Ellen. 1998. "Children's Desires/Mothers' Dilemmas: The Social Contexts of Consumption." In Henry Jenkins, ed., *The Children's Culture Reader*, pp. 297–317. New York: NYU Press.

Sennett, Richard, and Jonathan Cobb. 1972. *The Hidden Injuries of Class*. New York: Knopf.

Shapiro, Thomas M. 2004. *The Hidden Cost of Being African American: How Wealth Perpetuates Inequality*. New York: Oxford University Press.

Sherman, Rachel. 2007. *Class Acts: Service and Inequality in Luxury Hotels*. Berkeley: University of California Press.

Silbaugh, Katharine B. 1996. "Turning Labor into Love: Housework and the Law." *Northwestern University Law Review* 9:1–86.

———. 1997. "Commodification and Women's Household Labor." *Yale Journal of Law and Feminism* 9:81–120.

Skostak, Marjorie. 1981. *Nisa: The Life and Words of a !Kung Woman*. Cambridge: Harvard University Press.

Smith, Bonnie G. 1985. *Confessions of a Concierge: Madame Lucie's History of Twentieth-Century France*. New Haven: Yale University Press.

Stanton-Salazar, Ricardo. 2001. *Manufacturing Hope and Despair: The School and Kin Support Networks of U.S.-Mexican Youth*. New York: Teachers College Press.

Stearns, Peter N. 2003. *Anxious Parents: A History of Modern Childrearing in America*. New York: NYU Press.

Steinberg, Stephen. 1981. *The Ethnic Myth*. Boston: Beacon.

Stevens. Mitchell L. 2007. *Creating a Class: College Admissions and the Education of Elites*. Cambridge: Harvard University Press.

Strauss, Anselm L. 1987. *Qualitative Analysis for Social Scientists*. Cambridge: Cambridge University Press.

Susser, Ida. 1991. "The Separation of Mothers and Children." In John Hull Mollenkopf and Manuel Castells, eds., *Dual City: Restructuring New York*, pp. 207–225. New York: Russell Sage Foundation.

Tatum, Beverly Daniel. 1997. *"Why Are All the Black Kids Sitting Together in the Cafeteria?" and Other Conversations about Race*. 2d ed. New York: Basic Books.

Taylor, Samuel A. 1954. *Sabrina Fair, or, A Woman of the World: A Romantic Comedy*. New York: Random House.

Terkel, Studs. 1974. *Working: People Talk about What They Do All Day and How They Feel about What They Do*. New York: Pantheon.

Trepagnier, Barbara. 2006. *Silent Racism: How Well-Meaning White People Perpetuate the Racial Divide*. Boulder, CO: Paradigm.

Tronto, Joan C. 2002. "The 'Nanny' Question in Feminism." *Hypatia* 17 (2): 34–51.

UCLA-LOSH. 2002. "Voices from the Plant Floor." Los Angeles: Center for Occupational and Environmental Health and Center for Labor Research and Education, Institute for Labor and Employment, UCLA.

Valdés, Guadalupe. 1996. *Con Respeto: Bridging the Distances between Culturally*

Diverse Families and Schools; An Ethnographic Portrait. New York: Teachers College Press.

———. 2003. *Expanding Definitions of Giftedness: The Case of Young Interpreters from Immigrant Communities.* Mahwah, NJ: Erlbaum.

Valenzuela, Angela. 1999. *Subtractive Schooling: U.S.-Mexican Youth and the Politics of Caring.* Albany: SUNY Press.

Vélez-Ibañez, Carlos G. 2004. *Bonds of Mutual Trust: The Cultural Systems of Rotating Credit Associations among Urban Mexicans and Chicanos.* New Brunswick: Rutgers University Press.

Venkatesh, Sudhir Alladi. 2006. *Off the Books: The Underground Economy of the Urban Poor.* Cambridge: Harvard University Press.

Walkerdine, Valerie, and Helen Lucey. 1989. *Democracy in the Kitchen: Regulating Mothers and Socialising Daughters.* London: Virago.

Washington, Mary Helen. 1987. *Invented Lives: Narratives of Black Women, 1860–1960.* Garden City, NY: Anchor.

Weedon, Chris. 2004. *Identity and Culture: Narratives of Difference and Belonging.* New York: Open University Press.

Wells, Ryan. 2008. "Social and Cultural Capital, Race and Ethnicity, and College Student Retention." *Journal of College Student Retention: Research, Theory and Practice* 10 (2): 103–128.

Wong, Sau-ling C. 1994. "Diverted Mothering: Representations of Caregivers of Color in the Age of 'Multiculturalism.'" In Evelyn Nakano Glenn, Grace Chang, and Linda Rennie Forcey, eds., *Mothering Ideology, Experience, and Agency,* pp. 67–91. New York: Routledge.

Wrigley, Julia. 1996. *Other People's Children: An Intimate Account of the Dilemmas Facing Middle-Class Parents and the Women They Hire to Raise Their Children.* New York: Basic Books.

Zhou, Min. 2009. "Conflict, Coping, and Reconciliation: Intergenerational Relations in Chinese Immigrant Families." In Nancy Foner, ed., *Across Generations: Immigrant Families in America,* pp. 21–46. New York: NYU Press.

Zinn, Howard. 2005. *A People's History of the United States: 1492–Present.* New York: HarperPerennial.

Zlolniski, Christian. 2006. *Janitors, Street Vendors, and Activists: The Lives of Mexican Immigrants in Silicon Valley.* Berkeley: University of California Press.

REFERENCES

INDEX

Mary Romero is Professor of Justice and Social Inquiry at Arizona State University. She is the winner of the Lee Founders Award from the Society for the Study of Social Problems in 2004. She is the author or editor of many books, including *Maid in the U.S.A.*, *The Blackwell Companion to Social Inequalities*, and *Latino/a Popular Culture*.